Sew It Tonight, Give It Tomorrow

50 Fast, Fun and Fabulous Gifts to Make in an Evening

Edited by
Stacey L. Klaman

Rodale Press
Emmaus, Pennsylvania

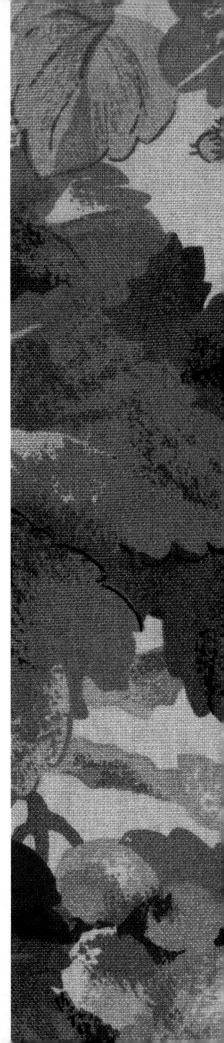

OUR MISSION

We publish books that empower people's lives.

RODALE BOOKS

SEW IT TONIGHT, GIVE IT TOMORROW EDITORIAL AND DESIGN STAFF

Editors: **Stacey L. Klaman**
 Jane Townswick
Book Designer: **Marta Mitchell Strait**
Technical Artist: **Tanya L. Lipinski**
Illustrators: **Jack Crane, Glenn Hughes, Charles M. Metz, and Ray Skibinski**
Photographer: **John P. Hamel**
Photo Stylist: **Marianne Grape Laubach**
Photographer's Assistant: **Troy Schnyder**
Studio Manager: **Mary Ellen Fanelli**
Copy Editor: **Maria Kasprenski Zator**
Editorial Assistance: **Susan Nickol and Stephanie Snyder**
Production Coordinator: **Patrick Smith**

RODALE BOOKS

Executive Editor, Home and Garden: **Margaret Lydic Balitas**
Senior Editor, Craft Books: **Cheryl Winters Tetreau**
Art Director, Home and Garden: **Michael Mandarano**
Copy Manager, Home and Garden: **Dolores Plikaitis**
Office Manager, Home and Garden: **Karen Earl-Braymer**
Editor-in-Chief: **William Gottlieb**

All of the photographs in this book, except for those on pages 2, 6, 20, 65, 159, 176, 186, 202, 217, and 231, were shot on location at Georgetown Manor, Ethan Allen Home Interiors, in Allentown, Pennsylvania.

The print on pages x–1 from the Color Works Collection© is used with permission from the Cranston Print Works Company. The Newstead Chintz fabric from the Bermuda collection, on pages 56–57, is used with permission from Waverly. The Plymouth print fabric in the color champagne on pages ii–iii and on pages 122–123 is used with permission from P. Kaufmann. The print on pages 174–175, Holiday Spirit 34 E-D by Jennifer Sampou, is used with permission from P&B Textiles.

If you have any questions or comments concerning this book, please write to:
 Rodale Press, Inc.
 Book Readers' Service
 33 East Minor Street
 Emmaus, PA 18098

Library of Congress Cataloging-in-Publication Data

Sew it tonight, give it tomorrow : 50 fast, fun and fabulous gifts to make in an evening / edited by Stacey L. Klaman.
    p.   cm.
  ISBN 0–87596–645–4 hardcover
  1. Sewing. 2. Gifts. I. Klaman, Stacey L.
TT715.S44 1995
646.2—dc20   94–38409
                                    CIP

Distributed in the book trade by St. Martin's Press

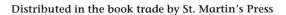

2 4 6 8 10 9 7 5 3 1 hardcover

CONTENTS

BAG IT—FOR PEOPLE ON THE GO

IT'S OH SEW CHRISTMAS

EMBELLISH IT!

Introduction

I love giving gifts even more than I enjoy receiving them. Nothing is more fun for me than surprising friends or family members with gifts that I've sewn especially for them. However, my busy life doesn't always leave me much spare time, so every minute I can devote to sewing is precious to me. I think that sewers everywhere share this feeling, along with a common wish to use our sewing talents for making beautiful and unique things to give to people we love. That desire is how the idea for *Sew It Tonight, Give It Tomorrow* was born.

As I started putting this book together, I gave much thought to the kinds of projects I'd like to see included in a book of gifts that could be sewn in an evening. I combed through magazines and catalogs, searching for ideas that would appeal to sewers who love classic designs and to those who enjoy making the "latest" in fashions, interior decoration, and fabric crafts.

As I began to sort through and select the projects for the book, the organization of the chapters unfolded easily and naturally. In "Family Affairs," you'll find gorgeous, one-of-a-kind gifts that will suit almost any special occasion, from graduations and anniversaries to weddings and christenings. They're sure to please everyone on your list—grandparents, siblings, special friends, neighbors, baby-sitters, and teachers—anyone close to your heart.

"Instant Interiors" shows you how easy it is to enhance the atmosphere in your home with simple, decorative projects that give any room a personal touch. Whether you enjoy soft florals, geometric patterns, or bold solids, the dynamite ideas in this chapter will complement any design.

"Bag It—For People on the Go" is overflowing with sensational solutions for carrying or storing many of life's necessary items. Whether you're off to the gym with exercise gear, packing for a weekend trip to visit friends, organizing important papers for a business trip, or just tucking fruit and sandwiches into a lunch bag, these innovative totes, duffels, bags, and carryalls will help you keep everything neatly and handily in its place.

If shopping for last-minute Christmas gifts sends you into an annual panic, you'll love the projects in "It's Oh Sew Christmas." Just think about how wonderful it would be to start sewing on December 1 and have 24 glorious gifts completed before Santa even leaves the North Pole!

The "Embellish It!" chapter will be a real lifesaver if you ever find yourself having to come up with a gift or two in a tight time crunch. All of these fast-and-fabulous projects start with a purchased item that magically transforms into a handcrafted gift with just a small investment in sewing time.

Looking back, I find it hard to believe that the last year and a half since I began this book has gone by so quickly. I hope that you enjoy making many or all of the exciting projects in the colorful pages of *Sew It Tonight, Give It Tomorrow*. Making someone feel special is what giving gifts is all about, and this book is my gift to you.

Stacey L. Klaman

How to Use This Book

Whether you're a beginner or an expert sewer, the colorful photographs, explicit step-by-step instructions, and detailed color illustrations in *Sew It Tonight, Give It Tomorrow* will allow you to duplicate all of the home decorations and garments just as the designers made them. If you're an advanced sewer, you may enjoy referring to the "General Instructions" beginning on page 240 to brush up on techniques that you've used in the past. If you're a newcomer to sewing, you'll want to read through them to learn about the basic tools and supplies necessary for a well-stocked sewing room. You'll also find everything you need to know about selecting and purchasing fabrics, preparing patterns and cutting fabric, machine-sewing basics, and embroidery and hand-sewing stitches, so you can sew with confidence from the first to the very last stitch.

The features listed below appear in each project. They'll make your sewing time more pleasurable and help you to achieve professional-looking results every time.

Full-size pattern pieces are provided wherever possible. For patterns too large to fit on one page, the pieces are shown in sections. Each section is clearly labeled with placement lines and numbers to make it easy to trace a complete pattern piece. The grain line helps you to lay out the pattern on the straight grain of the fabric. Seam lines on each pattern piece ensure that you will sew with accuracy.

Complete fabric requirements and supplies lists specify exactly how much fabric and what supplies are needed for each project. They also indicate where each fabric is used, making it easy to reproduce the look of the pictured project. Measurements in the cutting directions include the seam allowances, except with regard to the appliqué patterns.

A fabric options list is provided at the beginning of each project. The first fabric listed is the type used to make the project in the photograph. The remaining suggestions will help you to select other appropriate fabrics to produce equally effective and satisfying results.

The fabric key that follows will be helpful in identifying the common fabric used throughout this book. You can use this list so that it will be easy to position the fabrics together correctly. The right side of a fabric will always appear darker and the wrong side of the fabric will always appear lighter in each diagram of every project.

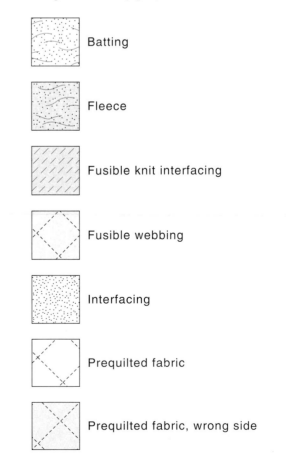

Batting

Fleece

Fusible knit interfacing

Fusible webbing

Interfacing

Prequilted fabric

Prequilted fabric, wrong side

Meet the Designers

Donna Babylon is the owner of Windsor Oak Publishing, a company that publishes books and leaflets on home-decorating projects. She is a regular contributor to magazines including *Sew News, Sewing Decor,* and *Woman's Day Weekend Decorating.*

For *Sew It Tonight, Give It Tomorrow,* Donna created the Crib Bumpers and the Bow, Rosette, and Butterfly Pillows.

Janis Bullis has been serving the home-decorating, apparel, and craft industries for more than 20 years as a consultant and designer. Her clients include companies involved with sewing patterns, craft supplies, fabrics, lace, and ribbons.

Alone and with others, Janis has contributed to more than 100 "how to" publications on topics ranging from bridal accoutrements and baby accessories to holiday decorating. She is the president of Creative Services of Central Valley, New York, a consulting and design company she founded more than a decade ago.

Janis is also a frequent contributor to well-known women's magazines including *Good Housekeeping, Family Circle, Sewing Decor,* and *Woman's Day.*

The projects Janis designed for this book are the Two-in-One Hostess Apron, the Braid-Trimmed Place Mats and Matching Napkins, and the Clown Sweatshirt.

Lynne Farris brings years of experience in the medium of soft sculpture to the world of sewing. She is the owner of Lynne Farris Designs, a creative services company that produces whimsical soft sculpture character costumes, puppets, and promotional displays for corporations, sports teams, and television commercials.

Lynne appears frequently on nationally televised craft programs such as the Discovery Channel's *Easy Does It.* She also contributes regularly to consumer craft publications including *McCall's Quilting* and *Better Homes and Gardens'* special interest magazines.

The projects Lynne designed for *Sew It Tonight, Give It Tomorrow* are the Keepsake Box with Soft Sculpture Flowers and the Soft Sculpture Flower Bouquet.

Barbara Field is a designer and illustrator who began her career at Rodale Press. Over the last 15 years she has accumulated a wealth of book and magazine credits for her outstanding cover designs and illustrations in the areas of woodworking, crafts, and cooking.

For the last five years Barbara has been combining her artistic talents with her love for sewing to create unique patterns and prototypes for such magazines as *Rodale's Quick & Easy Craft Collection* and *Holiday Gifts and Crafts.*

The projects Barbara designed for this book are the Bow Picture Decoration, the Rose Picture Decoration, the Lunch Bags, and the Farmer-and-Animal Sweatshirt.

Ellen Halloran brings 25 years of experience as a fine artist and jewelry designer to the field of sewing. Her work has been seen in numerous galleries in and around New York City and in publications such as the *New York Times, The San Francisco Chronicle,* and the *Dallas Morning News.*

The projects Ellen designed for *Sew It Tonight, Give It Tomorrow* are the Heart Garland, the Herbal Sleep Pillow, the Lingerie Bag, and the Christmas Show Towels.

Carol E. Kirby began designing a line of artistic bears in 1991. In just a few short years, her bears have become collector's items, and she can hardly keep up with the demand for them as she tours around the country. The popularity of Carol's bears has led to appearances in stores and at charity events. She also designed a special group of bears for a 1993 teddy bear calendar. All of her bears are fully jointed and handmade by Carol herself from superior-quality mohair. She will soon begin to design bears for worldwide distribution.

Exclusively for *Sew It Tonight, Give It Tomorrow,* Carol created Nicholas the Bear, her very first unjointed bear.

Patrick Lose began his successful career as a costume designer for stage and screen. His credits include more than 50 productions and work with celebrities such as Liza Minnelli and Jane Seymour.

As the owner of his own company, Out On A Whim, Patrick's fabric lines and patterns for clothing, dolls, and holiday crafts can be found at fabric and craft stores nationwide. In addition, Patrick's designs for crafts, clothing, and home-decorating accessories appear frequently in magazines including *Better Homes and Gardens, Country Crafts, Christmas Ideas, Decorative Woodcrafts,* and *Craft and Wear.*

The projects that Patrick designed for this book are the Lace and Appliquéd Hanger Covers, the Bottle Bags, the Jewelry Roll, and the Shoe Bag.

Linda McGehee is the owner of Ghee's, a mail-order sewing and notions company. She travels internationally, demonstrating and lecturing on sewing and texturing techniques. Her numerous teaching credits include Bernina University, Baby Lock Tech, Elna Impact, PFAFF Convention, Quilt Festival, Viking Convention, the Martha Pullen School, and the American Sewing Guild Conventions.

Texture With Textiles, Linda's first book, won first place in the sewing division of PCM's 1992 Product of Excellence Awards. *More...Texture With Textiles,* her second book, was a finalist for PCM's 1993 Product of Excellence Awards.

Linda's most popular mail-order patterns are the ones she designed for handbags with ready-to-wear handbag hardware. For *Sew It Tonight, Give It Tomorrow,* Linda designed the Drawstring Evening Bag, the Duffel Bag, and the Business Portfolio.

Laurie Pat McWilliams holds a degree in Clothing and Textiles and began her career as a supervisor in a garment factory. She has taught sewing techniques for over a decade and is currently a sewing specialist with Bernina.

Author of the book, *Keep It Sew Simple Garment Construction & Tailoring,* Laurie frequently contributes to publications such as *Crafts, Traditional Quilt,* and the *Bernina Magazine.*

For *Sew It Tonight, Give It Tomorrow,* Laurie designed the Bow Tie and Cummerbund and the Lacy Vest.

Nancy Reames is not a newcomer to Rodale Books. Many of her project designs appear in Rodale's *Scrap Basket Crafts.* In an encore performance, Nancy designed the Advent Calendar and the Christmas Wreath for *Sew It Tonight, Give It Tomorrow.*

Michele Reisch is an award-winning costume designer whose credits include an Emmy Award for the television soap opera *Ryan's Hope.* She has also designed costumes for other television shows such as *As the World Turns, Lifetime's Six Ladies Laughing,* and *Carol Leiffer at the Ed Sullivan Theatre.*

As a designer of Christmas ornaments, Michele's work has appeared in such publications as *New York Magazine* and the *New York Times.* Her designs have sold at Henri Bendel's in New York, the New York Public Library Gift Shop at Lincoln Center, and The John F. Kennedy Center for the Performing Arts in Washington, D.C.

For *Sew It Tonight, Give It Tomorrow,* Michele designed all three of the Merry Christmas Ornaments.

Gale Rose was destined for a career in the fashion industry after winning first place in a Singer sewing contest at the age of 17. Now, with more than 20 years of experience in the industry, her credits include such titles as manager of technical design at Macy's and fashion designer for companies such as Appletree Inc. and Russ Togs.

Recently Gale's designs have appeared in Rodale's *Scrap Basket Crafts.* For *Sew It Tonight, Give It Tomorrow,* Gale designed both whimsical and elegant projects—the Train Shoe Bags, the Sachet Bridal Pillow, the Beret, the Golf Club Covers, the Golf Tee Bag, the Sunflower Tea Cozy, the Tapestry Box, the Pillow Sachet, the Duvet Cover and Pillow Shams, the Christmas Tablecloth, the Soutache-Embellished Shirt, and the Eyelet Sheets and Pillowcases.

Wimpole Street Creations is the Battenberg lace brainchild of **Jeen Brown** and **Linda Thomas.** In just five short years, their company has grown from a small home-based business to one that employs 3 staff designers and 35 seamstresses. Over 150 different Battenberg lace shapes and sizes have been designed at Wimpole Street to produce unique gift and clothing ideas.

In addition to lace and lace kits, Wimpole Street publishes easy pattern books for making crafts with their lace creations. For more information about how to order a catalog, Battenberg lace, or a lace kit from Wimpole Street, see the "Buyer's Guide" on page 246.

For *Sew It Tonight, Give It Tomorrow,* Wimpole Street created the Battenberg Lace Dress and the Battenberg Lace Camisole and Tap Pants.

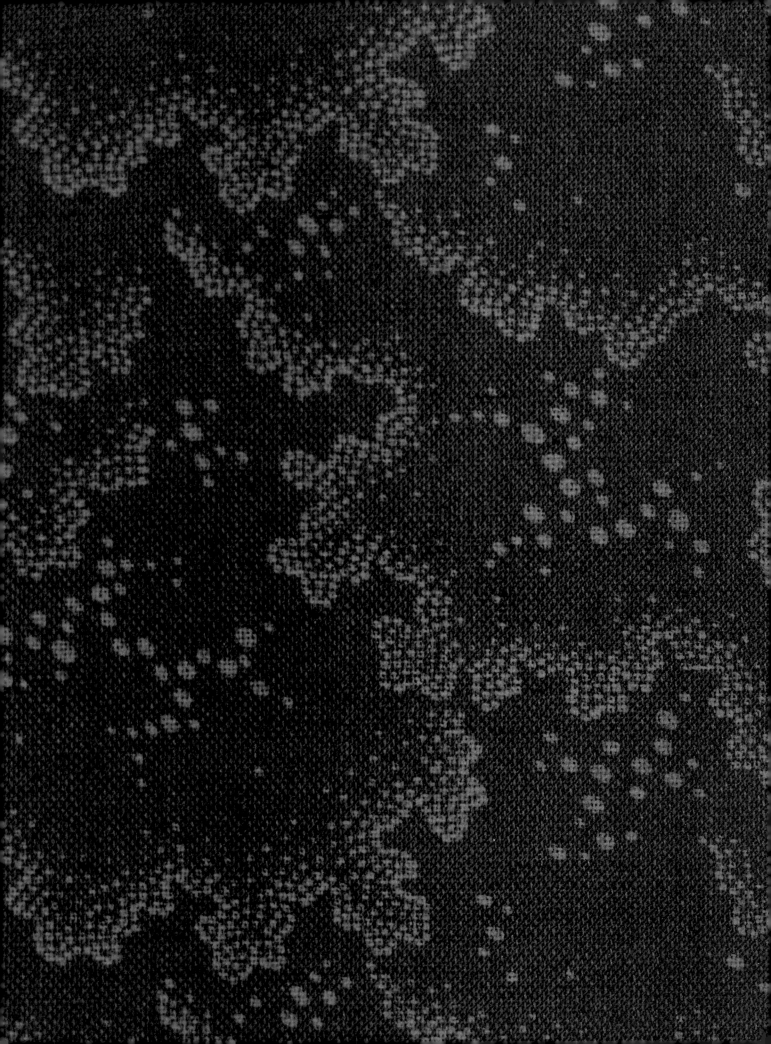

FAMILY AFFAIRS

Heart Garland

Show that your heart's in the right place when you make this adorable garland in soft pastel stripes. Hang it in the crib or on the nursery wall to let a little sweetheart know how much he or she is loved.

SIZE: The finished size of each heart is 5¼ inches wide and 5½ inches high. The finished garland is 27 inches long, excluding the ribbon ties.

NOTE: Measurements in the cutting directions include the seam allowances. Sew all the seams with ½-inch seam allowances.

CUTTING THE HEARTS, LACE, AND RIBBON

1. Trace the pattern on page 5 onto tracing paper and cut it out.

2. From each rectangle of fabric, cut two hearts.

3. Cut the lace into four 21-inch lengths.

4. Cut the grosgrain ribbon in half.

SEWING THE LACE TO THE HEARTS

1. With right sides together, pin and sew one length of lace around the edge of one heart, as shown in **Diagram 1**, making sure to overlap the ends of the lace. Repeat this step for one heart in each fabric.

Diagram 1

2. Referring to **Diagram 2**, with right sides together, pin and sew each pair of hearts together, leaving a 2-inch opening along the side for turning. Be careful not to catch the lace in the seam allowance when sewing the hearts together.

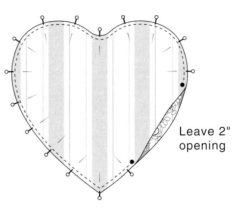

Leave 2" opening

Diagram 2

3. Turn each heart right side out and stuff firmly with polyester fiberfill. Turn under the seam allowance along the opening and blindstitch it closed. For more information, see "Embroidery and Hand-Sewing Stitches" on page 244.

FINISHING THE GARLAND

1. Join the hearts together by hand sewing 2 inches of the lace together between each heart, as shown in **Diagram 3**.

Diagram 3

MATERIALS LIST
FABRIC REQUIREMENTS
- 4 RECTANGLES OF STRIPED FABRIC, EACH 7 × 14 INCHES, FOR THE HEARTS IN THE FOLLOWING PASTEL COLORS: TEAL AND WHITE, PINK AND WHITE, PURPLE AND WHITE, ORANGE AND WHITE

OTHER SUPPLIES
- 2½ YARDS OF ¾-INCH-WIDE SHIRRED WHITE LACE
- 1½ YARDS OF 1-INCH-WIDE YELLOW GROSGRAIN RIBBON
- SEWING THREAD TO MATCH THE FABRIC
- HAND-SEWING NEEDLE
- 1-POUND BAG OF POLYESTER FIBERFILL
- TRACING PAPER

FABRIC OPTIONS
- COTTON
- POLISHED COTTON
- DOTTED SWISS
- GINGHAM
- EYELET
- CALICO
- MOIRÉ

2. Fold one 27-inch length of grosgrain ribbon in half crosswise and press. Thread a hand-sewing needle with matching thread and sew the fold to the end of the first heart, as shown in **Diagram 4.**

3. Referring to **Diagram 4**, with a sharp pair of shears, carefully make a V-shaped cut into each end of the ribbon. Repeat this step for the other length of grosgrain ribbon and the heart at the other end of the garland.

Diagram 4

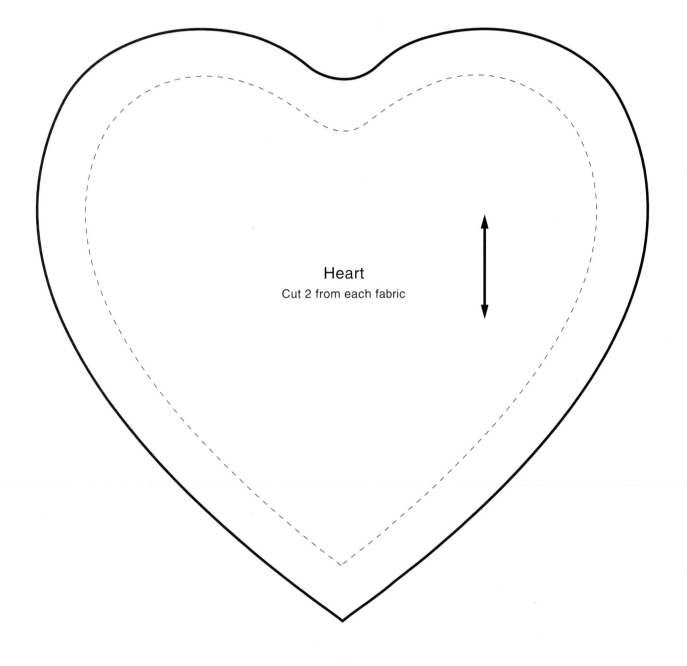

Heart
Cut 2 from each fabric

Crib Bumpers

Surround the newest little angel in the family with soft and sweet crib bumpers. They'll feel warm and cozy during a night of slumber. Trimmed with a coordinating ruffle, they'll send baby off to lullaby-land with a smile.

SIZE: The finished size of each side bumper is $9^1/_2 \times 51^1/_2$ inches. The finished size of each end bumper is $9^1/_2 \times 26^1/_2$ inches.

NOTE: Measurements in the cutting directions include the seam allowances. Sew all the seams with $^1/_2$-inch seam allowances.

CUTTING THE BUMPERS

1. Open the baby print to a single layer with the right side facing up. Referring to **Diagram 1**, cut four $8^1/_2 \times 27^1/_2$-inch end bumper strips. Cut four $8^1/_2 \times 52^1/_2$-inch side bumper strips.

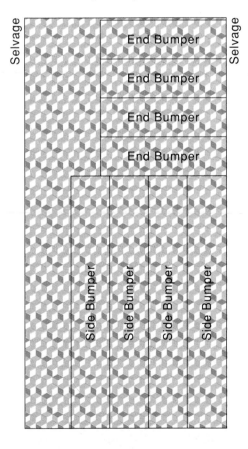

Diagram 1

2. From the coordinating fabric, cut seven $4^1/_2 \times 44$-inch ruffle strips. Cut one of these strips in half crosswise so there are two $4^1/_2 \times 22$-inch strips.

3. From the foam, cut two $7^1/_2 \times 51^1/_2$-inch strips. Cut two $7^1/_2 \times 26^1/_2$-inch strips.

4. From the ribbon, cut 28 pieces, each 24 inches long.

SEWING THE RUFFLES

Note: For each side bumper, $2^1/_2$ ruffle strips are needed. For each end bumper, only 1 ruffle strip is needed.

1. Referring to **Diagram 2**, to make the side bumper ruffles, with right sides together, pin and sew $2^1/_2$ ruffle strips together along the short ends. Press the seams open.

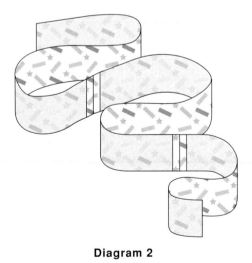

Diagram 2

2. With right sides together, fold the ruffle in half lengthwise. Pin and sew the short ends of the ruffle together, as shown in **Diagram 3** on page 8. Turn the ruffle right side out and press. Repeat Steps 1 and 2 for the remaining side bumper ruffle.

MATERIALS LIST

FABRIC REQUIREMENTS

• $2^1/_2$ YARDS OF BABY PRINT FOR THE BUMPERS

• $1^1/_8$ YARDS OF COORDINATING FABRIC FOR THE RUFFLE

OTHER SUPPLIES

• 19 YARDS OF $^1/_4$-INCH-WIDE COORDINATING SATIN RIBBON

• $1^1/_2$ YARDS OF $^3/_4$-INCH-THICK FOAM

• SEWING THREAD TO MATCH THE FABRICS

• HAND-SEWING NEEDLE

FABRIC OPTIONS

• COTTON

• DOTTED SWISS

• POLISHED COTTON

• GINGHAM

Know & Sew

FOR A QUICK-AND-EASY WAY TO MAKE GATHERS, CUT A PIECE OF DENTAL FLOSS OR FISHING LINE THE LENGTH OF A RUFFLE. SET YOUR SEWING MACHINE FOR A WIDE ZIGZAG STITCH AND A LONG STITCH LENGTH. PLACE THE DENTAL FLOSS OR FISHING LINE ON TOP OF THE FABRIC ⅜ INCH FROM THE EDGE OF THE RUFFLE. ZIGZAG OVER THE FLOSS OR THE FISHING LINE, MAKING SURE NOT TO CATCH THE FLOSS OR THE LINE IN THE STITCHING. PULL UP THE DENTAL FLOSS OR FISHING LINE AND GATHER THE RUFFLE TO THE SPECIFIED LENGTH. SECURE THE FLOSS OR FISHING LINE ENDS IN PLACE BY TYING THEM INTO A KNOT.

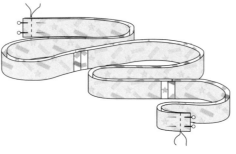

Diagram 3

3. To make the end bumper ruffles, with right sides together, fold one ruffle strip in half lengthwise. Pin and sew the short ends of the ruffle together, as shown in **Diagram 4.** Turn the ruffle right side out and press. Repeat this step for the remaining end bumper ruffle.

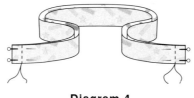

Diagram 4

4. To make two rows of gathering stitches on each ruffle, use the longest machine stitch and sew ¼ inch from the raw edges. Sew another line of stitches ¼ inch away from the first row of stitching.

5. Referring to **Diagram 5,** pull up the bobbin threads and evenly gather each ruffle. Secure the ends of the threads with a knot. Gather the side ruffles until they measure 51½ inches. Gather the end ruffles until they measure 26½ inches. Set all of the ruffles aside.

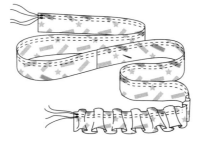

Diagram 5

ATTACHING THE RIBBON TIES

1. Fold each of the 28 ribbon ties in half crosswise and press.

2. Referring to **Diagram 6,** with the right side of one side bumper strip facing up, measure ½ inch from each end and mark with a pin. Divide the remaining length of the side bumper strip between the end pins into four equal sections and mark each section across the top and bottom with a pin.

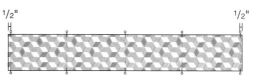

Diagram 6

3. Repeat Step 2 for one more side bumper strip.

4. Referring to **Diagram 7,** pin one ribbon to the right side of the fabric at each dividing mark. The ribbon's crease should be flush with the raw edges of the side bumper strip.

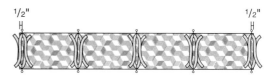

Diagram 7

5. With the right side of one end bumper strip facing up, measure ½ inch from each end and mark with a pin.

6. Repeat Step 5 for one more end bumper strip.

7. Referring to **Diagram 8,** pin one ribbon to the right side of the fabric at each dividing mark. The ribbon's crease should be flush with the raw edge of the end bumper strip.

Diagram 8

ASSEMBLING THE BUMPERS

1. With right sides together and raw edges even, pin one side ruffle to one side bumper strip with ribbons, as shown in **Diagram 9**. Making sure not to catch the ends of the ribbon in the stitching, machine baste the pieces together $1/4$ inch from the raw edges.

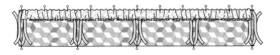

Diagram 9

2. With right sides together, pin one side bumper strip without ribbons to one side bumper–ruffle unit, as shown in **Diagram 10**.

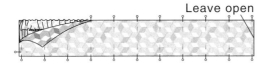

Leave open

Diagram 10

3. Sew the pieces together along three sides, leaving one short side open for turning. Back tack over each ribbon tie for additional reinforcement.

4. Clip the corners and trim the seam allowance to $1/4$ inch.

5. Turn the bumper right side out and press.

6. Repeat Steps 1 through 5 to make the remaining side bumper and the two end bumpers.

FINISHING THE BUMPERS

1. Insert a foam strip into each bumper through the side opening.

2. Turn under the seam allowance along the opening and blindstitch it closed. For information on blindstitching, see "Embroidery and Hand-Sewing Stitches" on page 244.

3. With the ruffle end facing up, and the ribbon ties facing out, fasten each bumper securely to the crib, as shown in the photograph on page 6.

Train Shoe Bags

All aboard! This train shoe bag is headed straight for fun in any little girl's or boy's room. Hang it on a wall, on a closet door, or even on the end of a bunk bed. You may never again have to remind your young ones to put away their shoes.

SIZE: The finished size is 44 inches long and 14¹/₂ inches high.

NOTE: Measurements in the cutting directions include the seam allowances. Sew all seams with ¹/₂-inch seam allowances, unless otherwise indicated. There is one pattern piece for all three cars. Transfer all markings to the right side of the fabric with a chalk pencil.

CUTTING THE TRAIN

1. To make the complete engine pattern, fold a sheet of tracing paper in half and trace the pattern piece on page 15 onto the paper, transferring all markings. Cut out the pattern and open it up.

2. Trace the engine top pattern piece on page 16 onto one layer of tracing paper and cut out the pattern.

3. Tape the engine top pattern to the right side of the engine pattern along the indicated lines.

4. To make the complete side engine and side engine reverse pattern, trace the pattern pieces on pages 16–17 onto tracing paper, transferring all markings and making sure to match the two sections of the side engine before cutting. Cut out the pattern.

5. To make the complete box car pattern, fold a sheet of tracing paper in half and trace the pattern piece on page 15 onto the paper, transferring all markings. Cut out the pattern and open it up.

6. To make the complete caboose pattern, fold a sheet of tracing paper in half. Trace the pattern piece on page 15 and the caboose top pattern piece on page 14 onto the paper, transferring all markings and making sure to match the caboose top to the caboose before cutting. Cut out the pattern and open it up.

7. To make the complete pocket pattern, trace the pattern pieces on pages 18–19 onto tracing paper, transferring all markings and making sure to match the two sections of the pocket before cutting. Cut out the pattern.

8. Trace the remaining pattern pieces on pages 14–17 onto tracing paper and cut them out.

9. From the turquoise solid, cut one engine, one engine reverse, one side engine, one side engine reverse, and one pocket.

10. From the yellow solid, cut one box car, one box car reverse, and one pocket.

11. From the red solid, cut one caboose, one caboose reverse, and one pocket.

12. From the interfacing, cut one engine, one side engine, one box car, and one caboose.

13. Fold the felt in half lengthwise and cut it in half along the fold. Following the manufacturer's directions, iron the fusible webbing onto one side of one piece of felt.

14. Remove the paper backing from the fusible webbing and iron the other piece of felt onto the fusible webbing, making sure that the raw edges of both pieces of felt align.

15. From the double layer of felt, cut the following:

- 1 smokestack
- 1 cow catcher
- 6 wheels, each 3³/₈ inches diameter
- 1 side engine roof, 2 × 5³/₄ inches
- 1 caboose roof, 1 × 6¹/₄ inches
- 2 connectors, each 1 × 2 inches

MATERIALS LIST
FABRIC REQUIREMENTS
- ¹/₂ YARD OF TURQUOISE SOLID FOR THE ENGINE AND SIDE ENGINE
- ¹/₂ YARD OF YELLOW SOLID FOR THE BOX CAR
- ¹/₂ YARD OF RED SOLID FOR THE CABOOSE
- ¹/₃ YARD OF BLACK FELT FOR THE WHEELS, SMOKE-STACK, SIDE ENGINE ROOF, COW CATCHER, CABOOSE ROOF, AND CONNECTORS
- ¹/₂ YARD OF FUSIBLE WEBBING
- ³/₄ YARD OF STIFF INTER-FACING

OTHER SUPPLIES
- SEWING THREAD TO MATCH THE FABRICS
- 9 PLASTIC OR METAL RINGS, EACH ³/₄ INCH DIAMETER
- HAND-SEWING NEEDLE
- TRACING PAPER
- CHALK PENCIL

FABRIC OPTIONS
- CANVAS
- DENIM
- HEAVYWEIGHT COTTON TWILL
- HEAVYWEIGHT POLISHED COTTON

Know & Sew

FOR PRECISION POCKET PLEATING, TRY MARKING THE PLEAT LINES WITH TWO DIFFERENT COLORS. USE A WATER-SOLUBLE FABRIC MARKER OR A CHALK PENCIL TO MARK THE FOLD LINE. THEN USE A DIFFERENT COLOR FABRIC MARKER OR CHALK PENCIL TO MARK THE MEET LINE. THIS WILL MAKE IT EASIER TO SET AND PRESS THE PLEATS.

SEWING THE CARS

1. Pin the interfacing onto the wrong side of the engine reverse.

2. Machine baste the interfacing and engine reverse together using a $1/4$-inch seam allowance.

3. With right sides together, pin the engine to the engine reverse. Sew the pieces together, leaving a 4-inch opening at the bottom for turning.

4. Clip the corners. Turn the engine right side out and press.

5. Turn under the seam allowance along the opening and press. Slip stitch the opening closed. For more information, see "Embroidery and Hand-Sewing Stitches" on page 244.

6. Repeat Steps 1 through 5 for the box car and caboose.

7. Repeat Step 1 for the side engine.

8. Referring to **Diagram 1**, with right sides together, pin the side engine to the side engine reverse. Sew the pieces together, leaving a 4-inch opening along the side for turning.

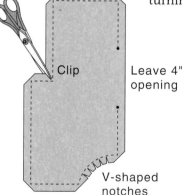

Clip

Leave 4" opening

V-shaped notches

Diagram 1

9. Referring to **Diagram 1**, clip the corners and cut several V-shaped notches in the curve.

10. Turn the side engine right side out and press.

11. Turn under the seam allowance along the opening and press. Slip stitch the opening closed.

SEWING THE POCKETS

1. With the wrong side of the turquoise pocket facing up, fold down $1^1/2$ inches from the top and press. Fold down and press $1/2$ inch along the sides and bottom of the pocket.

2. Turn the pocket over. Following the pleat markings, fold and press all four pleats in place to form two pockets, as shown in **Diagram 2**.

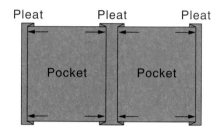

Pleat   Pleat   Pleat

Pocket   Pocket

Diagram 2

3. Pin the pocket to the engine along the placement lines. Pin the center of the pocket to the engine. Edge stitch the pocket to the engine down the center and along the sides, as shown in **Diagram 3**. For more information, see "Edge Stitching and Topstitching" on page 242.

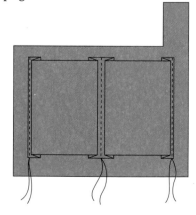

Diagram 3

4. Fold and pin the pleats in place along the bottom of the pocket.

5. Edge stitch the bottom of the pocket to secure it to the engine, as shown in **Diagram 4.**

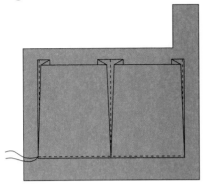

Diagram 4

6. Repeat Steps 1 through 5 to sew the corresponding pockets to the box car and to the caboose.

ASSEMBLING THE TRAIN

1. Referring to **Diagram 5**, with right sides facing up, overlap ¹/₂ inch of the engine onto the side engine. Edge stitch the pieces together.

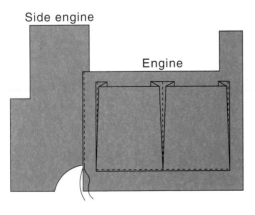

Diagram 5

2. Referring to **Diagram 6** for placement, pin the wheels to the engine, box car, and caboose. Edge stitch com-

pletely around each wheel, making sure to catch the train cars as you sew.

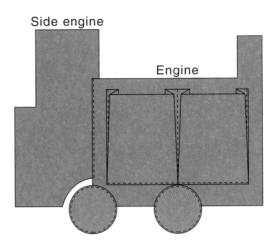

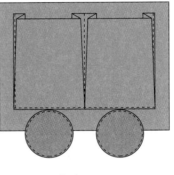

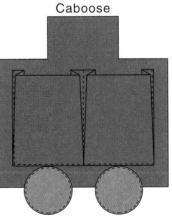

Diagram 6

3. Referring to **Diagram 7** on page 14, pin the side engine roof, smokestack, cow catcher, and caboose roof in place. Pin one connector between each set of cars, leaving a ¹/₂-inch space between each car. Edge stitch around each piece, catching the cars as you sew.

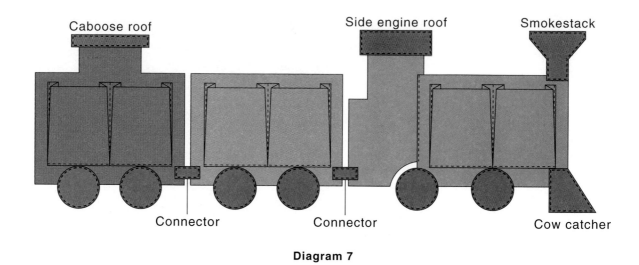

Caboose roof

Side engine roof

Smokestack

Connector

Connector

Cow catcher

Diagram 7

FINISHING THE TRAIN

Thread a hand-sewing needle with matching thread and sew one ring to the back of each car at the upper corner of each pocket. Sew one ring to the center back of the smokestack, side engine roof, and caboose roof.

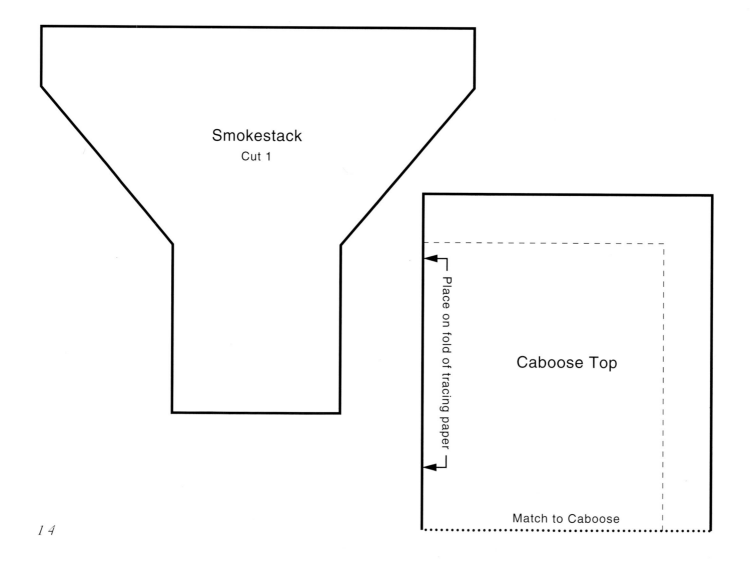

Smokestack
Cut 1

Place on fold of tracing paper

Caboose Top

Match to Caboose

Match to Caboose Top

Match to Engine Top

Place on fold of tracing paper

Pocket placement line

Engine and Engine Reverse

Cut 1 of each from fabric
Cut 1 from interfacing

Box Car and Box Car Reverse

Cut 1 of each from fabric
Cut 1 from interfacing

Caboose and Caboose Reverse

Cut 1 of each from fabric
Cut 1 from interfacing

Pocket placement line

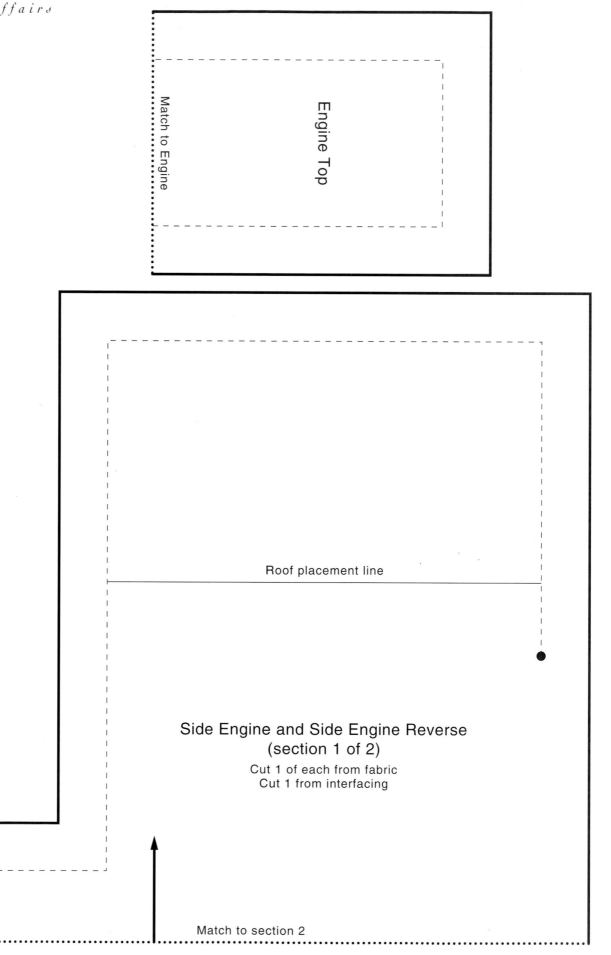

Engine Top

Match to Engine

Roof placement line

**Side Engine and Side Engine Reverse
(section 1 of 2)**

Cut 1 of each from fabric
Cut 1 from interfacing

Match to section 2

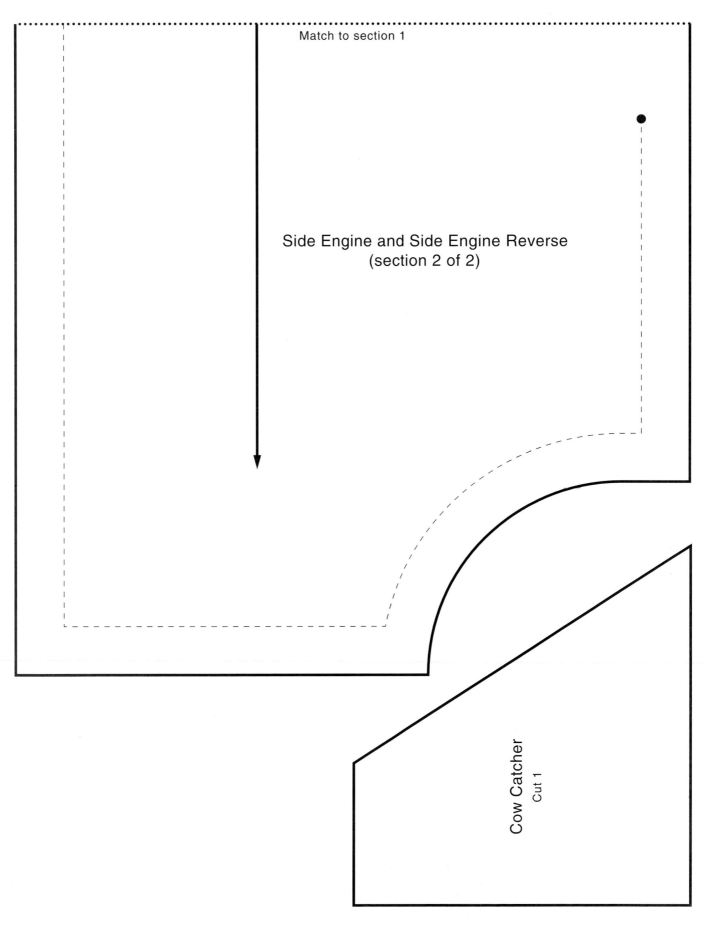

Match to section 1

Side Engine and Side Engine Reverse
(section 2 of 2)

Cow Catcher
Cut 1

Pleat

Pocket
(section 1 of 2)
Cut 1 from each fabric

Match to section 2

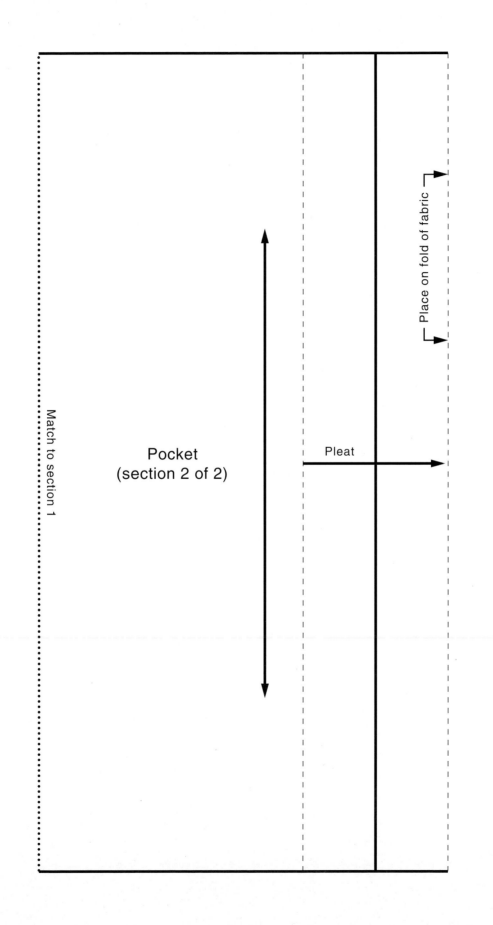

Match to section 1

Pocket
(section 2 of 2)

Pleat

Place on fold of fabric

Keepsake Box with Soft Sculpture Flowers

A soft sculpture nosegay adorns this beautiful fabric-covered keepsake box. Use colors that complement a room to create a one-of-a-kind gift for holding treasured love notes or cherished mementos.

SIZE: The finished size is approximately 7 inches long and 3 inches high.

NOTE: Measurements in the cutting directions include the seam allowances. Sew all seams with $1/2$-inch seam allowances, unless otherwise indicated.

CUTTING THE FABRIC FOR THE BOX

Note: The following formula will help you to figure out how much velour is necessary for covering any size box.

1. To find the length you need to cover the box lid, determine the height of the box lid. Then, double that measurement and add $1/2$ inch. To find the width you need, measure the circumference of the box lid and add 1 inch. For example, the height of the box lid shown in the photograph is $1/2$ inch, so the length of the velour needed is $1/2 + 1/2 + 1/2 = 1 1/2$ inches. The circumference of the box lid is 21 inches, so the width of the velour needed is $21 + 1 = 22$ inches.

2. Use the same formula in Step 1 to determine how much velour you need to cover the bottom portion of the box. For example, the height of the bottom portion of the box shown in the photograph is $2 1/2$ inches, so the length of the velour needed is $2 1/2 + 2 1/2 + 1/2 = 5 1/2$ inches. The circumference of the box is $20 1/2$ inches, so the width of the velour needed is $20 1/2 + 1 = 21 1/2$ inches.

3. If you are using a different size box, use the formula in Steps 1 and 2 to fill in the following blanks with your own measurements. From the velour, cut one ____ × ____-inch piece for the box lid. Cut one ____ × ____-inch piece for the bottom portion of the box.

4. Trace the shape of the lid four times on the velour. Cut out the pieces for lining the inside and outside of the lid and the bottom portion of the box.

CUTTING THE FLOWERS

1. Trace the pattern pieces on page 24 onto template plastic, transferring all markings. Cut out the pattern pieces. Transfer all markings onto the right side of the fabric using a chalk pencil.

2. From the medium green solid, cut one $1 1/2 × 9$-inch bias strip for the stems. Cut three leaves.

3. From the light green solid, cut three leaves.

4. From the medium peach solid, cut three buds and one flower.

5. From the light peach solid, cut three buds and one flower.

6. From the wire, cut three 4-inch lengths for the stems.

COVERING THE BOX AND LID

1. Following the manufacturer's directions, apply the Peel 'N Stick velour to the outside of the box, extending $1/4$ inch of the fabric below the box bottom and the remaining fabric above the top edge. Fold over $1/2$ inch where the velour overlaps along the side of the box for a nice, clean finish. Turn the $1/4$-inch extension to the underside of the box and finger press to smooth the raw edges flat.

2. Fold the excess fabric above the top edge to the inside of the box to form the lining, repositioning it as necessary for a smooth finish, as shown in **Diagram 1** on page 22.

MATERIALS LIST

FABRIC REQUIREMENTS

• $1/8$ YARD OF MEDIUM GREEN SOLID FOR THE LEAVES AND STEMS

• $1/8$ YARD OF LIGHT GREEN SOLID FOR THE LEAVES

• $1/8$ YARD OF MEDIUM PEACH SOLID FOR THE BUDS AND FLOWER

• $1/8$ YARD OF LIGHT PEACH SOLID FOR THE BUDS AND FLOWER

OTHER SUPPLIES

• CARDBOARD OVAL BOX, $7 × 6$ INCHES

• ROLL OF CREAM-COLORED VELOUR PEEL 'N STICK FABRIC

• CREAM-COLORED OVAL LACE DOILY, $5 × 6$ INCHES

• $1 1/2$ YARDS OF 1-INCH-WIDE CREAM-COLORED PLEATED SATIN RIBBON

• $1/4$ YARD OF $1/4$-INCH YELLOW RATTAIL CORDING

• 12-INCH LENGTH OF MEDIUM-GAUGE WIRE

• SEWING THREAD TO MATCH THE FABRICS

• HAND-SEWING NEEDLE

• TEMPLATE PLASTIC

• FINE-POINT, PERMANENT MARKER

• CHALK PENCIL

• FABRIC GLUE

FABRIC OPTIONS

• MOIRÉ

• VELVET

• VELVETEEN

• CHINTZ

• VELOUR

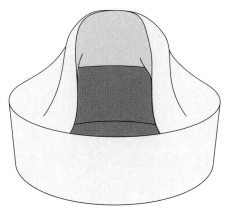

Diagram 1

3. Before removing the paper backing from the Peel 'N Stick velour, place one piece of lid-shaped velour inside the bottom of the box. If necessary, trim the edges of the velour. Remove the paper backing and apply the velour to cover the inside bottom of the box. Repeat this step to cover the outside bottom of the box.

4. Repeat Steps 1 through 3 to apply the velour to the lid.

APPLYING THE RIBBON

Use fabric glue to apply the pleated ribbon to the upper edge of the lid and the lower edge of the box bottom, making sure to cover the seams, as shown in **Diagram 2.**

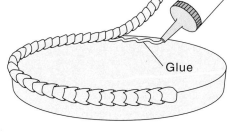

Glue

Diagram 2

SEWING THE FLOWER

1. With right sides together, pin and sew the medium peach flower and the light peach flower together, leaving one side open for turning, as shown in **Diagram 3.**

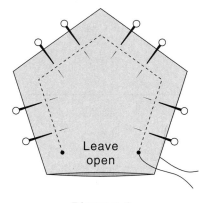

Leave open

Diagram 3

2. Clip the corners and turn the flower right side out. Turn under the seam allowance along the opening and blindstitch it closed. For information on blindstitching, see "Embroidery and Hand-Sewing Stitches" on page 244.

3. Tie several knots close together in one 5-inch length of rattail, leaving a 1-inch tail on either side, as shown in **Diagram 4.** Trim the ends of the cording close to the knots and apply a little fabric glue to prevent the ends from unraveling.

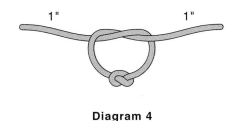

1"   1"

Diagram 4

4. Glue the knotted rattail to the center of the flower. Gather the petals around the rattail and glue them in place for a three-dimensional look, as shown in **Diagram 5.**

Diagram 5

SEWING THE LEAVES, BUDS, AND STEMS

1. With right sides together, pin and sew one medium green leaf and one light green leaf together, leaving the bottom edge open between the dots for turning. Clip the edges and turn the leaf right side out. Turn under the seam allowance along the opening and blindstitch it closed. Repeat this step for the remaining two leaves.

2. Topstitch each leaf along the indicated vein lines. For more information, see "Edge Stitching and Topstitching" on page 242.

3. Place a small amount of fabric glue on either side of the center vein of each leaf and pinch together for a three-dimensional look, as shown in **Diagram 6**.

Diagram 6

4. With right sides together, pin and sew one peach bud and one light peach bud together, leaving the bottom edge open for turning. Clip the edges and turn the bud right side out. Turn under the seam allowance along the opening and finger press. Repeat this step for the remaining two buds.

5. With right sides together, fold the bias strip in half lengthwise. Sew the long sides of the strip together, ³/₈ inch from the edge, leaving the short ends open for turning. Turn the strip right side out and press.

6. Cut the strip into thirds and insert one piece of wire into each strip. Use fabric glue to attach one bud to the end of one stem, as shown in **Diagram 7**. Repeat this step for the remaining buds and stems.

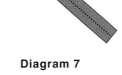

Diagram 7

FINISHING THE BOX

1. Referring to **Diagram 8**, glue the lace doily to the top of the box lid.

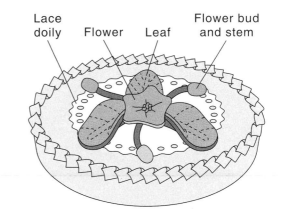

Diagram 8

2. Glue the leaves to the lace, as shown in **Diagram 8**.

3. Bend each stem into desired position and glue one between each leaf. Glue the flower to the center of the lid on top of the leaves, as shown in **Diagram 8**.

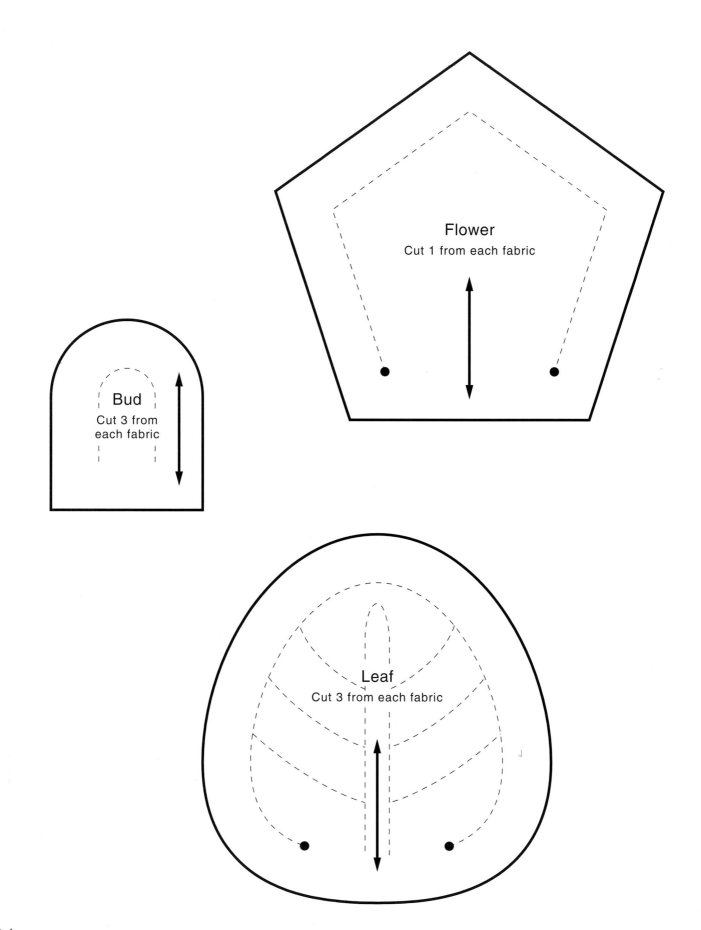

Bud
Cut 3 from
each fabric

Flower
Cut 1 from each fabric

Leaf
Cut 3 from each fabric

Beret

Hats off to a timeless classic! This beret can be worn for a dressed-down weekend of fun, or it can add a little sizzle of style to an outfit for a night on the town. Sew versatile, you'll want to make it in an array of colors.

Beret

❖

SKILL LEVEL: EASY

SIZE: The finished size is 13 inches in diameter. One size fits all.

NOTE: Measurements in the cutting directions include the seam allowances. Sew all the seams with ½-inch seam allowances.

CUTTING THE BERET

1. To make the complete rim pattern, fold a sheet of tracing paper in half and trace the pattern pieces on pages 28–29 onto the paper, making sure to match the two pattern pieces before cutting. Cut out the pattern and open it up. Mark one short end of the complete pattern for the center back and the other short end to place on the fold of the fabric.

2. From the black solid, cut one 13¾-inch-diameter circle for the crown of the beret. Place the complete rim pattern on the fold of the fabric and cut one rim.

3. From the black lining, cut one 13¾-inch-diameter circle for lining the crown. Place the complete rim pattern on the fold of the fabric and cut one rim for the lining.

SEWING THE RIM

1. With right sides together, fold the rim in half crosswise. Pin and sew the center back ends together, as shown in **Diagram 1**. Press the seam open. Repeat this step for the rim lining.

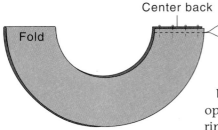

Center back / Fold

Diagram 1

2. With right sides together, pin and sew the rim lining to the rim along the inner circle, as shown in **Diagram 2**.

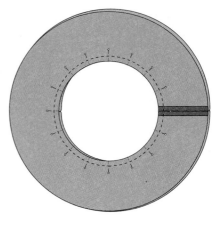

Diagram 2

3. Trim the seam allowance to ¼ inch.

4. Turn the rim right side out and press.

5. Topstitch around the inner circle ⅜ inch from the edge, leaving a 1-inch opening to insert the elastic, as shown in **Diagram 3**. For more information, see "Edge Stitching and Topstitching" on page 242.

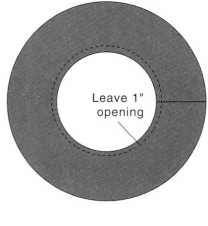

Leave 1" opening

Diagram 3

6. Insert a safety pin into one end of the elastic and weave it through the

casing on the rim. Adjust the elastic to fit the circumference of the head. Overlap and sew the ends of the elastic together, as shown in **Diagram 4.** Topstitch the opening closed.

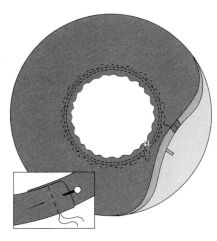

Diagram 4

SEWING THE CORDING TO THE BERET

With the right side facing up, pin and sew the cording along the edge of the crown, as shown in **Diagram 5.**

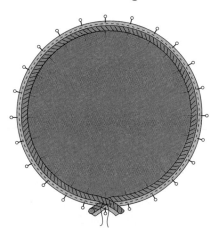

Diagram 5

SEWING THE RIM TO THE BERET

1. With right sides together, pin and sew the rim to the crown, as shown in

Diagram 6, making sure not to catch the rim lining in the seam allowance. Trim the seam allowance to ¼ inch.

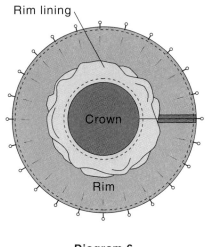

Diagram 6

2. With right sides together, pin and sew the crown lining to the rim lining, leaving a 3-inch opening for turning, as shown in **Diagram 7**. Trim the seam allowance to ¼ inch.

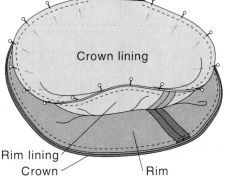

Diagram 7

FINISHING THE BERET

Turn the beret right side out. Turn under the seam allowance along the opening and whipstitch it closed. For information on whipstitching, see "Embroidery and Hand-Sewing Stitches" on page 244.

Know&Sew

TO PRESS THE WOOL BERET WHEN IT IS COMPLETE, SOAK A MAN'S COTTON HANDKERCHIEF IN WATER AND PLACE IT ON TOP OF THE BERET. WITH AN IRON ON THE DRY SETTING, PRESS THE FABRIC THROUGH THE HANDKERCHIEF UNTIL THE HANDKERCHIEF IS DRY. THIS WILL ELIMINATE SHINE AND WRINKLES ON THE BERET.

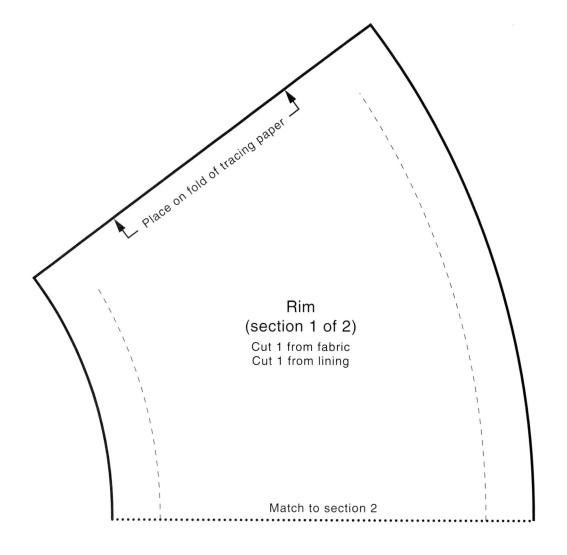

Rim
(section 1 of 2)

Cut 1 from fabric
Cut 1 from lining

Place on fold of tracing paper

Match to section 2

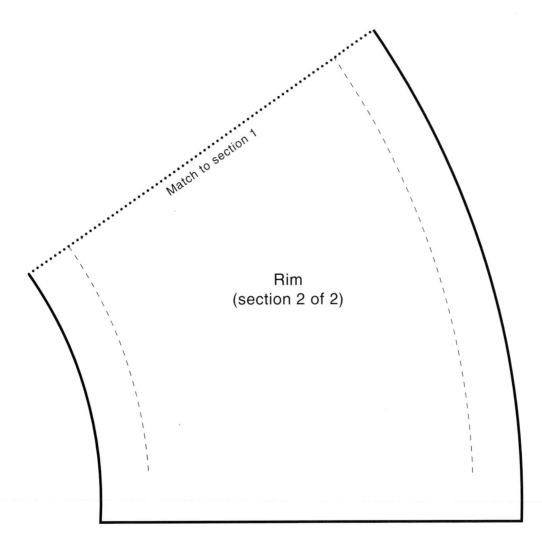

Match to section 1

Rim
(section 2 of 2)

Lace and Appliquéd Hanger Covers

Who says that hangers can't be as charming as the clothes they display? These handy hanger accessories will never go out of style, especially when they are custom-made. The lace and pearls dress up any woman's closet, while the moon and stars are a perfect accessory for a man's wardrobe.

SIZE: The covers are custom-made to fit any size hanger.

NOTE: Measurements in the cutting directions include the seam allowances. Sew all the seams with $1/2$-inch seam allowances.

CUTTING THE COVER

1. To make the cover pattern, place the plastic hanger on top of the tracing paper. Referring to **Diagram 1**, and beginning at the neck of the hanger, trace around the outside of the hanger. Remove the hanger and add $3/4$ inch around the sides and 2 inches along the bottom of the pattern. The base of the neck should be $1^1/4$ inches wide. Cut out the pattern.

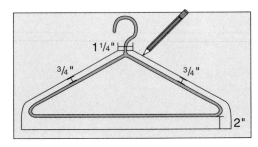

Diagram 1

2. From the peach or blue print, cut four covers. Two will be used for the outside cover and two will be used for the lining.

3. From the fusible fleece, cut four covers.

Note: If making the lace cover, go directly from here to "Sewing the Lining to the Cover." If making the appliquéd cover, follow Steps 4 through 6 here as well as the section on "Appliquéing the Stars and Moon."

4. Trace the pattern pieces on page 33 onto template plastic and cut them out.

5. Trace the templates onto the paper side of the fusible webbing and cut out the pieces.

6. Following the manufacturer's directions, iron the three stars from the webbing onto the wrong side of the yellow-orange print. Iron the moon from the webbing onto the wrong side of the white print.

APPLIQUÉING THE STARS AND MOON

1. Remove the paper backing from the fusible webbing on the three stars and the moon. Following the manufacturer's directions, iron the stars and moon to the right side of one cover, as shown in **Diagram 2**.

Diagram 2

2. Set the machine for a narrow stitch width and a short stitch length. Referring to **Diagram 2**, with matching thread, satin stitch around each star. With matching thread, satin stitch around the moon. For additional information, see "Machine Appliqué" on page 242.

SEWING THE LINING TO THE COVER

1. Following the manufacturer's directions, iron the fusible fleece onto the

wrong side of each cover piece and each lining piece.

2. With right sides together, pin and sew the two cover pieces together along the sides, as shown in **Diagram 3.** Clip the corners and trim the seam allowance to $^1/_4$ inch. Press the seams open. Repeat this step for the two lining pieces.

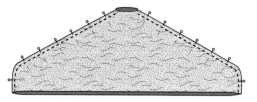

Diagram 3

3. Turn down the $^1/_2$-inch seam allowance along the edge of the neck on the cover and press, as shown in **Diagram 4.** Repeat this step for the lining.

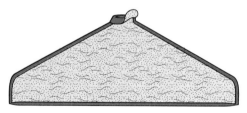

Diagram 4

4. With wrong sides together, insert the lining into the cover, as shown in **Diagram 5.**

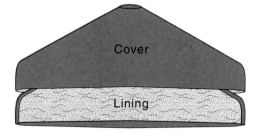

Diagram 5

5. Making sure that the neck edges are even, blindstitch the lining to the cover around the neck edge. For more information about blindstitching, see

"Embroidery and Hand-Sewing Stitches" on page 244.

6. Machine baste the lining to the cover inside the seam allowance along the bottom edge, as shown in **Diagram 6.**

Diagram 6

CUTTING THE BINDING

1. Measure around the bottom edge of the cover. For the binding, cut a lengthwise strip of fabric, $2^1/_4$ inches wide and $1^1/_4$ inches longer than the bottom edge measurement.

2. With right sides together, fold the binding in half crosswise. Pin and sew the short raw edges together, as shown in **Diagram 7.** Press the seam open.

Diagram 7

3. Turn up a $^1/_2$-inch hem along one long side of the binding and press, as shown in **Diagram 8.**

Diagram 8

4. With right sides together, pin and sew the raw edge of the binding to the bottom edge of the hanger, as shown in **Diagram 9.**

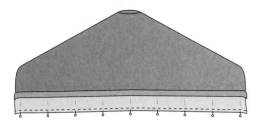

Diagram 9

5. Trim the seam allowance to $\frac{1}{4}$ inch.

FINISHING THE COVER

1. Turn the hemmed edge of the binding to the inside of the cover and pin it to the lining.

2. Thread a hand-sewing needle with matching thread and blindstitch the binding to the lining.

TRIMMING THE LACE COVER

1. Cut out several floral motifs from the lace and arrange them on one side of the cover.

2. Referring to the photograph on page 30, thread a hand-sewing needle with matching thread and hand sew the lace motifs in place.

3. Randomly sew the pearls on top of the lace.

4. Insert a hanger into the cover.

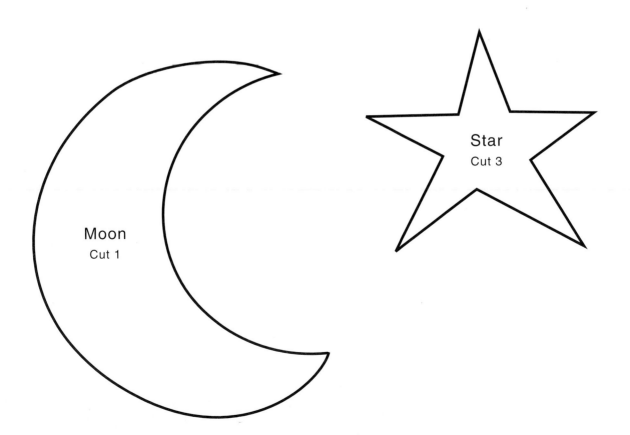

Moon
Cut 1

Star
Cut 3

Bow Tie and Cummerbund

What can you make for the man in your life? Start with a printed fabric and whip up this bow tie and matching cummerbund for a New Year's Eve formal or a special celebration out on the town!

Bow Tie

SKILL LEVEL: *EASY*

SIZE: The bow tie can be custom-made to fit a neck size of up to 17 inches.

NOTE: Measurements in the cutting directions include the seam allowances. Sew all the seams with ¹/₂-inch seam allowances.

CUTTING THE TIE

1. From the geometric print, cut one 5 × 6-inch rectangle for the small bow. Cut one 6 × 7-inch rectangle for the large bow. Cut one 2 × 4-inch rectangle for the knot. Cut one 3 × 20-inch strip for the neckband.

2. From the interfacing, cut one 2¹/₂ × 4-inch rectangle for the small bow. Cut one 3 × 5-inch rectangle for the large bow. Cut one 1 × 4-inch rectangle for the knot.

FUSING THE TIE

1. Following the manufacturer's directions, iron the 2¹/₂ × 4-inch piece of interfacing onto the lower half of the wrong side of the small bow, as shown in **Diagram 1**.

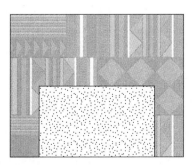

Diagram 1

2. Repeat Step 1 for the large bow and the knot and their corresponding pieces of interfacing.

SEWING THE TIE

1. With right sides together, fold and pin the small bow in half lengthwise, as shown in **Diagram 2**.

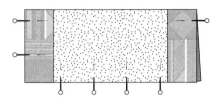

Diagram 2

2. Sew the edges of the small bow together, leaving a 2-inch opening along the bottom edge, as shown in **Diagram 3**. Clip the corners and trim the seam allowance to ¹/₄ inch. Turn the small bow right side out and press. Turn under the seam allowance along the opening and blindstitch it closed. For information on blind-stitching, see "Embroidery and Hand-Sewing Stitches" on page 244.

3. Repeat Steps 1 and 2 for the large bow.

4. With right sides together, fold and pin the neckband in half lengthwise. Sew the raw edges together, leaving one short side open for turning, as shown in **Diagram 4** on page 36. Clip the corners and trim the seam allowance to ¹/₄ inch. Turn the neckband right side out and press. Turn under the seam allow-ance along the opening and blindstitch it closed. Repeat this step for the knot.

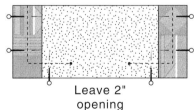

Leave 2" opening

Diagram 3

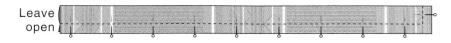

Leave open

Diagram 4

ASSEMBLING THE TIE

1. Referring to **Diagram 5**, place the large bow on top of the neckband so that the right side of the neckband is $7^1/_2$ inches long and the left side of the neckband is $5^1/_2$ inches long. Center the large bow on the neckband.

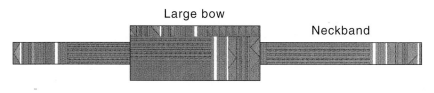

Large bow

Neckband

Diagram 5

2. Center the small bow on top of the large bow. Pin both bows to the neckband. Referring to **Diagram 6**, and starting at the top of the large bow, sew a straight line down the center of the bow, catching the small bow and neckband as you stitch.

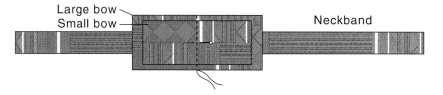

Large bow
Small bow

Neckband

Diagram 6

3. Center the knot over the bow stitching line. Wrap each end of the knot tightly over the bows, carefully

scrunching the bows together, as shown in **Diagram 7.**

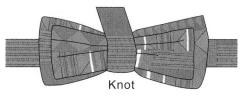

Knot

Diagram 7

4. Turn the neckband over. Overlap the ends of the knot tightly and whipstitch them in place, as shown in **Diagram 8.** For information on whipstitching, see "Embroidery and Hand-Sewing Stitches" on page 244.

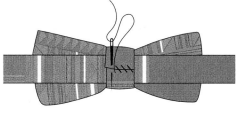

Diagram 8

FINISHING THE TIE

Note: The exact placement of each half of the Velcro coin on the neckband will depend on the neck measurement of the wearer. If possible, baste each half of the coin onto the ends of the neckband and try it on to see if the placement is correct before sewing.

Referring to **Diagram 9**, sew the loop half of the Velcro coin onto the front side of the long end of the neckband. Sew the hook half of the Velcro coin to the back side of the short end of the neckband.

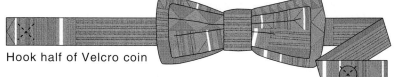

Hook half of Velcro coin

Loop half of Velcro coin

Diagram 9

Cummerbund

SKILL LEVEL: *INTERMEDIATE*

SIZE: The cummerbund can be custom-made to fit any size waist up to 50 inches.

NOTE: Measurements in the cutting directions include the seam allowances. Sew all the seams with $1/2$-inch seam allowances.

CUTTING THE CUMMERBUND

1. Use these equations to determine the measurements for the cummerbund front, front facing, back, and interfacing. Then fill in the blanks in Steps 2 through 4.
- for the front and front facing:
  waist size ÷ 2 + 8 = ____
- for the back:
  waist size ÷ 2 - 4 = ____
- for the front and front-facing interfacing:
  waist size ÷ 2 + 7 = ____
- for the back interfacing:
  waist size ÷ 2 - 5 = ____

2. From the geometric print, cut one 12 ×____-inch rectangle for the cummerbund front. Cut one 6 ×____-inch rectangle for the cummerbund front facing.

3. From the geometric print, cut two 6 ×____-inch rectangles for the cummerbund back pieces.

4. From the fusible interfacing, cut two 5 × ____-inch rectangles, one for the cummerbund front and one for the cummerbund front facing. Cut two 5 × ____-inch rectangles for the cummerbund back pieces.

5. Trace the cummerbund template on page 39 onto template plastic with a fine-point, permanent marker.

6. Cut out the template and set it aside for now.

FUSING THE CUMMERBUND

1. Following the manufacturer's directions, iron the fusible interfacing for the cummerbund front facing onto the wrong side of the cummerbund front facing and inside the seam allowance.

2. Iron the interfacing for each cummerbund back piece onto the wrong side of each cummerbund back piece and inside the seam allowance.

FOLDING THE FRONT

1. With straight pins, mark both edges of the wrong side of the cummerbund front according to the measurements shown in **Diagram 10**. Using a yardstick and a chalk pencil, draw a line between each set of straight pins. Do not remove the pins.

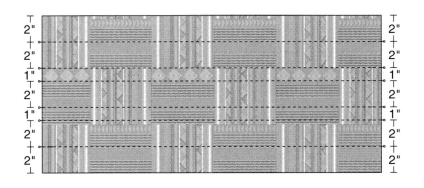

Diagram 10

2. Referring to **Diagram 11** on page 38, and starting at the bottom edge, fold the fabric upward and iron a crease along the first line. Remove the pair of pins that marked this line. Then iron a crease along every other line, removing the pair of pins that mark each crease line. When finished, three sets of pins will have been removed, and three sets of pins will remain to mark the pleat lines. Turn the cummerbund front to the right side. There should be a total of three crease lines.

MATERIALS LIST FOR THE CUMMERBUND

FABRIC REQUIREMENTS
- 1 YARD OF GEOMETRIC PRINT (ENOUGH FOR A 50-INCH WAIST)
- 1 YARD OF HEAVYWEIGHT FUSIBLE INTERFACING

OTHER SUPPLIES
- 5-INCH VELCRO STRIP TO MATCH THE FABRIC
- SEWING THREAD TO MATCH THE FABRIC
- HAND-SEWING NEEDLE
- YARDSTICK
- TEMPLATE PLASTIC
- FINE-POINT, PERMANENT MARKER
- CHALK PENCIL

FABRIC OPTIONS
- COTTON
- LINEN
- SATIN

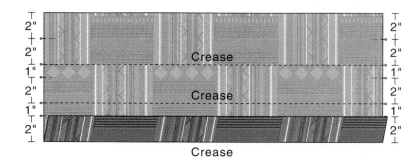

Diagram 11

3. To create the first pleat, bring the first crease line up to the first set of pins. Pin the pleat in place, as shown in **Diagram 12.** Repeat this step with the remaining two crease lines. When pinning is complete, there should be three pleats on the cummerbund front. Press them well and remove all of the remaining pins.

Diagram 12

4. Following the manufacturer's directions, iron the interfacing for the cummerbund front onto the wrong side of the cummerbund front and inside the seam allowance.

SEWING THE CUMMERBUND

1. With right sides together, fold and pin one cummerbund back piece in half lengthwise, matching the raw edges. Sew the raw edges together,

leaving one short side open for turning, as shown in **Diagram 13.** Repeat this step for the remaining back piece.

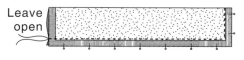

Diagram 13

2. Referring to **Diagram 14,** and measuring from the open end, cut 4 inches of fabric off the length of one back piece.

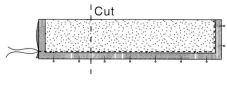

Diagram 14

3. Clip the corners and trim the seam allowance to $1/4$ inch. Turn the cummerbund back piece right side out and press. Turn under the seam allowance along the opening and blindstitch it closed. For information on blindstitching, see "Embroidery and Hand-Sewing Stitches" on page 244. Repeat this step for the remaining back piece.

ASSEMBLING THE CUMMERBUND

1. With right sides together, center and pin the long cummerbund back piece to the right side edge of the cummerbund front, as shown in **Diagram 15.** Make sure the pleats are facing down. Sew the back piece in place. Repeat this step to sew the short cummerbund back piece to the left side edge of the cummerbund front.

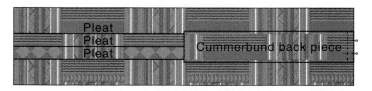

Diagram 15

2. Turn the cummerbund front piece to the wrong side so that the interfacing is facing up. Referring to **Diagram 16**, trace the cummerbund template onto each corner of the interfacing.

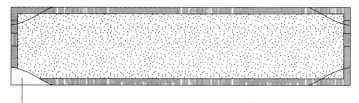

Template

Diagram 16

3. With right sides together, pin the cummerbund front to the cummerbund front facing, making sure not to catch the cummerbund back pieces in the seam allowances.

4. Referring to **Diagram 17**, sew the pieces together by following the ¹/₂-inch seam allowance and the lines created by the template, leaving a 6-inch opening at the bottom center for turning. Clip the curves and trim the seam allowance to ¹/₄ inch. Turn the cummerbund right side out and press.

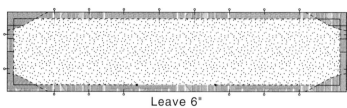

Leave 6"
opening

Diagram 17

FINISHING THE CUMMERBUND

1. Referring to **Diagram 18**, center and pin the loop half of the Velcro strip onto the front side of the long cummerbund back piece, 1 inch from the end. Sew it in place.

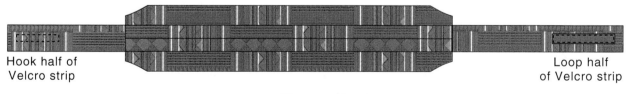

Hook half of
Velcro strip

Loop half
of Velcro strip

Diagram 18

2. Center and pin the hook half of the Velcro strip to the back side of the short cummerbund back piece, ¹/₂ inch from the end. Sew it in place.

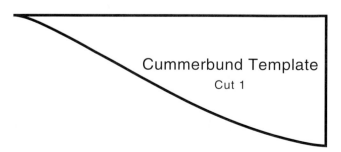

Cummerbund Template
Cut 1

Sachet Bridal Pillow

*Sew a wedding gift that newlyweds will treasure happily ever after.
Use new lace or the remnants of a treasured wedding gown and fill this Sachet
Bridal Pillow with rosebuds. The scent will drift down the aisle as
the wedding bands are carried to the altar.*

SIZE: The finished size is 11 inches square.

NOTE: Measurements in the cutting directions include the seam allowances. Sew all the seams with $1/2$-inch seam allowances.

CUTTING THE PILLOW

1. Referring to **Diagram 1**, with the right side facing up, cut off the scalloped edges of the fabric $3^1/2$ inches from the top and bottom. These two strips will be used for the ruffle.

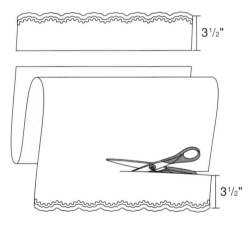

$3^1/2$"

$3^1/2$"

Diagram 1

2. From the remaining fabric, cut one $6^1/2$-inch square for the pillow front. Cut two $6 \times 6^1/2$-inch rectangles for the pillow backs.

SEWING THE RUFFLE

1. With right sides together, pin the ruffle strips together along the short ends and sew them together, as shown in **Diagram 2**.

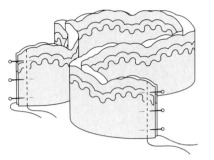

Diagram 2

2. Finish the raw edges with a zigzag stitch, as shown in **Diagram 3**. Press the seams to one side.

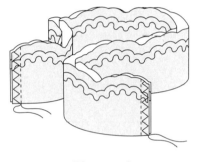

Diagram 3

3. To make one row of gathering stitches, use the longest machine stitch and sew $1/4$ inch from the unfinished edge of the ruffle, as shown in **Diagram 4**.

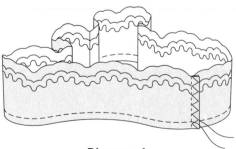

Diagram 4

4. Pull up the bobbin thread and evenly gather the ruffle to fit around the pillow front. Secure the ends of the threads with a knot.

MATERIALS LIST

FABRIC REQUIREMENT
- $1/2$ YARD OF WHITE BEADED LACE WITH SCALLOPED EDGES

OTHER SUPPLIES
- SEWING THREAD TO MATCH THE FABRIC

FABRIC OPTIONS
- BEADED LACE
- REMNANT OF A WEDDING GOWN
- SATIN
- MOIRÉ
- TAFFETA

SEWING THE RUFFLE TO THE FRONT

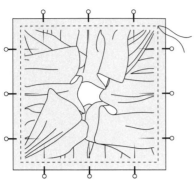

Diagram 5

With right sides together, pin the ruffle to the pillow front, making sure the raw edges are even. Sew the ruffle to the pillow front, as shown in **Diagram 5.**

HEMMING THE BACKS

1. Turn under and pin a $1\frac{1}{2}$-inch hem along one 6-inch side of one pillow back.

2. Topstitch the hem in place $1\frac{1}{4}$ inches from the edge, as shown in **Diagram 6.** For more information, see "Edge Stitching and Topstitching" on page 242.

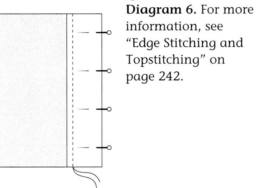

Diagram 6

3. Repeat Steps 1 and 2 to hem the remaining pillow back.

ASSEMBLING THE PILLOW

1. With the right side of the pillow front facing up, fold the ruffle toward the center of the pillow front.

2. Referring to **Diagram 7,** with right sides facing, pin the pillow backs to the pillow front, matching the raw edges and making sure the pillow backs overlap in the center.

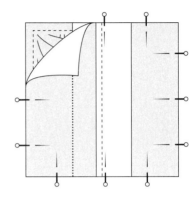

Diagram 7

3. Sew the pillow backs to the pillow front, making sure not to catch the ruffle in the seam.

4. Clip the corners and trim the seam allowance to $\frac{1}{4}$ inch.

5. Turn the pillow right side out.

FINISHING THE PILLOW

Fill the sachet bridal pillow with rosebuds or your favorite potpourri.

Golf Club Covers

*Your favorite golf enthusiast will be off to a roaring start with
a set of Numbered and Lucky the Lion Golf Club Covers. Both practical and
fun, they'll protect the most prized golf clubs and show other
golfers who's king of the course.*

Golf Club Covers

❖

Numbered Golf Club Covers

SKILL LEVEL: EASY

SIZE: The finished size is 5 inches wide and 11 inches high.

NOTE: Measurements in the cutting directions include the seam allowances. Sew all seams with $^1/_2$-inch seam allowances, unless otherwise indicated.

CUTTING THE COVERS

Note: To save time, cut and sew all of the covers at the same time.

1. Trace the pattern pieces on page 48 onto tracing paper, making sure to match the two sections before cutting. Cut out the pattern.

2. From the brown solid, cut six covers. Three will be used for the cover fronts and three for the cover backs.

3. From the brown solid, cut three 3 × 27-inch strips for the cover sides.

4. From the prequilted fabric, cut six covers for lining the cover fronts and cover backs.

5. From the prequilted fabric, cut three 3 × 27-inch strips for lining the cover sides.

6. Using a chalk pencil, transfer one number from the number patterns on page 49 onto the right side of each of the three cover fronts. Do not transfer the number placement box.

LINING THE COVERS

1. With wrong sides together, pin one lining cover to one cover front, as shown in **Diagram 1**. Machine baste these pieces together using a $^1/_4$-inch seam allowance. Repeat this step to sew the remaining lining covers to the remaining cover fronts and cover backs.

Diagram 1

2. With wrong sides together, pin one lining side to one cover side. Machine baste these pieces together using a $^1/_4$-inch seam allowance. Repeat this step to sew the remaining lining sides to the remaining cover sides.

SATIN STITCHING THE NUMBERS

1. Thread the sewing machine with dark brown thread. Set the machine for a wide zigzag stitch and a short stitch length.

2. Satin stitch the number 1 on the right side of one cover front, as shown in **Diagram 2**. Satin stitch the numbers 3 and 5 onto the remaining cover fronts.

Diagram 2

SEWING THE COVERS TOGETHER

1. With right sides together, pin and sew one cover side to one cover front. Clip several V-shaped notches into the seam allowance, as shown in **Diagram 3**. Repeat this step for the remaining cover sides and cover fronts.

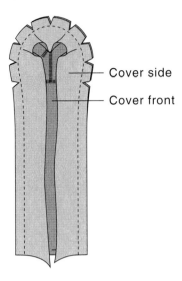

Cover side

Cover front

Diagram 3

2. Repeat Step 1 to sew the cover sides to the cover backs.

FINISHING THE COVERS

Turn up a 1½-inch hem along the unfinished bottom edge and blindstitch it in place. For information on blindstitching, see "Embroidery and Hand-Sewing Stitches" on page 244. Turn the cover right side out. Repeat this step to finish the remaining covers.

Lucky the Lion Golf Club Cover

SKILL LEVEL: *ADVANCED*

SIZE: The finished size is 5 inches wide and 12 inches high.

NOTE: Measurements in the cutting directions include the seam allowances. Sew all seams with ½-inch seam allowances, unless otherwise indicated. Transfer all the dart markings to the wrong side of the fabric using a chalk pencil. Transfer all other markings to the right side of the fabric using a chalk pencil.

CUTTING THE LION

1. Trace the pattern pieces on pages 49–53 onto tracing paper, making sure to match the two sections of the front shaft before cutting. Transfer all the markings and cut out the pattern pieces.

2. From the brown solid, cut four ears.

3. From both the brown solid and prequilted fabric, cut the following:
- 1 center face
- 1 side face and 1 side face reverse
- 1 center snout
- 1 side snout and 1 side snout reverse
- 1 front shaft
- 1 back shaft

4. From the synthetic fur, cut one center head, one side head, and one side head reverse.

5. From the black felt, cut 1 nose.

SEWING THE LINING

1. Sew the dart on the brown side snout and the side snout reverse. Sew the dart on the lining side snout and the side snout reverse.

Know&Sew

TO REMOVE WRINKLES OR CREASES FROM SYNTHETIC SUEDE, AVOID PRESSING ON THE RIGHT SIDE OF THE FABRIC BECAUSE IT MIGHT RUIN THE NAP. PRESS ON THE WRONG SIDE USING A PRESS CLOTH AND AN IRON ON THE SYNTHETIC SETTING. OR, FOR EXTRA PROTECTION AGAINST FLATTENING THE NAP, PRESS SYNTHETIC SUEDE FACE DOWN ON ANOTHER PIECE OF SYNTHETIC SUEDE. IF THE FABRIC BECOMES FLATTENED ACCIDENTALLY, YOU CAN BRUSH IT WITH A TOOTHBRUSH OR A TERRY CLOTH TOWEL TO RESTORE THE NAP.

2. With wrong sides together, pin all the lining pieces to the corresponding brown pieces. Using a ¼-inch seam allowance, machine baste the lining pieces and brown pieces together.

SEWING THE FACE

1. With right sides together, pin and sew the side snout to the center snout, as shown in **Diagram 4.** Clip several V-shaped notches in the seam allowance so that it will curve properly when turned. To complete the snout, pin and sew the side snout reverse to the other side of the center snout.

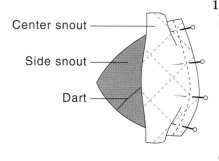

Center snout

Side snout

Dart

Diagram 4

2. With right sides together, pin the side face to the center face, as shown in **Diagram 5.** Sew the pieces together and press the seam open. To complete the face, pin and sew the side face reverse to the other side of the center face and press the seam open.

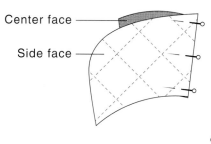

Center face

Side face

Diagram 5

3. With right sides together, pin the completed face to the completed snout, as shown in **Diagram 6.** Sew the pieces together. Clip several V-shaped notches into the seam allowance and turn the unit right side out.

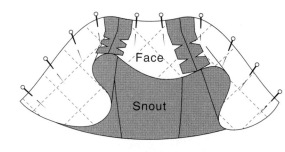

Face

Snout

Diagram 6

4. Following the manufacturer's directions, attach the eyes to the face. Set this unit aside.

SEWING THE EARS

1. With right sides together, pin and sew two ears together, leaving the bottom edge open. Trim the seam allowance to ¼ inch. Turn the ear right side out and press. Repeat this step to sew the remaining ear.

2. Fold in the sides of one ear so they meet at the center, as shown in **Diagram 7.** Machine baste the folds in place along the bottom edge with a ¼-inch seam allowance. Repeat this step for the other ear.

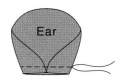

Ear

Diagram 7

SEWING THE EARS TO THE HEAD

1. Cut open the dart on the side head and the side head reverse along the cutting line.

2. Pin one ear into the dart seam of the side head, as shown in **Diagram 8.** Sew the ear into the dart seam along the stitching line. Repeat this step for the other ear and the side head reverse.

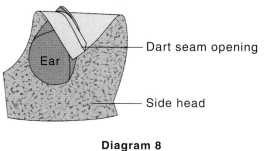

Dart seam opening

Ear

Side head

Diagram 8

SEWING THE HEAD

1. With right sides together, pin the center head to the side head. Sew the pieces together. Clip several V-shaped notches in the seam allowance along the curve, as shown in **Diagram 9,** and press the seams open.

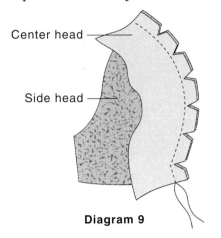

Diagram 9

2. To complete the head, pin and sew the side head reverse to other side of the center head.

SEWING THE FACE AND HEAD TOGETHER

1. With right sides together, pin the face to the head. Sew the pieces together, making sure not to catch the ears in the seam allowance. Clip several V-shaped notches into the seam allowance along the curve, as shown in **Diagram 10.**

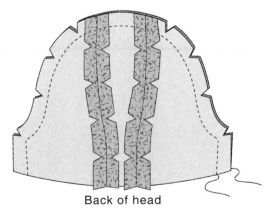

Back of head

Diagram 10

2. With right sides together, pin one short side of the back shaft to the bottom

of the back of the head. Sew the pieces together, as shown in **Diagram 11.**

Back shaft

Diagram 11

3. With right sides together, pin the front shaft to the back shaft and bottom of the face. Sew the pieces together. Trim the seam allowance to ¼ inch. Clip several V-shaped notches into the seam allowance along the curve, as shown in **Diagram 12.**

Front shaft

Diagram 12

FINISHING THE LION

1. Turn up a 1½-inch hem along the unfinished bottom edge and blindstitch it in place. For information on blindstitching, see "Embroidery and Hand-Sewing Stitches" on page 244.

2. Turn the lion right side out. Refer to the photograph on page 43 for placement of the nose and glue it to the snout.

Know&Sew

BECAUSE SYNTHETIC FURS ARE BULKY, IT'S HELPFUL TO BRUSH THE PILE AWAY FROM THE RAW EDGES TO MAKE IT EASIER TO HANDLE WHEN YOU SEW SEAMS. SET YOUR MACHINE AT A STITCH LENGTH OF 10 TO 12 STITCHES PER INCH FOR SEWING THE CENTER AND SIDE HEAD PIECES TOGETHER, AS WELL AS FOR SEWING THE FACE AND HEAD TOGETHER.

Numbered Golf Club Cover
(section 1 of 2)
Cut 6 from fabric
Cut 6 from lining

Match to section 2

Number
placement

Numbered Golf Club Cover
(section 2 of 2)

Match to section 1

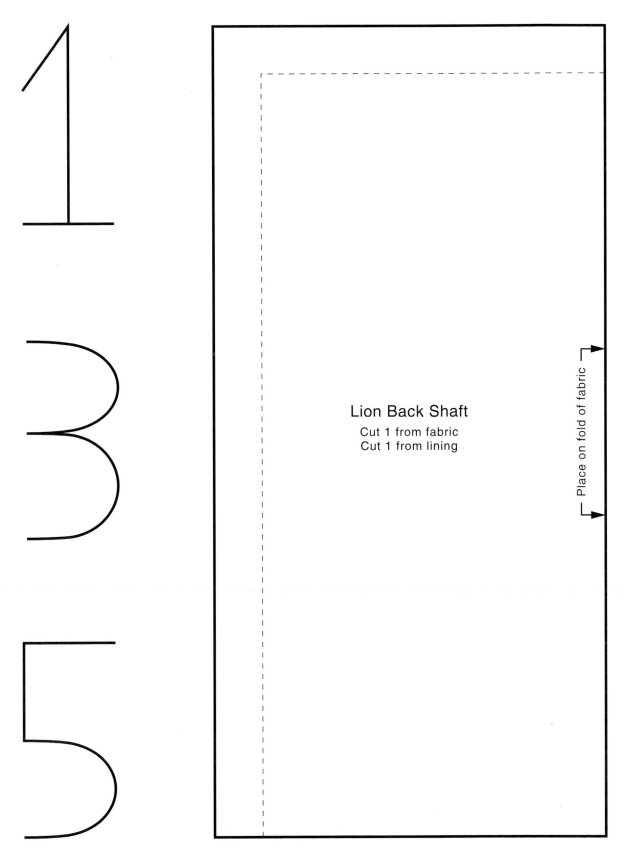

Lion Back Shaft

Cut 1 from fabric
Cut 1 from lining

Place on fold of fabric

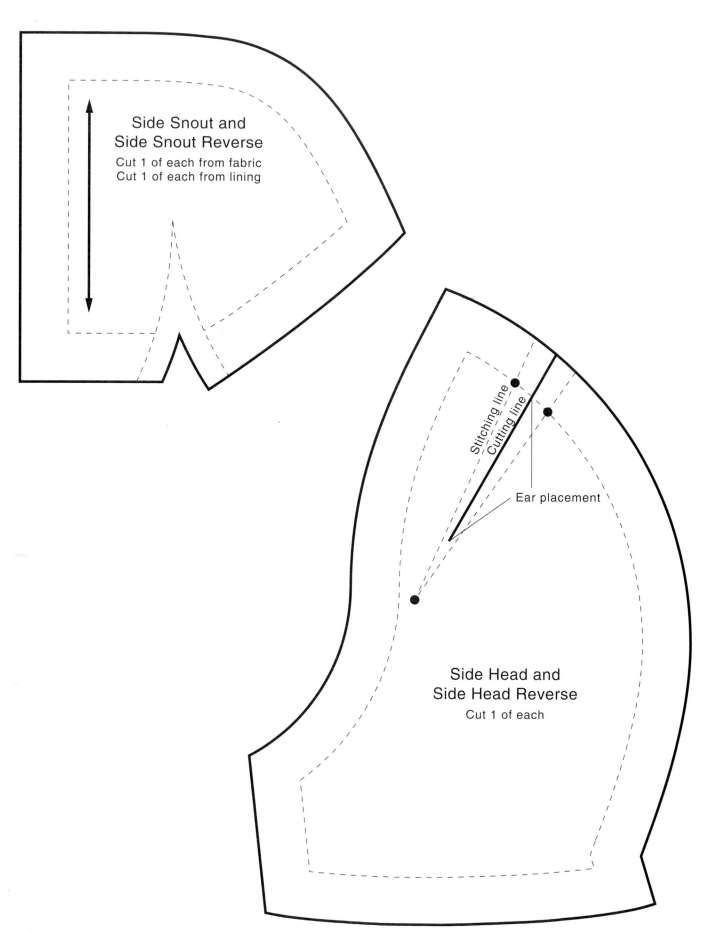

Side Snout and
Side Snout Reverse

Cut 1 of each from fabric
Cut 1 of each from lining

Stitching line

Cutting line

Ear placement

Side Head and
Side Head Reverse

Cut 1 of each

Lion Front Shaft
(section 1 of 2)

Cut 1 from fabric
Cut 1 from lining

Match to section 2

Match to section 1

Lion Front Shaft
(section 2 of 2)

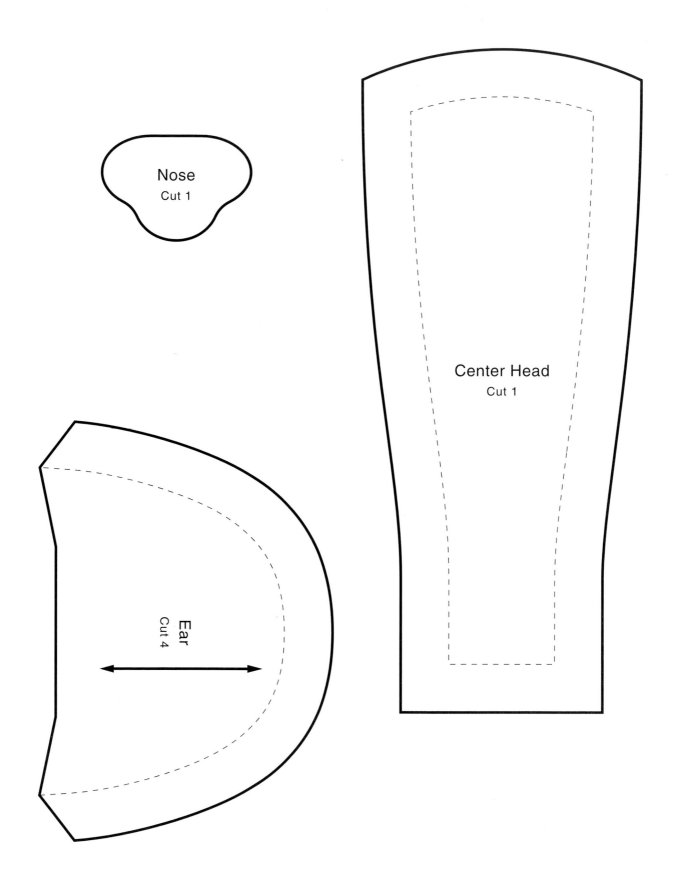

Nose
Cut 1

Center Head
Cut 1

Ear
Cut 4

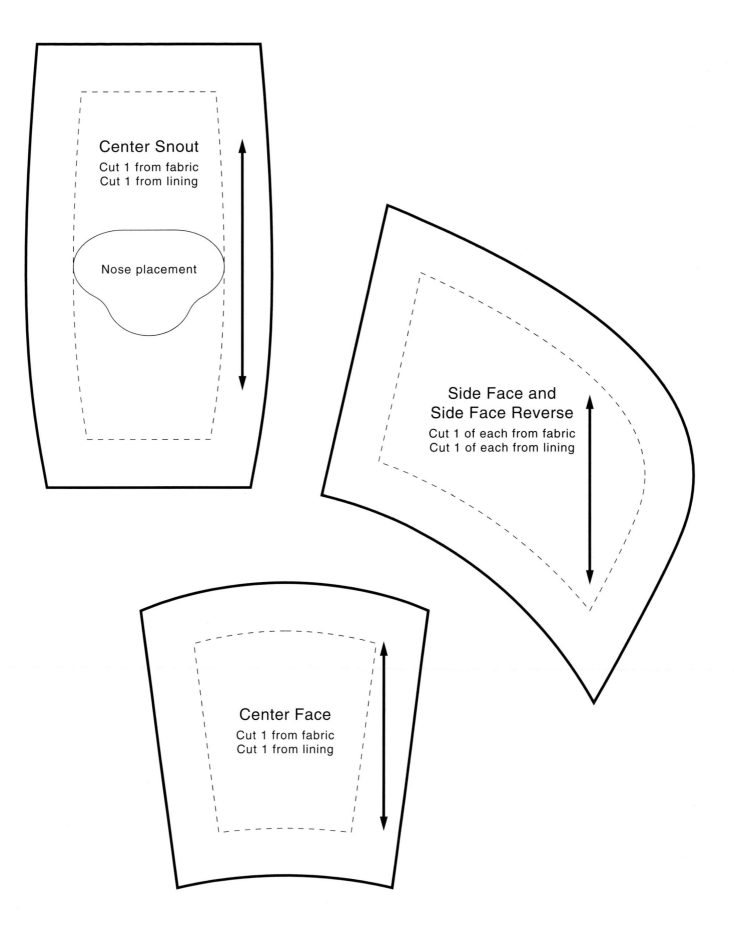

Center Snout

Cut 1 from fabric
Cut 1 from lining

Nose placement

Side Face and
Side Face Reverse

Cut 1 of each from fabric
Cut 1 of each from lining

Center Face

Cut 1 from fabric
Cut 1 from lining

Golf Tee Bag

Lucky the Lion Golf Club Cover wouldn't be complete without a matching golf tee bag. Ideal for keeping extra tees on hand, this soft pouch with drawstring tie can be easily attached to the outside of a golf bag.

SIZE: The finished size is 6$\frac{1}{2}$ inches wide and 7$\frac{1}{2}$ inches high.

NOTE: Measurements in the cutting directions include the seam allowances. Sew all the seams with $\frac{1}{2}$-inch seam allowances.

CUTTING THE BAG

From the brown solid, cut one 9$\frac{1}{2}$ × 14-inch rectangle for the bag.

SEWING THE BAG

1. With right sides together, fold the bag in half crosswise and pin.

2. Referring to **Diagram 1**, sew along the bottom of the bag. Pivot and turn the corner, then sew to within 2$\frac{1}{2}$ inches of the top of the bag. Backstitch and stop.

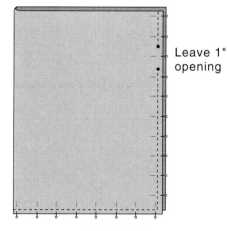

Leave 1" opening

Diagram 1

3. Referring to **Diagram 1**, finish the side seam by sewing 1$\frac{1}{2}$ inches down from the top of the bag, leaving a 1-inch opening. Backstitch and stop.

4. Clip the bottom corners and press the side seam open.

5. To form the drawstring casing, fold down 1$\frac{1}{2}$ inches from the top of the bag, as shown in **Diagram 2**. Sew the casing closed 1 inch from the top edge. Turn the bag right side out.

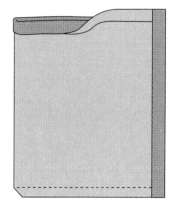

Diagram 2

FINISHING THE BAG

1. Knot one end of the cording and insert a safety pin through the knot.

2. Insert the safety pin into the opening at the side seam and thread it through the casing, as shown in **Diagram 3**.

3. Remove the safety pin. Knot the remaining end of the cording. Pull the cording tightly to close the bag.

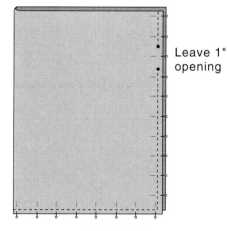

Diagram 3

MATERIALS LIST

FABRIC REQUIREMENT
• 11 × 15-INCH REC-TANGLE OF BROWN SOLID FOR THE BAG

OTHER SUPPLIES
• $\frac{3}{4}$ YARD OF BROWN CORDING
• SEWING THREAD TO MATCH THE FABRIC
• SAFETY PIN

FABRIC OPTIONS
• ULTRASUEDE
• WOOL FLANNEL

INSTANT
INTERIORS

Sunflower Tea Cozy

Brighten any breakfast with a burst of sunflower fun! For a lifelike look, this three-dimensional tea cozy has a textured center of coiled fringe and petals that hold their shape with floral wire. A snap to sew, it will create such a stir that sipping tea may never be the same again.

SIZE: The finished size is 11½ inches high and 13 inches wide.

NOTE: Measurements in the cutting directions include the seam allowances. Sew all the seams with ¼-inch seam allowances. Transfer all markings to the right side of the fabric with a chalk pencil.

CUTTING THE TEA COZY

1. Trace the pattern pieces on pages 62–64 onto tracing paper, making sure to match the two sections of the tea cozy before cutting. Transfer all markings and cut out the pattern pieces.

2. From the green solid, cut two tea cozies. One will be used for the front and one will be used for the back.

3. From the prequilted fabric, cut two tea cozies for the lining.

4. From the brown solid, cut one flower center.

5. From the bright yellow solid, cut 64 petals. To do this, fold the fabric in half so that the right sides are facing. Fold it in half again so that the wrong sides are now facing. There will be 4 layers of fabric. Trace 16 petals onto the fabric. Place one or two straight pins in each petal, penetrating all 4 layers so that the fabric does not shift when cutting. When you cut, you will have 64 petals.

6. From the fusible interfacing, cut 32 petals. To do this, repeat Step 5 and trace 8 petals onto the interfacing. When you cut, you will have 32 petals.

7. From the floral wire, cut 32 pieces, each 4¾ inches long.

MAKING THE PETALS

Note: To save time, make all the petals at the same time.

1. With wrong sides facing up, place 32 yellow petals on an ironing board.

2. Center one piece of floral wire lengthwise on each petal.

3. Following the manufacturer's directions, with the fusible side facing down, iron one interfacing petal onto each yellow petal, keeping the wire as straight as possible, as shown in **Diagram 1**.

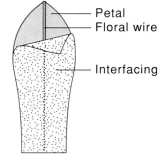

Petal
Floral wire
Interfacing

Diagram 1

4. With right sides together, pin the remaining 32 petals to the wired-and-fused petals. Leaving the bottom edge open, sew each petal together using a ¼-inch seam allowance, as shown in **Diagram 2**. Turn the petals right side out and press.

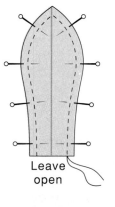

Leave open

Diagram 2

ASSEMBLING THE SUNFLOWER

1. With wrong sides together, pin the tea cozy front to one piece of lining, as shown in **Diagram 3.** Machine baste these pieces together with a $1/4$-inch seam allowance, making sure to leave the bottom, straight edge open.

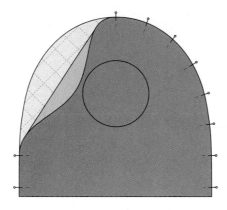

Diagram 3

2. Pin 16 petals evenly around the center circle on the tea cozy front, making sure that the open end of each petal is $1/4$ inch inside the circle, as shown in **Diagram 4.** This will form the first layer of petals.

Diagram 4

3. Sew the petals to the tea cozy front, stitching $1/4$ inch from the open edge of each petal.

4. Referring to **Diagram 5,** make the second layer of petals by staggering

and pinning the remaining 16 petals on top of the first layer.

Diagram 5

5. Repeat Step 3 to sew these petals to the tea cozy front.

6. With the right side facing up, pin the flower center to the tea cozy front, making sure the raw edges of the petals are covered by the flower center, as shown in **Diagram 6.**

Diagram 6

7. Sew the edge of the flower center to the tea cozy front using a medium-width zigzag stitch.

8. Beginning at the middle of the flower center, and using a small whip-stitch, sew the fringe to the flower center following the spiral placement marking, as shown in **Diagram 7.** For information on whipstitching, see

"Embroidery and Hand-Sewing Stitches" on page 244.

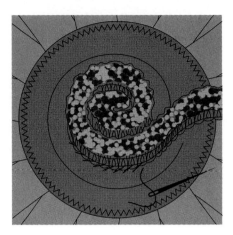

Diagram 7

ASSEMBLING THE TEA COZY

1. With wrong sides together, pin the tea cozy back to the remaining piece of lining. Machine baste these pieces together with a $1/4$-inch seam allowance, making sure to leave the bottom, straight edge open.

2. Gently fold each of the petals toward the center of the flower on the tea cozy front.

3. With right sides together, pin and sew the tea cozy back to the front, leaving the bottom, straight edge open, as shown in **Diagram 8.**

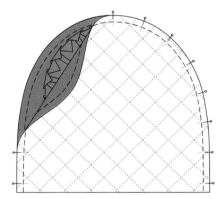

Leave open

Diagram 8

4. Finish the bottom edge of the tea cozy with a medium-width zigzag stitch. Make sure to sew close to the raw edge through one layer of fabric and one layer of lining.

5. Turn up a $1^1/_2$-inch hem along the bottom of the tea cozy.

6. Blindstitch the hem of the tea cozy in place, as shown in **Diagram 9.** For information on blindstitching, see "Embroidery and Hand-Sewing Stitches" on page 244.

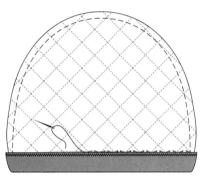

Diagram 9

7. Press the hem of the tea cozy and turn it right side out.

FINISHING THE TEA COZY

Referring to **Diagram 10,** randomly bend the petals of both layers of the sunflower. This will give the tea cozy a three-dimensional effect.

Diagram 10

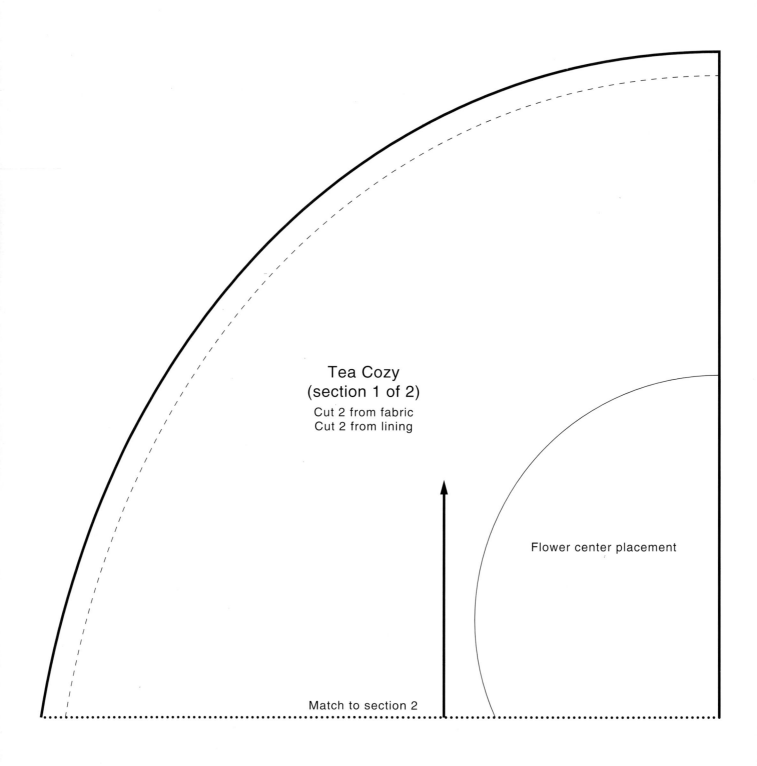

Tea Cozy
(section 1 of 2)

Cut 2 from fabric
Cut 2 from lining

Flower center placement

Match to section 2

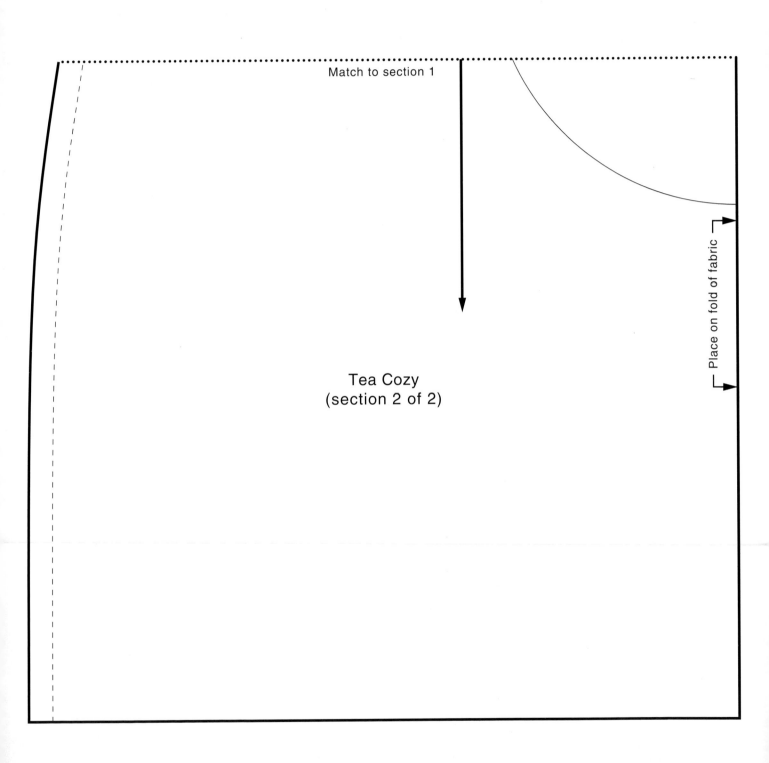

Match to section 1

Tea Cozy
(section 2 of 2)

Place on fold of fabric

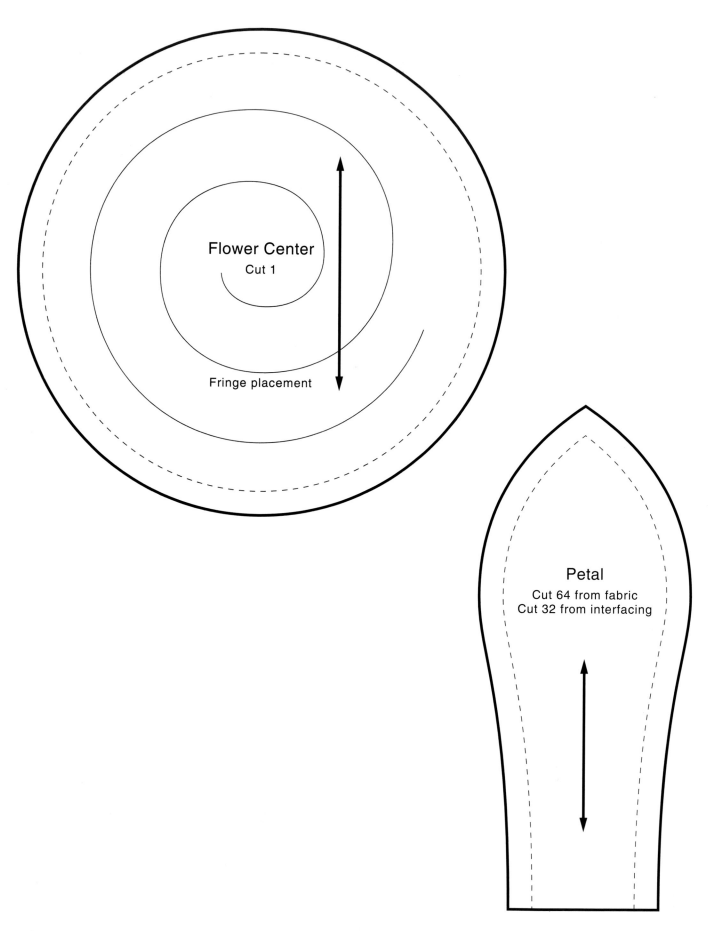

Flower Center
Cut 1

Fringe placement

Petal
Cut 64 from fabric
Cut 32 from interfacing

Bottle Bags

Make gift giving twice as nice when you wrap a bottle in one of these fanciful bags. They're perfect for holding herbed vinegar and oil or for bringing a special beverage to a party. And the best part of all is they're reusable!

Bottle Bags

❖

SKILL LEVEL: EASY

SIZE: The finished size of each bottle bag is 5 inches wide and 14 inches high.

NOTE: Measurements in the cutting directions include the seam allowances. Sew all seams with $5/8$-inch seam allowances, unless indicated otherwise.

CUTTING THE HEARTS-AND-STARS BAG

1. Trace the heart and star pattern pieces on page 69 onto template plastic and cut them out.

2. Following the manufacturer's directions, iron a 6-inch square of fusible webbing onto the wrong side of the yellow print.

3. Trace around the star pattern on the paper side of the fusible webbing and cut out six stars.

4. Following the manufacturer's directions, iron a 6-inch square of webbing onto the wrong side of the red print.

5. Trace around the heart pattern on the paper side of the fusible webbing and cut out six hearts.

6. From the green print, cut one $7^1/4 \times 27$-inch rectangle for the bag.

7. From the yellow solid, cut one $2^1/4 \times 13^1/4$-inch strip for the binding.

8. From the red print, cut one $2^3/4 \times 27$-inch strip for the tie.

CUTTING THE STARS-AND-MOONS BAG

1. Trace the star and moon pattern pieces on page 69 onto template plastic and cut them out.

2. Following the manufacturer's directions, iron a 6-inch square of fusible webbing onto the wrong side of the yellow print.

3. Trace around the star pattern on the paper side of the fusible webbing and cut out six stars.

4. Following the manufacturer's directions, iron a 6-inch square of fusible webbing onto the wrong side of the white print.

5. Trace around the moon pattern on the paper side of the fusible webbing and cut out six moons.

6. From the blue print, cut one $7^1/4 \times 27$-inch rectangle for the bag.

7. From the yellow print, cut one $2^1/4 \times 13^1/4$-inch strip for the binding.

8. From the white print, cut one $2^3/4 \times 27$-inch strip for the tie.

APPLIQUÉING THE SHAPES

1. With wrong sides together, fold the bag in half crosswise and turn so the fold is along the bottom.

2. Arrange three of each appliqué shape on one side of the bag, inside the seam allowances, as shown in **Diagram 1.**

Diagram 1

3. Following the manufacturer's directions, iron the appliqué shapes onto one side of the bag. Repeat Steps 2 and 3 to iron the remaining six appliqué shapes onto the other side of the bag. Unfold the bag.

4. Set the sewing machine for a narrow zigzag stitch and a short stitch length. Using sewing thread to match the fabric of the shape to be appliquéd, satin stitch around each shape, as shown in **Diagram 2**. For more information, see "Machine Appliqué" on page 242.

Diagram 2

SEWING THE BAG

1. With wrong sides together, fold the bag in half crosswise. Pin and sew the side seams, as shown in **Diagram 3**.

Diagram 3

2. Trim the seam allowance for each of the side seams to $1/4$ inch.

3. Turn the bag wrong side out and press. Sew the side seams again, $3/8$ inch from the edge, as shown in **Diagram 4**.

Diagram 4

SEWING THE BINDING

1. With right sides together, fold the binding in half crosswise, matching the raw edges. Pin and sew the short ends together, as shown in **Diagram 5**. Press the seam open.

Diagram 5

2. Turn under a $5/8$-inch seam allowance along one edge of the binding and press, as shown in **Diagram 6**.

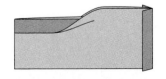

Diagram 6

Know&Sew

YOU CAN APPLIQUÉ THE HEARTS, STARS, AND MOONS EVEN IF YOU DON'T HAVE A ZIGZAG STITCH ON YOUR MACHINE. USE PINKING SHEARS TO TRIM THE EDGES OF EACH APPLIQUÉ SHAPE AND TOPSTITCH THEM IN PLACE ON THE RIGHT SIDE OF THE BAG. OR, CUT THE APPLIQUÉ SHAPES OUT OF A FABRIC, SUCH AS FELT, THAT WILL NOT FRAY.

3. With right sides together, insert the bag into the circle of the binding, matching the binding seam to one side seam of the bag. Pin the raw edge of the binding to the top of the bag, as shown in **Diagram 7**.

Diagram 7

4. Sew the binding to the bag. Trim the seam allowance to ³/₈ inch.

5. Turn the bag wrong side out. Fold the binding out to the wrong side of the bag and press, as shown in **Diagram 8**.

Diagram 8

6. Sew the binding in place by stitching directly over the previous line of stitching.

SEWING THE TIE

1. With right sides together, fold the strip for the tie in half lengthwise and press. Sew along one short side and the long side, leaving the other short side open for turning. Turn the tie right side out and press.

2. Turn under a ⁵/₈-inch seam allowance along the remaining side and blindstitch it closed. For information on blindstitching, see "Embroidery and Hand-Sewing Stitches" on page 244.

FINISHING THE BAG

1. Fold the tie in half crosswise and press a crease along the fold.

2. Referring to **Diagram 9**, center the crease of the tie on the right side of the bag back, 3 inches from the top and pin it. Topstitch the tie in place through only one thickness of the bag. For more information, see "Edge Stitching and Topstitching" on page 242.

Diagram 9

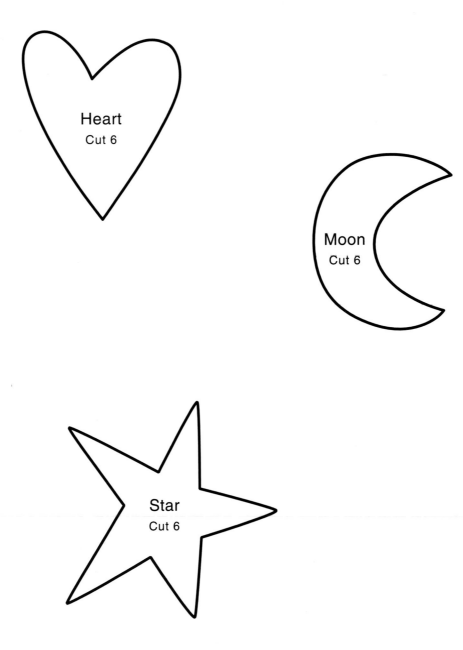

Heart
Cut 6

Moon
Cut 6

Star
Cut 6

Two-in-One Hostess Apron

For elegant holiday entertaining or festive occasions, this hostess apron is the perfect touch. It also makes a wonderful gift for a special friend or for Mom on Mother's Day.

SIZE: The bibbed hostess apron is 32 inches long and will fit a small, medium, or large waist.

NOTE: Measurements in the cutting directions include the seam allowances. Sew all the seams with $1/2$-inch seam allowances.

CUTTING THE APRON

1. Referring to **Diagram 1**, from the peach solid, cut the following:

- 1 apron skirt, 23 × 44 inches
- 1 bib, 7 × 25 inches
- 1 waistband, 4 × 22 inches
- 4 strap pieces, each $2^{1}/_2$ × 44 inches
- 4 ruffles, each 4 × 35 inches, cut on the bias
- 2 pockets, each 7 × $9^{1}/_2$ inches

2. From the satin ribbon, cut three 7-inch strips. Cut one 44-inch strip.

3. From the fusible webbing, cut three 7-inch strips. Cut one 44-inch strip.

4. From the grosgrain ribbon, cut two 1-yard strips.

SEWING THE POCKETS

1. To make a hem at the top of one pocket, turn under $1/2$ inch along one short side and press. Turn under $1^{1}/2$ inches more and press again. Machine baste the hem in place.

2. Following the manufacturer's directions, use one 7-inch strip of fusible webbing to fuse one 7-inch strip of satin ribbon onto the right side of the pocket, $1/2$ inch from the top. Edge stitch the ribbon in place along the top and bottom of the ribbon, as shown in

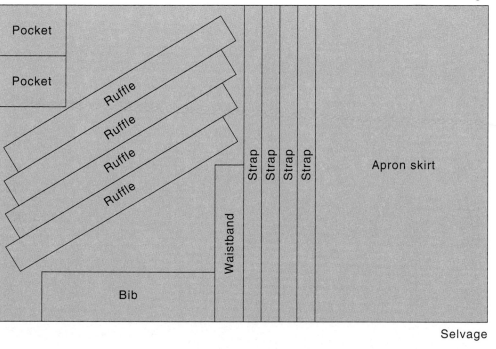

Diagram 1

Diagram 2. For more information, see "Edge Stitching and Topstitching" on page 242.

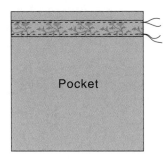

Diagram 2

3. Turn under $^1/_2$ inch on each of the remaining sides of the pocket and press.

4. Repeat Steps 1 through 3 for the remaining pocket.

5. Place each pocket on the apron skirt, 6 inches down from the top edge and 8 inches from the side edges, as shown in **Diagram 3**. Topstitch the sides and bottom of each pocket to the skirt. For more information, see "Edge Stitching and Topstitching" on page 242.

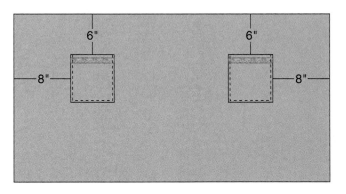

Diagram 3

SEWING THE SKIRT

1. Following the manufacturer's directions, iron the strip of fusible interfacing onto the wrong side of the waistband.

2. With the wrong side facing up, use a chalk pencil to mark a $^1/_2$-inch seam al-

lowance on each short end of the waistband, as shown in **Diagram 4.** Set the waistband aside.

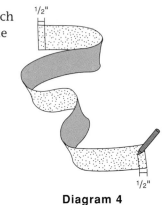

Diagram 4

3. To hem the skirt, turn under $^1/_2$ inch along the bottom and press. Turn under 2 inches more and press again. Machine baste the hem in place.

4. Following the manufacturer's directions, use the 44-inch strip of fusible webbing to iron the 44-inch strip of satin ribbon onto the right side of the skirt hem, 1 inch from the bottom. Edge stitch the ribbon in place along the top and bottom of the ribbon.

5. To make a double hem along one side of the skirt, turn under $^1/_4$ inch and press. Turn under $^1/_4$ inch more and press again. Topstitch the hem in place $^1/_4$ inch from the edge. Repeat for the remaining side of the skirt.

6. To make two rows of gathering stitches along the top of the skirt, use the longest machine stitch and sew $^1/_4$ inch from the raw edge. Sew another line of stitches $^1/_4$ inch away from the first row of stitching.

7. Pull up the bobbin threads and evenly gather the top of the skirt until it is 21 inches wide. Secure the ends of the threads with a knot.

8. With right sides together, pin the waistband to the top of the skirt, as shown in **Diagram 5.** Ease the gathers to fit between the ½-inch seam allowance marks on the waistband. Sew the waistband to the skirt between the two rows of gathering stitches. Remove the second row of gathering stitches and press the seam toward the waistband.

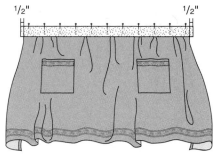

Diagram 5

9. Pin one end of one grosgrain ribbon to the right side of one end of the waistband, as shown in **Diagram 6.**

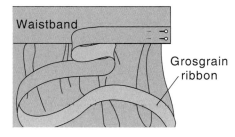

Diagram 6

10. With right sides together, fold the waistband in half lengthwise over the ribbon. Sew the end of the waistband along the seam line, catching the ribbon between the two layers of fabric, as shown in **Diagram 7.** Trim the seam allowance to ¹⁄₄ inch.

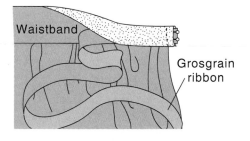

Diagram 7

11. Repeat Steps 9 and 10 to sew the remaining grosgrain ribbon to the opposite side of the waistband. Turn the waistband right side out.

12. Turn under ¹⁄₂ inch along the unfinished edge of the waistband and press.

Whipstitch this edge to the waistband, as shown in **Diagram 8.** For information on whipstitching, see "Embroidery and Hand-Sewing Stitches" on page 244.

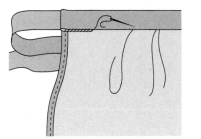

Diagram 8

SEWING THE BIB

1. With wrong sides together, fold the bib in half crosswise and press. Machine baste the raw edges together inside the seam allowance, as shown in **Diagram 9.**

Folded edge

Diagram 9

2. Following the manufacturer's directions, use the remaining 7-inch strip of fusible webbing to fuse the remaining 7-inch strip of satin ribbon onto one side of the bib, 1 inch from the folded edge. Edge stitch the ribbon in place through both layers of fabric along the top and bottom of the ribbon, as shown in **Diagram 10.**

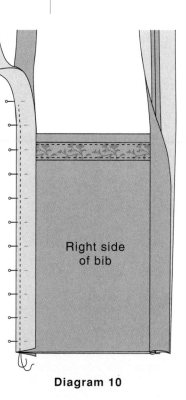

Right side of bib

Diagram 10

Know&Sew

TO GUARANTEE GATHERS THAT ARE PERFECTLY SPACED, DIVIDE THE APRON SKIRT AND THE WAISTBAND INTO QUARTERS AND MARK EACH QUARTER WITH A PIN. WHEN PULLING UP THE BOBBIN THREADS, MATCH THE PINS ON THE SKIRT WITH THE PINS ON THE WAISTBAND AND EVENLY ADJUST THE GATHERS BEFORE PINNING THEM IN PLACE.

ATTACHING THE STRAPS

1. Referring to **Diagram 10** on page 73, sandwich one side of the bib between the right sides of two strap pieces, matching the outside raw edges to the raw edge of the bib. Pin and sew the three layers together along the outside long edge. Trim the seam allowance to $1/4$ inch. Turn the straps to the right side and press.

2. Repeat Step 1 to sew the remaining strap pieces to the other side of the bib.

SEWING THE RUFFLES

1. To make one ruffle, with right sides together, pin and sew two ruffle strips together along one set of short ends. Press the seam open.

2. With wrong sides together, fold the ruffle in half lengthwise and pin the short ends together. With a chalk pencil, mark a gradual 3-inch curve at one end, beginning at the raw edges and ending at the fold, as shown in **Diagram 11.** Cut along the marked line and repin the curved ends together. To make both ends symmetrical, fold the ruffle in half crosswise to cut the curve at the other end.

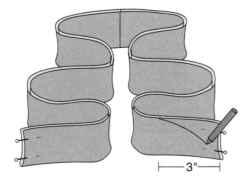

Diagram 11

3. Repeat Steps 1 and 2 for the two remaining ruffle strips.

4. To make two rows of gathering stitches along the raw edge of one

ruffle, use the longest machine stitch and sew $1/4$ inch from the raw edges. Sew another line of stitches $1/4$ inch away from the first row of stitching.

5. Pull up the bobbin threads and evenly gather the ruffle until it is 43 inches long. Secure the ends of the threads with a knot.

6. Repeat Steps 4 and 5 for the remaining ruffle.

7. Referring to **Diagram 12,** pin and sew the gathered edge of one ruffle to the right side and along the raw edge of one strap front, allowing $1/2$ inch of the strap ends to extend beyond the ends of the ruffle. Trim the seam allowance to $1/4$ inch. Turn the ruffle toward the outside.

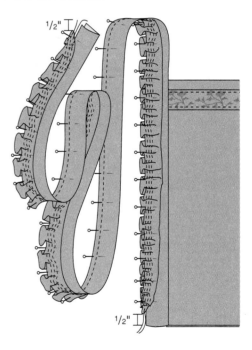

Diagram 12

8. Turn under and press $1/2$ inch along the raw edge of the corresponding strap back. Sandwich the seam allowance of the ruffle between the front and back of the strap. Whipstitch the opening closed along the length of the strap.

9. Repeat Steps 7 and 8 and sew the remaining ruffle to the other side of the bib.

Know & Sew

TO GIVE A MORE TAILORED LOOK TO THE HOSTESS APRON, SIMPLY ELIMINATE THE RUFFLES. AFTER SEWING THE STRAPS TO THE BIB, TURN UNDER AND PRESS A $1/2$-INCH SEAM ALLOWANCE ALONG THE THREE UNFINISHED SIDES OF EACH STRAP. THEN TOPSTICH AROUND ALL FOUR SIDES OF EACH STRAP.

FINISHING THE APRON

1. To make a double hem along the bottom edge of the bib and the straps, turn under ¼ inch and press. Topstitch. Turn under another ¼ inch and press again. Topstitch the hem.

2. Sew a ⅞-inch buttonhole ½ inch from the bottom of each strap on the bib front. Sew a ⅞-inch buttonhole at the other end of each strap according to the height of the wearer, as shown in **Diagram 13**.

3. Center the bib on the waistband and pin it in place.

4. Referring to **Diagram 14**, sew four buttons onto the inside of the waistband, aligning each button so that it corresponds with a buttonhole on the bib and at each end of the straps. Button the ends of the straps by criss-crossing them across the back of the apron.

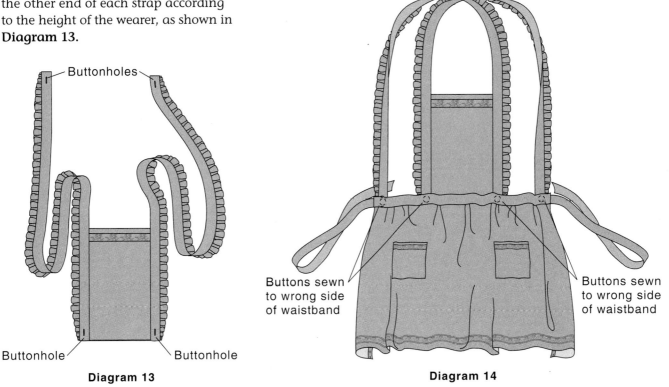

Buttonholes

Buttonhole   Buttonhole

Diagram 13

Buttons sewn to wrong side of waistband

Buttons sewn to wrong side of waistband

Diagram 14

Braid-Trimmed Place Mats and Matching Napkins

Nothing short of a romantic dinner for two deserves to be served on these rich cream-and-burgundy place mats with matching napkins and rings. Their easy elegance may tempt you to dine in style every night of the week.

SIZE: The finished size of each place mat is 12 × 18 inches. The finished size of each napkin is 18 inches square.

NOTE: Measurements in the cutting directions include the seam allowances. Sew all seams with $1/2$-inch seam allowances, unless indicated otherwise.

CUTTING THE PLACE MATS AND NAPKINS

1. From the beige solid, cut four 13 × 19-inch rectangles. Two will be used for the place mat fronts and two will be used for the place mat backs. Cut two 19-inch squares for the napkins.

2. From the interfacing, cut two 13 × 19-inch rectangles for the place mats.

SEWING THE PLACE MATS

1. Following the manufacturer's directions, iron one piece of interfacing to the wrong side of each front.

2. With right sides together, pin and sew one front to one back, leaving a 3-inch opening along the bottom for turning, as shown in **Diagram 1.**

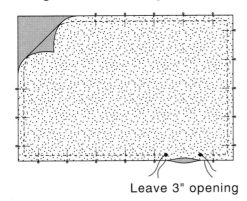

Leave 3" opening

Diagram 1

3. Clip the corners and trim the seam allowance to $1/4$ inch. Turn the place mat right side out and press.

4. Turn under the seam allowance along the opening and slip stitch it closed. For information on slip stitching, see "Embroidery and Hand-Sewing Stitches" on page 244.

5. Repeat Steps 2 through 4 to sew the remaining place mat front and back together.

TRIMMING THE PLACE MATS

1. Referring to **Diagram 2,** whipstitch the $3/16$-inch cording around the edge of one front. For information on whipstitching, see "Embroidery and Hand-Sewing Stitches" on page 244.

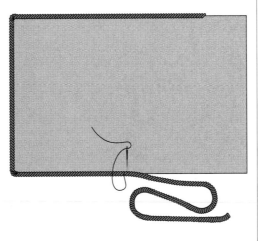

Diagram 2

2. To secure the ends of the cording together, cut the cording so that the ends meet. Match the ends together to make them look like one continuous piece of cording. Wrap sewing thread around the ends to prevent unraveling and to join the ends together. Finish by sewing the ends to the place mat, as shown in **Diagram 3** on page 78.

MATERIALS LIST FOR TWO PLACE MATS AND NAPKINS

FABRIC REQUIREMENTS

- $1^3/8$ YARD OF BEIGE SOLID FOR THE PLACE MATS AND NAPKINS

- $1^1/4$ YARDS OF 20-INCH-WIDE MEDIUM-WEIGHT FUSIBLE INTERFACING

OTHER SUPPLIES

- $3^1/2$ YARDS OF $3/16$-INCH BURGUNDY CORDING FOR TRIMMING THE PLACE MATS

- 3 YARDS OF $1/2$-INCH-WIDE BURGUNDY SCROLL BRAID FOR THE PLACE MATS

- 1 YARD OF $3/8$-INCH BURGUNDY CORDING FOR THE NAPKIN RINGS

- 4 BURGUNDY TASSELS, EACH 3 INCHES LONG

- SEWING THREAD TO MATCH THE FABRICS, CORDING, AND BRAID

- 2 SILK ROSES

- 2 WOODEN NAPKIN RINGS, EACH $1^1/2$ INCHES DIAMETER

- HAND-SEWING NEEDLE

- CHALK PENCIL

- FABRIC GLUE

- TRANSPARENT TAPE

FABRIC OPTIONS

- LINEN

- SHEETING

- CANVAS

- COTTON

- POLISHED COTTON

- DAMASK

Know & Sew

BEFORE SEWING THE BRAID TO THE PLACE MAT, IT'S A GOOD IDEA TO PRESHRINK THE BRAID. YOU CAN EASILY DO THIS BY HOLDING AN IRON JUST ABOVE EACH LENGTH OF BRAID SO THAT IT'S LIGHTLY STEAMED. THEN USE A FABRIC GLUE STICK TO SECURE THE BRAID IN PLACE ON THE PLACE MAT SO THAT YOU CAN SEW IT WITHOUT WORRYING ABOUT SLIPPING.

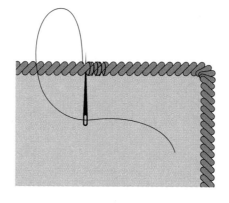

Diagram 3

3. Using a chalk pencil, mark the scroll braid placement line around the entire place mat 1½ inches from the edge.

4. To add the scroll braid, begin by turning under ¼ inch at the end of the braid so that the raw edge is not showing. Starting along the bottom of the place mat, whipstitch the braid in place until you come to a corner.

5. At the corner, fold and overlap the braid, as shown in **Diagram 4**. Continue attaching the braid to the place mat, folding and overlapping the braid at each corner.

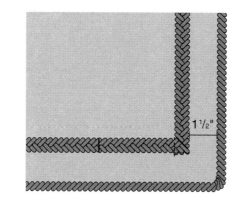

Diagram 4

6. To finish, match the ends of the braid together and add ¼ inch. Cut the braid, turn under the ¼ inch, and sew it in place, as shown in **Diagram 4**.

7. Repeat Steps 1 through 6 for the remaining place mat.

SEWING THE NAPKINS

1. With the wrong side of one napkin facing up, use a chalk pencil and mark each corner of the napkin with a dot, placing it ½ inch from either edge, as shown in **Diagram 5**.

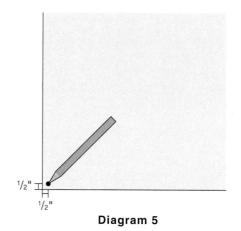

Diagram 5

2. Fold each corner to this dot and toward the wrong side of the napkin. Trim each corner, as shown in **Diagram 6**.

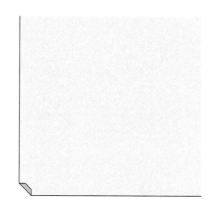

Diagram 6

3. To create a double hem around all four edges, turn under ¼ inch toward the wrong side of the napkin and press.

4. Turn under ¼ inch more and press again.

5. Pin the hem in place. The corners will automatically be mitered, as shown in **Diagram 7**.

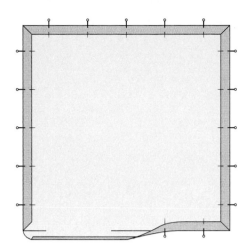

Diagram 7

MAKING THE NAPKIN RINGS

1. Cut the 3/8-inch cording in half to create two 18-inch pieces.

2. Wrap transparent tape near the ends of one piece of cording, as shown in **Diagram 9**.

3. Referring to **Diagram 9**, wrap matching thread around the ends of the cording, close to the tip, to prevent unraveling. Carefully remove the transparent tape.

4. Wrap the cording around one napkin ring. Tie it into a knot, slipping two tassels onto the cording before completing the knot.

5. Secure the cording and the knot to the napkin ring with fabric glue.

6. Repeat Steps 2 through 5 for the remaining piece of cording, napkin ring, and tassels.

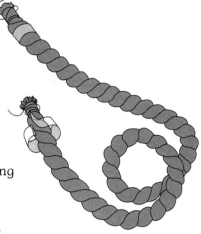

Diagram 9

6. Edge stitch the hem in place and hand tack the mitered corners closed, as shown in **Diagram 8**. For more information, see "Edge Stitching and Topstitching" on page 242.

Diagram 8

FINISHING THE NAPKIN RINGS

Referring to **Diagram 10**, glue a silk rose over the knot on each napkin ring. Tie a knot at the ends of each piece of cording.

Diagram 10

7. Repeat Steps 1 through 6 for the remaining napkin.

Bow, Rosette, and Butterfly Pillows

Add a breath of spring to your living room any time of the year with a tremendous trio of floral-accented pillows. Make one or all three to create a coordinated, custom look worthy of a professional decorator.

Bow Pillow

SKILL LEVEL: *INTERMEDIATE*

SIZE: The finished size is 14 inches square.

NOTE: Measurements in the cutting directions include the seam allowances. Sew all the seams with $\frac{1}{2}$-inch seam allowances.

CUTTING THE PILLOW

1. From the green solid, cut two 15-inch squares. One will be used for the pillow front and one for the pillow back.

2. From the floral print, cut four 6 × 44-inch-long strips for the ruffle. Cut one 22-inch square for the bow. Cut one 5 × 6-inch rectangle for the tie.

SEWING THE BOW

1. With right sides together, fold the square for the bow in half and pin. Sew the long sides together, as shown in **Diagram 1**.

Diagram 1

2. Center the seam between the two folded edges and press the seam open, as shown in **Diagram 2**. Turn the bow right side out, keeping the seam centered, and press the folds in place.

Diagram 2

3. With the seam side facing down, fold the bow in half crosswise and press. Open it up and hand baste a row of stitches along the creased fold line, as shown in **Diagram 3**, leaving a tail of thread at each end.

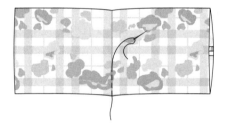

Diagram 3

4. Gently pull up the thread and loosely gather the bow along the creased fold line. Secure the thread at each end with a knot.

SEWING THE TIE

1. To make the tie, repeat Steps 1 and 2 under "Sewing the Bow."

2. Wrap the tie securely around the center of the bow, making sure the seam of the tie is on the underside.

3. Insert one end of the tie into the other end, making sure the tie remains around the center of the bow, as shown in **Diagram 4** on page 82. Turn under the seam allowance on the end of the tie that shows and whipstitch the tie

MATERIALS LIST FOR THE BOW PILLOW

FABRIC REQUIREMENTS

• $\frac{1}{2}$ YARD OF GREEN SOLID FOR THE PILLOW FRONT AND BACK

• $1\frac{1}{2}$ YARDS OF BLUE, PINK, AND GREEN FLORAL PRINT FOR THE BOW AND RUFFLE

OTHER SUPPLIES

• 14 × 14-INCH SQUARE PILLOW FORM

• SEWING THREAD TO MATCH THE FABRICS

• HAND-SEWING NEEDLE

• 4 SAFETY PINS

• CHALK PENCIL

FABRIC OPTIONS

• COTTON

• POLISHED COTTON

• MOIRÉ

• LIGHTWEIGHT DAMASK

closed. For information on whip-stitching, see "Embroidery and Hand-Sewing Stitches" on page 244.

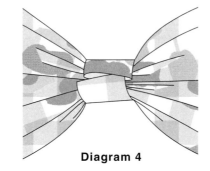

Diagram 4

Know&Sew

YOU CAN SAVE TIME AND CHANGE THE LOOK OF THE PILLOW IN TWO EASY STEPS. FIRST, ELIMINATE THE SECTION ABOUT SEWING THE TIE AND MOVE DIRECTLY TO THE SECTION ABOUT SEWING THE BOW TO THE PILLOW FRONT. THEN, WHEN THE PILLOW IS COMPLETELY FINISHED, COVER THE GATHERING STITCHES AT THE CENTER OF THE BOW WITH A CLUSTER OF SILK FLOWERS. JUST TIE THE WIRE STEMS SECURELY AROUND THE CENTER OF THE BOW AND CLIP OFF THE EXCESS WIRE.

4. Hand tack the tie to the bow to secure it in place.

SEWING THE BOW TO THE PILLOW FRONT

1. Referring to **Diagram 5**, pin the bow to the right side of the pillow front on the diagonal. Machine baste each end of the bow to the pillow front inside the seam allowance.

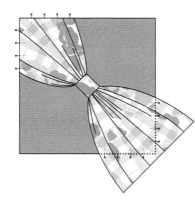

Diagram 5

2. Trim away the excess fabric so that the raw edges are even. Set the pillow front aside.

SEWING THE RUFFLE

1. Referring to **Diagram 6**, with right sides together, form a 90-degree angle with two ruffle strips. With a chalk

pencil, draw a diagonal line, as shown in the diagram.

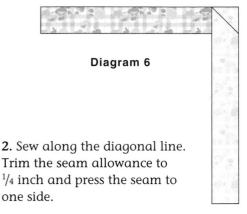

Diagram 6

2. Sew along the diagonal line. Trim the seam allowance to $1/4$ inch and press the seam to one side.

3. Repeat Steps 1 and 2 to sew the remaining two ruffle strips together. Then repeat these steps once again to sew the strips into one continuous circle, as shown in **Diagram 7**. Be careful not to twist the ruffle when sewing the two longer strips together.

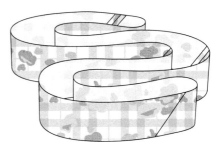

Diagram 7

4. With wrong sides together, fold and pin the ruffle in half lengthwise, maintaining the circular shape and matching the raw edges. Press along the fold.

5. To make two rows of gathering stitches, use the longest machine stitch and sew $1/4$ inch from the raw edges. Sew another line of stitches $1/4$ inch away from the first row of stitches.

6. Referring to **Diagram 8**, divide the pillow front into quarters and mark each quarter along the edges with a straight pin. Divide the ruffle into quarters and mark each quarter with a safety pin. This will help to distribute the ruffle evenly.

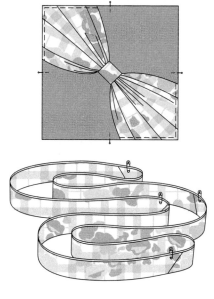

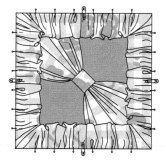

Diagram 8

distributed evenly. If necessary, remove the stitches in the area to be adjusted, redistribute the gathers, and resew.

5. Remove the row of gathering stitches that shows on the pillow front.

SEWING THE PILLOW TOGETHER

1. Fold the ruffle to the center of the pillow front. With right sides together, pin the pillow back to the pillow front, making sure the ruffle is sandwiched between the layers of fabric, as shown in **Diagram 10**.

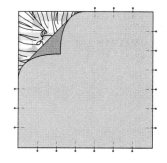

Diagram 10

SEWING THE RUFFLE TO THE PILLOW FRONT

1. With right sides together, pin the ruffle to the pillow front, matching the raw edges and the quarter-mark pins, as shown in **Diagram 9**.

Diagram 9

2. Referring to **Diagram 9**, pull up the bobbin threads on the ruffle and evenly gather the strip between each set of quarter-mark pins. Make sure to gather the ruffle closely at each corner.

3. Sew the ruffle to the pillow front between the first and second row of gathering stitches.

4. Turn the ruffle toward the outside of the pillow and make sure the gathers are

2. Turn the pillow over so that the wrong side of the pillow front is facing up. Sew the front to the back on top of the row of stitches on the pillow front that is furthest from the raw edge, leaving an 8-inch opening for turning, as shown in **Diagram 11**. To reinforce the seams, sew again directly on top of the previous stitching.

Leave 8" opening

Diagram 11

3. Clip the corners and the trim seam allowance to $1/4$ inch. Turn the pillow right side out.

FINISHING THE PILLOW

1. Carefully press the ruffle, the front, and the back of the pillow.

2. Insert the pillow form. Turn under the seam allowance along the opening and slip stitch it closed. For information on slip stitching, see "Embroidery and Hand-Sewing Stitches" on page 244.

Rosette Pillow

SKILL LEVEL: *EASY*

SIZE: The finished size is 14 inches in diameter.

NOTE: Measurements in the cutting directions include the seam allowances. Sew all the seams with ½-inch seam allowances.

MAKING THE PATTERN

1. To make a 36-inch-diameter circle pattern, fold the 40-inch square of paper into quarters.

2. Referring to **Diagram 12**, and starting at the corner where the folds meet, use the yardstick and pencil to measure and mark a curve 18 inches from the corner. Cut on the marked line and open up the pattern.

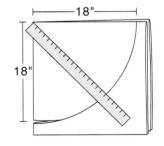

Diagram 12

CUTTING THE PILLOW

1. From the floral print, cut one circle for the pillow.

2. From the green solid, cut one circle for the lining.

ADDING THE TAPED CORDING

1. Referring to **Diagram 13**, pin the taped cording along the edge of the

right side of the floral circle. Overlap and carefully match the ends of the cording.

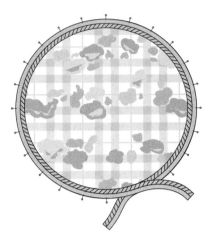

Diagram 13

2. Machine baste the cording to the fabric. Trim the excess from the ends of the cording.

SEWING THE PILLOW

1. With right sides together, pin the lining circle to the floral circle, as shown in **Diagram 14**. Sew the circles together directly over the machine basting stitches, leaving a 4-inch opening for turning.

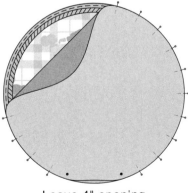

Leave 4" opening

Diagram 14

2. Referring to **Diagram 15**, clip several V-shaped notches around the edge of the circle, making sure not to cut through the stitching.

Diagram 15

3. Turn the circle right side out and press. Turn under the seam allowance along the opening and slip stitch it closed. For more information on slip stitching, see "Embroidery and Hand-Sewing Stitches" on page 244.

FORMING THE ROSETTE

1. With the lining facing up, place the pillow form in the center of the circle.

2. Referring to **Diagram 16**, gather the circle around the pillow form. Wrap a rubber band around the gathers to secure them in place.

Diagram 16

3. Arrange the fabric at the top of the pillow so that it resembles the petals of a rose. To do this, gently manipulate the fabric so that both the floral side and the lining show, as shown in **Diagram 17**.

Diagram 17

FINISHING THE PILLOW

1. Wrap the green cording around the rubber band two times and tie it into a secure bow.

2. Remove the rubber band from the neck of the pillow by carefully lifting up the fabric and cutting it with a pair of scissors.

3. Trim the ends of the cording if they are too long.

4. Tie each end of the cording into a secure knot to prevent unraveling, as shown in **Diagram 18**.

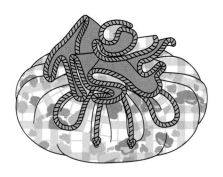

Diagram 18

Know & Sew

IF YOU DON'T LIKE TO SEW OVER PINS, YOU CAN STILL PREVENT THE FLORAL AND LINING LAYERS FROM SHIFTING AS YOU SEW THEM TO-GETHER. SIMPLY CHANGE THE PIN PLACEMENT SO THAT THE PINS ARE PARALLEL TO THE SEAM LINE AND 1 INCH FROM THE RAW EDGE. THIS WILL SECURELY HOLD THE LAYERS TOGETHER AND ALLOW THE PRESSER FOOT TO PASS BY EACH PIN WITHOUT HAVING TO REMOVE IT.

Butterfly Pillow

SKILL LEVEL: *EASY*

SIZE: The finished size of the large pillow is 14 × 18 inches. The finished size of the small pillow is 14 inches square.

NOTE: Measurements in the cutting directions include the seam allowances. Sew all the seams with 1/2-inch seam allowances.

CUTTING THE PILLOWS

1. From the floral print, cut two 15 × 19-inch rectangles for the rectangular pillow.

2. From the green solid, cut two 15-inch squares for the square pillow.

3. From the white solid, cut two 15 × 19-inch rectangles for the lining. Cut two 15-inch squares for the lining.

SEWING THE PILLOWS

1. For the rectangular pillow, with wrong sides together, pin each lining rectangle to each print rectangle, making sure the raw edges are even. Sew the pieces together inside the seam allowance.

2. Referring to **Diagram 19**, with the right sides of the print facing, pin and sew the rectangles together, leaving a 6-inch opening along one side for turning.

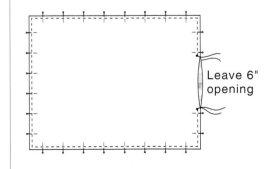

Leave 6" opening

Diagram 19

3. Clip the corners and trim the seam allowance to 1/4 inch.

4. Turn the pillow right side out and press.

5. To create perfect corner points on the pillow, firmly place small amounts of polyester fiberfill into each corner.

6. Continue to stuff the rest of the pillow by inserting small handfuls of polyester fiberfill until the pillow is firm and smooth.

7. Turn under the seam allowance along the opening and slip stitch it closed. For information on slip stitching, see "Embroidery and Hand-Sewing Stitches" on page 244.

8. To make the square pillow, repeat Steps 1 through 7 with the square pieces of fabric.

FINISHING THE PILLOWS

1. Group the white, green, and blue cording together, making sure the ends align. Tie a knot into one end of the grouping. Braid the white, green, and blue cording together. Tie a knot at the end of the braid to prevent the braid and the ends of the cording from unraveling, as shown in **Diagram 20.** For more information, see "Braiding" on page 243.

Diagram 20

2. Center the square pillow on top of the rectangular pillow.

3. Center the two pillows as a unit on top of the braided cording.

4. Referring to **Diagram 21**, bring each end of the braid toward the center of the pillows, twist them around one another, and pull them tightly to give the pillows a butterfly look.

Diagram 21

5. Pull each end of the braid back toward the direction from which it came.

While doing so, wrap the braid several times around the braid already in place, as shown in **Diagram 22**.

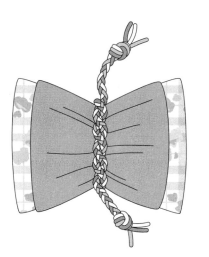

Diagram 22

6. Turn the pillow over. Match the ends of the braid together on the back side of the pillows. Twist the braids together once more.

7. Wrap each end of the braid several times around the braid on the back of the pillow to secure the twist.

8. Tuck the ends of the braid between the pillows.

Know&Sew

IF THE PILLOW PROVES TOO LARGE FOR AN ARMCHAIR, HERE IS A WAY TO MAKE TWO BUT-TERFLY PILLOWS FROM ONE. INSTEAD OF ONE LONGER BRAID TO WRAP AROUND BOTH PILLOWS, MAKE TWO SHORTER ONES. THEN WRAP ONE BRAIDED PIECE AROUND ONE PILLOW AND THE RE-MAINING PIECE AROUND THE OTHER PILLOW. BECAUSE THEY TAKE UP LESS SPACE, THESE SMALLER BUTTERFLIES CAN EVEN BE USED FOR A CHILD'S CHAIR.

Soft Sculpture Flower Bouquet

These "everlasting" lilies instantly add a soft touch to a special corner in any room. Simply a pleasure to behold on a writing desk, dressing table, or curio shelf, they're a welcome reminder of warm days in the sun.

SIZE: The finished bouquet is approximately 10 inches high and is seen in the photograph in a 3-inch vase.

NOTE: Measurements in the cutting directions include the seam allowances. Sew all seams with $1/2$-inch seam allowances, unless indicated otherwise.

CUTTING THE FLOWERS, LEAVES, AND STEMS

1. Trace the pattern pieces on pages 91–93 onto template plastic, transferring all markings, and cut them out.

2. From the medium green solid, cut one round leaf. Cut three large, one medium, and three small leaves. Cut the following for the stems:
   - one $1^{1}/2 \times 8$-inch bias strip
   - one $1^{1}/2 \times 7$-inch bias strip
   - one $1^{1}/2 \times 6$-inch bias strip
   - one $1^{1}/2 \times 5$-inch bias strip
   - one $1^{1}/2 \times 4$-inch bias strip

3. From the light green solid, cut one round leaf. Cut three large, one medium, and three small leaves. Using a chalk pencil, transfer the vein lines onto the right side of the fabric.

4. From the medium peach solid, cut three large lilies and two small lilies.

5. From the light peach solid, cut three large lilies and two small lilies.

6. From the polyester fleece, cut three large lilies and two small lilies.

7. From the yellow rattail cording, cut three 5-inch pieces. These will be used for the flower centers.

8. From the medium-gauge wire, cut three 8-inch, three 7-inch, three 6-inch, three 5-inch, and three 4-inch lengths.

9. From the floral wire, cut three 15-inch, one 10-inch, three 8-inch, and one 6-inch lengths.

SEWING THE FLOWERS

1. Pin and sew one large fleece lily onto the wrong side of one large medium peach lily. Then, with right sides together, pin and sew these pieces to one large light peach lily, leaving the bottom edge open between the dots, as shown in **Diagram 1**.

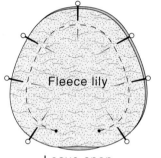

Leave open

Diagram 1

2. Trim the seam allowance to $1/4$ inch and turn the lily right side out. Turn under the seam allowance along the opening and finger press. Do not stitch it closed.

3. Repeat Steps 1 and 2 to sew the remaining large and small lilies.

MAKING THE FLOWER CENTERS

1. Tie several knots close together on one 5-inch piece of yellow rattail, leaving a 1-inch tail on either side, as shown in **Diagram 2** on page 90. Trim the ends close to the knots and apply fabric glue to prevent the ends from unraveling. Repeat this step for the remaining lengths of rattail cording.

MATERIALS LIST
FABRIC REQUIREMENTS
- $3/8$ YARD OF MEDIUM GREEN SOLID FOR THE LEAVES AND STEMS
- $3/8$ YARD OF LIGHT GREEN SOLID FOR THE LEAVES
- 22-INCH SQUARE OF MEDIUM PEACH SOLID FOR THE LILIES
- 22-INCH SQUARE OF LIGHT PEACH SOLID FOR THE LILIES
- $1/8$ YARD OF $1/4$-INCH-THICK POLYESTER FLEECE

OTHER SUPPLIES
- $1/2$ YARD OF $1/4$-INCH YELLOW RATTAIL CORDING
- SEWING THREAD TO MATCH THE FABRICS
- HAND-SEWING NEEDLE
- $2^{1}/2$ YARDS OF FLORAL WIRE FOR THE LEAVES
- 3 YARDS OF MEDIUM-GAUGE WIRE FOR THE STEMS
- TEMPLATE PLASTIC
- FINE-POINT, PERMANENT MARKER
- CHALK PENCIL
- FABRIC GLUE
- VASE
- PEBBLES, MARBLES, OR GLASS PEBBLES

FABRIC OPTIONS
- MOIRÉ
- VELVET
- SATIN
- POLISHED COTTON
- RAW SILK
- TAFFETA

Diagram 2

Know&Sew

TURNING NARROW
STRIPS RIGHT SIDE OUT
CAN BE A BREEZE IF YOU
KNOW HOW. THREAD A
TAPESTRY OR LARGE-
EYED EMBROIDERY
NEEDLE WITH A LENGTH
OF TAPESTRY YARN AND
KNOT ONE END OF THE
THREAD. THE LENGTH OF
YARN SHOULD BE AT
LEAST 2 INCHES LONGER
THAN THE STRIP YOU'RE
TURNING. INSERT THE
NEEDLE THROUGH THE
WRONG SIDE OF ONE
LAYER OF FABRIC AT ONE
SHORT END OF THE STRIP.
LET THE NEEDLE DROP
THROUGH THE STRIP AND
OUT THE OTHER SHORT
END. GENTLY PULL THE
NEEDLE SO THAT THE
STRIP TURNS RIGHT SIDE
OUT. WHEN YOU'RE FIN-
ISHED, CLIP THE KNOT
AND REMOVE THE
NEEDLE AND YARN.

2. Glue one knotted rattail to the
end of one 8-inch length of
medium-gauge wire, as
shown in **Diagram 3.**
Repeat this step for
one 7-inch and one
6-inch length of
medium-
gauge wire.

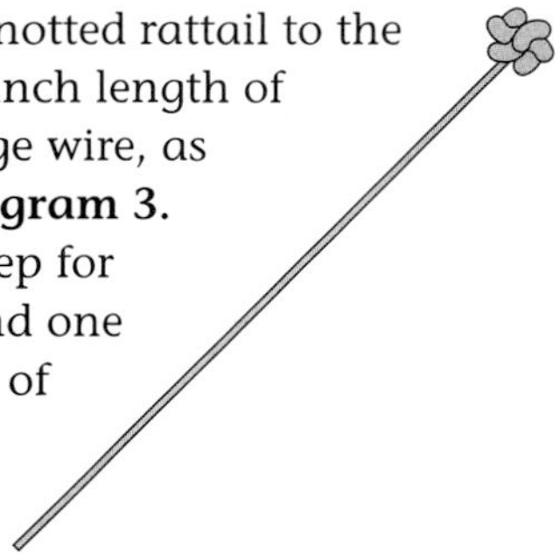

Diagram 3

MAKING THE STEMS

1. With right sides together, fold the
8-inch bias strip in half lengthwise,
making sure the raw edges are even.
Sew the long sides together ³/₈ inch
from the edge, leaving the ends open
for turning, as shown in **Diagram 4.**
Turn the stem right side out. Repeat this
step for the remaining four bias strips.

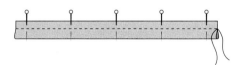

Diagram 4

2. Insert the 8-inch rattail-and-wire
unit and two 8-inch lengths of
medium-gauge wire into the
8-inch stem, as shown in
Diagram 5. Glue the rattail
to the open end at the top
of the stem. Repeat this
step for the 7-inch
and 6-inch stems.

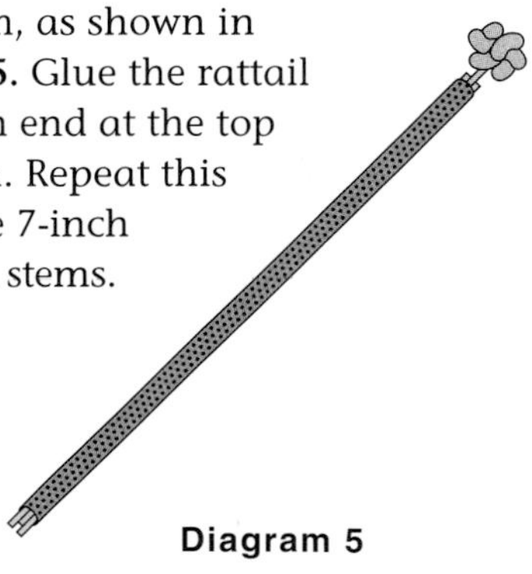

Diagram 5

3. Insert three 5-inch lengths of
medium-gauge wire into the 5-inch stem
and three 4-inch lengths of medium-
gauge wire into the 4-inch stem.

COMPLETING THE LILIES

1. Insert the wires of the 8-inch stem
into the opening of one large lily,
making sure that the knotted rattail is
placed on the outside of the lily, as
shown in **Diagram 6.**

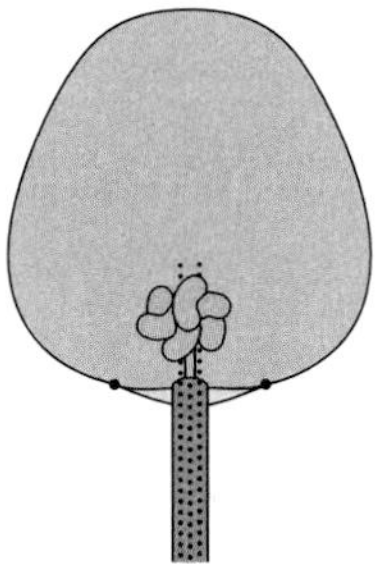

Diagram 6

2. Wrap and glue the lily around the
flower center, as shown in **Diagram 7.**
Trim the excess wire that extends beyond the fabric. Repeat Steps 1 and 2
for the 7-inch and 6-inch stems and the
remaining two large lilies.

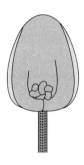

Diagram 7

3. Insert the wires of the 5-inch stem
into the opening of one small lily.
Wrap and glue the lily together to form
a bud, as shown in **Diagram 8.** Repeat

this step for the 4-inch stem and the remaining small lily.

Diagram 8

SEWING THE LEAVES

1. With right sides together, pin and sew one large medium green and one large light green leaf together, leaving the bottom edge open. Trim the seam allowance to ¼ inch and turn the leaf right side out. Turn under the seam allowance along the opening and finger press. Do not stitch it closed. Repeat this step for the remaining leaves.

2. Topstitch each leaf along the indicated vein lines. For more information, see "Edge Stitching and Topstitching" on page 242.

3. Fold the floral wires in half and insert the folded end into each leaf. Cut off the excess wire extending beyond the edge of the leaf.

FINISHING THE BOUQUET

1. Arrange the various leaves and lilies into a bouquet, and twist the wire stems together at the bottom. Secure the arrangement together with several dabs of fabric glue.

2. Glue the stems of the bouquet to the bottom of the vase. Fill the vase with pebbles, marbles, or glass pebbles to hold the bouquet in place.

3. Referring to the photograph on page 88, gently bend the leaves and the stems to give the bouquet a lifelike appearance.

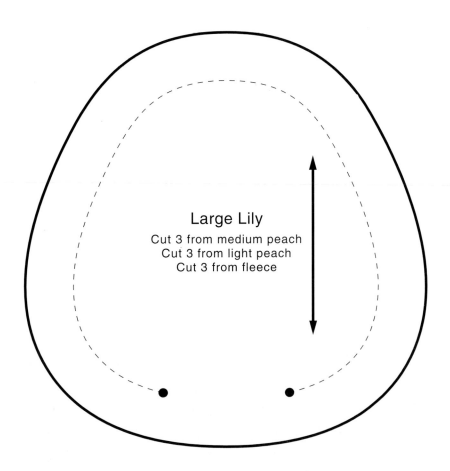

Large Lily
Cut 3 from medium peach
Cut 3 from light peach
Cut 3 from fleece

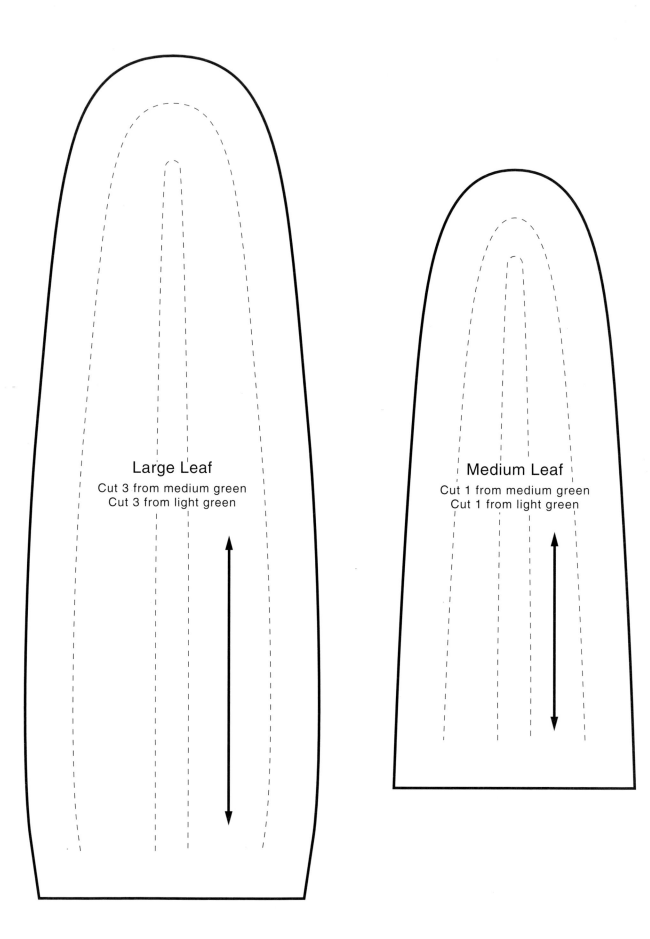

Large Leaf
Cut 3 from medium green
Cut 3 from light green

Medium Leaf
Cut 1 from medium green
Cut 1 from light green

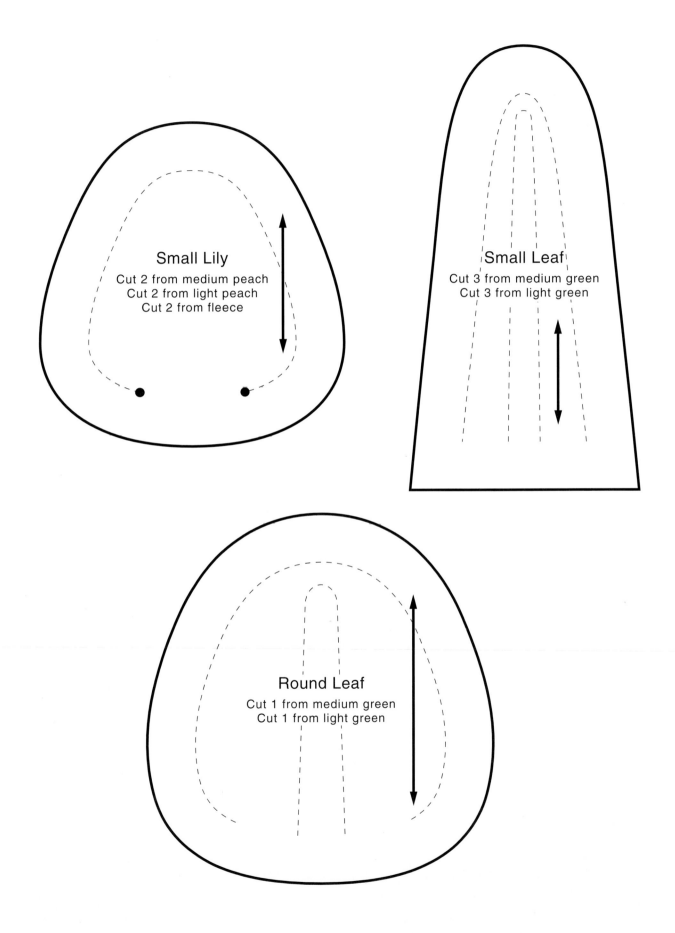

Small Lily

Cut 2 from medium peach
Cut 2 from light peach
Cut 2 from fleece

Small Leaf

Cut 3 from medium green
Cut 3 from light green

Round Leaf

Cut 1 from medium green
Cut 1 from light green

Rose Picture Decoration

Add a hint of English country charm to any decorating scheme with this lovely decoration. You can make several of them to mix or match with the Bow Picture Decoration on page 112.

SIZE: The finished size is approximately 13 inches wide and 30 inches long.

NOTE: Measurements in the cutting directions include the seam allowances. Sew all the seams with $1/2$-inch seam allowances.

Cutting the Decoration

1. Trace the pattern piece on page 98 onto tracing paper and cut it out.

2. From the plaid, cut one 7×54-inch piece for the petal strip.

3. From the dark green print, cut one 10×17-inch piece for the horizontal leaf strip and one 10×33-inch piece for the vertical leaf-and-tail strip.

4. From the burgundy, cut one $7^{1}/_{2}$-inch-diameter circle for the rose center.

Sewing the Petal Strip

1. With right sides together, fold the petal strip in half lengthwise and pin. Press the fold.

2. To form a curve, place the plate upside down on the strip $1/2$ inch from the end, as shown in **Diagram 1**. Align the rim of the plate with the lengthwise edge of the strip.

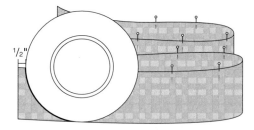

Diagram 1

3. Referring to **Diagram 1**, trace around the rim of the plate onto the fabric with a chalk pencil.

4. Cut along the traced line through both layers of fabric.

5. Repeat Steps 2 through 4 for the other end of the strip.

6. With right sides together, pin the curved edges of the strip together, making sure the raw edges are even.

7. Set the machine for a wide stitch width and a short stitch length. Sew the curved edges of the strip together. Turn the strip right side out and press.

8. Pin the raw edges of the strip together. Sew the raw edges together using a zigzag stitch.

9. To make two rows of gathering stitches, use the longest machine stitch and sew along the inside edge of the zigzag stitching.

10. Sew another line of stitches $1/4$ inch away from the first row of long machine stitching.

11. Pull up the bobbin threads and loosely gather the strip. Secure the bobbin threads in place at each end of the strip with a knot, as shown in **Diagram 2**.

Diagram 2

12. Set the sewing machine for a small stitch length, 10 to 12 stitches per inch. Secure the gathering stitches in place by sewing between the two rows of gathering stitches.

MATERIALS LIST

FABRIC REQUIREMENTS

- $3/8$ YARD OF 54-INCH-WIDE DARK GREEN-AND-BURGUNDY PLAID FOR THE PETAL STRIP

- $3/8$ YARD OF 54-INCH-WIDE DARK GREEN PRINT FOR THE LEAVES AND TAIL

- $1/4$ YARD OF 45-INCH-WIDE BURGUNDY SOLID FOR THE ROSE CENTER

OTHER SUPPLIES

- SEWING THREADS TO MATCH THE FABRICS

- 7- OR 8-INCH-DIAMETER PLATE

- $1/2$-INCH-WIDE METAL OR PLASTIC RING

- HAND-SEWING NEEDLE

- TRACING PAPER

- CHALK PENCIL

FABRIC OPTIONS

FOR THE PETAL STRIP

- COTTON PLAID

- COTTON JACQUARD

- POLISHED COTTON

- VELVET

- SATIN

- MOIRÉ

FOR THE ROSE CENTER, LEAVES, AND TAIL

- COTTON JACQUARD

- COTTON PLAID

- POLISHED COTTON

- VELVET

- SATIN

- MOIRÉ

SEWING THE ROSE CENTER

1. With wrong sides together, fold the circle for the rose center in half. Pin and sew the raw edges together using a zigzag stitch.

2. To make two rows of gathering stitches, repeat Steps 9 through 11 under "Sewing the Petal Strip" on page 95.

ASSEMBLING THE ROSE

1. Thread a needle with burgundy thread and knot the end. Pull the needle through the gathered side of the rose center. Accordian pleat the rose center, as shown in **Diagram 3.** Secure in place with a few hand-tack stitches.

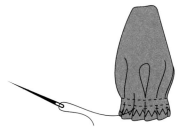

Diagram 3

2. Hand tack the gathered side of the rose center to one end of the gathered side of the petal strip. Begin wrapping the petal strip around the rose center, tacking as you go, as shown in **Diagram 4.**

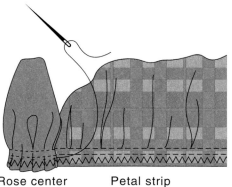

Rose center   Petal strip

Diagram 4

3. Continue to wrap and hand tack until the entire strip has been wrapped around the rose center, as shown in **Diagram 5.** Set the unit aside.

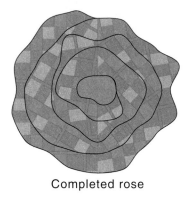

Completed rose

Diagram 5

SEWING THE HORIZONTAL STRIP

1. With right sides together, fold the horizontal leaf strip in half lengthwise. Pin and sew along the length of the strip, leaving a 3-inch opening near the middle of the strip. Remove the pins.

2. Center the seam between the two folded edges and press the seam open, as shown in **Diagram 6.**

Leave 3" opening

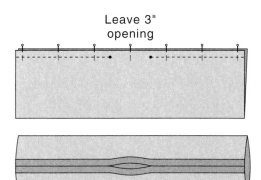

Diagram 6

3. With the seam facing up, use a chalk pencil to trace the leaf pattern 1/2 inch from each end of the strip, as shown in **Diagram 7.** Pin and sew along each line through all the layers of fabric.

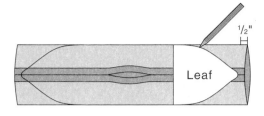

Diagram 7

4. Clip the curves and trim the seam allowance to ¼ inch. Turn the strip right side out and press.

5. Slip stitch the 3-inch opening closed. For information on slip stitching, see "Embroidery and Hand-Sewing Stitches" on page 244.

6. With the seam side facing down, fold the strip in half lengthwise. Measure and mark the center of the strip with a pin. Then measure 1³/₄ inches on either side of the center pin and 1 inch up from the fold. Mark these points with straight pins, as shown in **Diagram 8.** Remove the center pin.

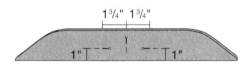

Diagram 8

7. Hand tack through all the layers at each pin. Remove the pins.

8. Unfold the strip and finger press to form two box pleats and a center cup, as shown in **Diagram 9.**

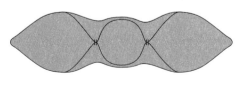

Diagram 9

9. Hand tack the box pleats in place by stitching through all the layers at the previous tacking points, as shown in **Diagram 9.**

SEWING THE VERTICAL STRIP

1. Using the vertical leaf-and-tail strip, repeat Steps 1 and 2 under "Sewing the Horizontal Strip."

2. Trace the leaf pattern onto one end of the strip. Pin along the leaf pattern line through all the layers of fabric.

3. At the other end of the strip, measure a 45-degree angle, ½ inch from the end, and mark with straight pins, as shown in **Diagram 10.** This will become the tail.

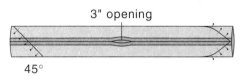

Diagram 10

4. Sew along the pattern line and the 45-degree angle. Clip the curves and trim the seam allowance to ¼ inch. Turn the strip right side out and press. Slip stitch the opening closed.

5. Referring to **Diagram 8,** with the seam side facing down, fold the strip in half lengthwise. Measure and mark a point 6 inches from the leaf end of the strip and 1 inch up from the fold with a pin.

6. Hand tack through all the layers at this point. Remove the pin. Unfold the strip and finger press to form one box pleat. Hand tack the box pleat in place by stitching through all the layers at the previous tacking point, as shown in **Diagram 9.**

FINISHING THE DECORATION

1. With the cup of the horizontal leaf strip facing right side up, place the bottom of the rose in the cup. Working from underneath the strip, hand tack the rose to the cup. Stitch all around the base of the rose to secure it in place.

2. Place the horizontal leaf strip on top of the vertical leaf-and-tail strip at the base of the vertical box pleat, as shown in **Diagram 11.** Hand tack the strips securely together all the way around the base of the rose.

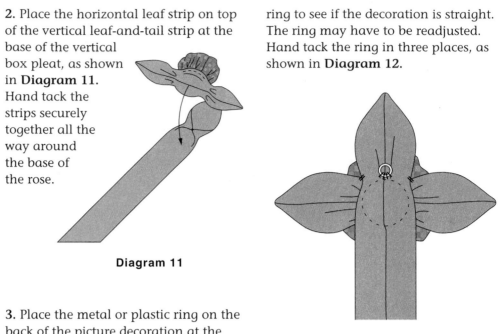

Diagram 11

3. Place the metal or plastic ring on the back of the picture decoration at the base of the vertical leaf. Hold up the ring to see if the decoration is straight. The ring may have to be readjusted. Hand tack the ring in three places, as shown in **Diagram 12.**

Diagram 12

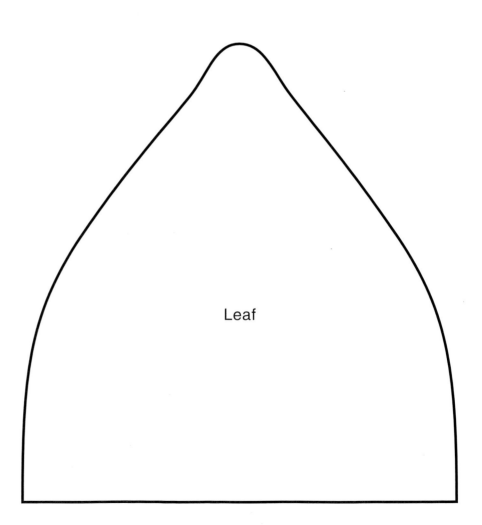

Leaf

Duvet Cover and Pillow Shams

You can almost smell the floral fragrance of a summer bouquet when you spread this duvet cover and matching pillow shams over your bed. Sewing this sumptuous set is as satisfying as walking down a garden path.

Duvet Cover and Pillow Shams

❖

Duvet Cover

SKILL LEVEL: ADVANCED

SIZE: The finished size of the duvet cover shown in the photograph on page 99 will fit a full-size comforter. For information on the fabric and cording requirements for a twin-, queen-, or king-size duvet cover and matching pillow shams, see the chart on page 105.

NOTE: Measurements in the cutting directions include the seam allowances. Sew all seams with $\frac{1}{2}$-inch seam allowances, unless indicated otherwise.

CUTTING THE COVER

Note: The front and back of the duvet cover are each made from three sections of fabric.

From the floral print, cut the following pieces:

- 1 rectangle, 39 × 89 inches, for the center front
- 1 rectangle, 39 × 89 inches, for the center back
- 2 strips, each 20 × 89 inches, for the side fronts
- 2 strips, each 20 × 89 inches, for the side backs

SEWING THE COVER FRONT

1. With right sides together, pin one side front to the center front along the longest side.

2. Sew the side front to the center front, as shown in **Diagram 1**. For durability, sew another line of stitches directly on top of the previous line of stitching. Trim the seam allowance to $\frac{1}{4}$ inch. Press the seam open.

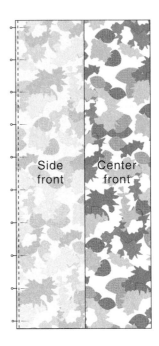

Diagram 1

3. Repeat Steps 1 and 2 to sew the remaining side front to the other side of the center front.

4. To hem the top of the cover front, turn under the $\frac{1}{2}$-inch seam allowance along the top and press, as shown in **Diagram 2**.

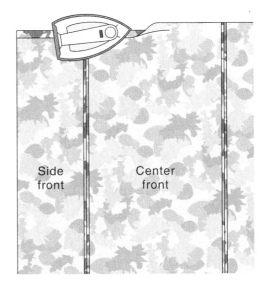

Diagram 2

5. Turn under 1 inch more and press the hem again.

6. Referring to **Diagram 3**, topstitch the hem. For information on topstitching, see "Edge Stitching and Topstitching" on page 242.

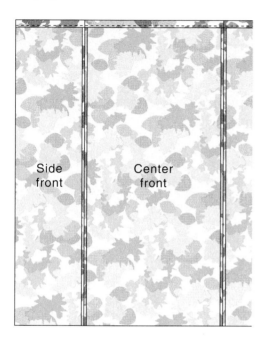

Diagram 3

Diagram 4

2. Use a zipper foot to sew the taped cording to the cover back ¼ inch from the raw edges.

SEWING THE COVER BACK

1. To sew the duvet cover back, repeat Steps 1 through 3 under "Sewing the Cover Front."

2. To hem the top of the cover back, repeat Steps 4 through 6 under "Sewing the Cover Front."

SEWING THE TAPED CORDING

1. With the right side of the cover back facing up, pin the taped cording around the sides and bottom of the cover back, rounding the cording at the corners, as shown in **Diagram 4**. Make sure the raw edges of the taped cording and the cover back are even. Do not pin the taped cording to the side that has been hemmed.

SEWING THE COVER TOGETHER

1. With right sides together, pin the cover front to the cover back, making sure the raw edges are even, and leaving the center sections open, as shown in **Diagram 5**.

Diagram 5

2. Referring to **Diagram 6**, continue using a zipper foot to sew the cover front to the cover back along the two sides and the bottom using a ¹/₂-inch seam allowance. For added durability, sew again directly on top of the previous line of stitching.

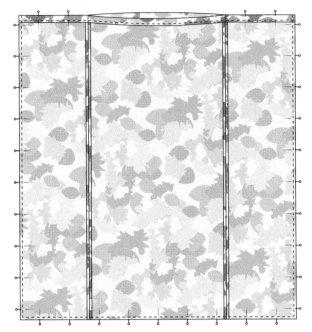

Diagram 6

3. Change to a regular presser foot and referring to **Diagram 7**, pin and sew the cover front to the cover back along the top, hemmed edges of the side sections using a 1-inch seam allowance. Before you sew, make sure the edges are even.

Diagram 7

4. Trim the bottom corners to a ¹/₂-inch seam allowance. Turn the cover right side out.

5. Turn under the 1-inch hem along the top of the center front and center back sections and press the hems. Press the entire cover.

FINISHING THE COVER

1. Unfold the 1-inch hem along the center front and center back sections.

2. Referring to **Diagram 8**, evenly space three buttons along the hem on the right side of the center back section. Thread a hand-sewing needle with matching thread and sew the buttons in place.

Diagram 8

3. Sew three buttonholes onto the right side of the center front section, making sure they align with the buttons.

4. Turn under the 1-inch hem of the center front and center back sections to button the cover.

Pillow Shams

SKILL LEVEL: *INTERMEDIATE*

SIZE: The finished size of the shams will fit standard-size pillows.

NOTE: Measurements in the cutting directions include the seam allowances. Sew all the seams with ¹/₂-inch seam allowances.

CUTTING THE SHAMS

Note: These instructions are for two pillow shams.

From the floral print, cut the following:
- 2 rectangles, each 21 × 27 inches, for the sham fronts.
- 4 rectangles, each 17 × 21 inches, for the sham back pieces.
- 4 strips, each 9 × 89 inches, for the ruffles

SEWING THE SHAM BACKS

1. Turn under a ¹/₂-inch seam allowance along one 21-inch side of one sham back piece and press the fold. Turn under 1 inch more and press the fold again.

2. Topstitch the hem ³/₄ inch from the edge, as shown in **Diagram 9.** For more information, see "Edge Stitching and Topstitching" on page 242.

Diagram 9

3. Repeat Steps 1 and 2 to form a hem on the three remaining sham back pieces.

4. To complete the sham back, with the right sides facing up, overlap 4 inches of two sham back pieces along the hemmed edges and pin them in place, as shown in **Diagram 10.** Make sure the overlapped edges along the top and bottom are even.

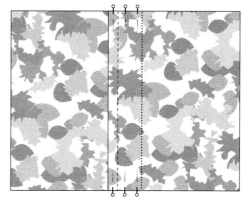

Overlap 4"

Diagram 10

5. Sew the overlapped sections in place ¹/₄ inch from the top and bottom edges, as shown in **Diagram 11.**

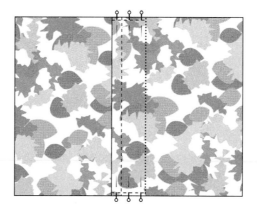

Diagram 11

6. Repeat Steps 4 and 5 to sew the two remaining sham back pieces together.

SEWING THE RUFFLES

1. With right sides together, pin and sew two ruffle strips together along the short ends, as shown in **Diagram 12**. Press the seams open.

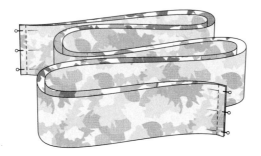

Diagram 12

2. With wrong sides together, fold the ruffle in half lengthwise, making sure to keep the circular shape and that the raw edges are even.

3. Press along the length of the fold.

4. To make one row of gathering stitches, use the longest machine stitch and sew $1/4$ inch from the raw edges of the ruffle, as shown in **Diagram 13**.

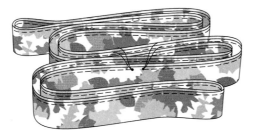

Diagram 13

5. Pull up the bobbin thread and evenly gather the ruffle to fit around the edges of one sham back. Make sure to secure the ends of the gathering threads with a knot.

6. Repeat Steps 1 through 5 to sew the remaining ruffle.

SEWING THE RUFFLES TO THE SHAM BACKS

1. With right sides together, pin one ruffle to one sham back, easing the

ruffle around the corners. Make sure the raw edges are even.

2. Sew the ruffle to the sham back with a $1/4$-inch seam allowance, as shown in **Diagram 14.**

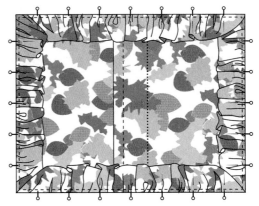

Diagram 14

3. Repeat Steps 1 and 2 to sew the remaining ruffle to the other sham back.

SEWING THE TAPED CORDING

1. With the right side of one sham back facing up, pin the taped cording around the edges of the sham back on top of the ruffle, rounding the cording at the corners, as shown in **Diagram 15**. Make sure the raw edges of the sham, ruffle, and cording are even. Overlap the ends of the cording where they meet.

Diagram 15

2. Using a zipper foot, sew the taped cording to the sham back ¹/₄ inch from the raw edges. Carefully trim the excess cording where the two ends overlap.

3. Repeat Steps 1 and 2 to sew the taped cording to the remaining pillow sham back.

FINISHING THE SHAMS

1. With right sides together, pin one sham front to one sham back, as shown in **Diagram 16**. Make sure that the ruffle and the taped cording will not get caught in the seam allowance when you sew.

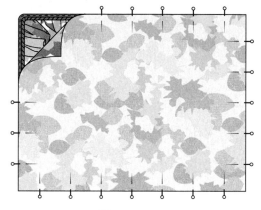

Diagram 16

2. Sew the front to the back. Turn the pillow sham right side out and press.

3. Repeat Steps 1 and 2 for the remaining sham front and sham back.

SIZE	YARDAGE		CUTTING	
	CORDING (yards)	FABRIC (yards)	CENTER FRONT AND CENTER BACK (cut 1 of each)	SIDE FRONT AND SIDE BACK (cut 2 of each)
TWIN	13¹/₂	13¹/₂	35" × 89"	18" × 89"
QUEEN	14	16¹/₄	43" × 95"	22" × 95"
KING	14¹/₄	16¹/₄	51" × 95"	26" × 95"
NOTE: PILLOW SHAMS ARE CUT FROM THE LEFTOVER FABRIC. YARDAGES ARE VERY GENEROUS.				

Tapestry Box

Fill this tapestry box with the scent of an old-fashioned bouquet to evoke warm thoughts of days gone by. A charming accent to any bedroom, dining room, or living room, a pair of them can be made in just one evening!

SIZE: The finished size of the box is 5½ inches wide, 7½ inches long, and 4 inches high.

NOTE: Measurements in the cutting directions include the seam allowances. Sew all the seams with ½-inch seam allowances.

CUTTING THE FABRIC FOR THE BOX

From the floral print, cut the following:

- 1 strip, 5 × 27 inches, for the side
- 1 strip, 4¾ × 26½ inches, for the side lining
- 1 rectangle, 6½ × 8½ inches, for the base
- 1 rectangle, 6 × 8 inches, for the base lining

SEWING THE SIDE AND SIDE LINING

With right sides together, fold the side strip in half crosswise. Pin and sew the ends together, as shown in **Diagram 1.** Press the seam open. Repeat this step for the side lining strip.

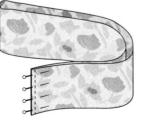

Diagram 1

SEWING THE BOX AND LINING

1. Referring to **Diagram 2**, with right sides together, pin and sew the side to the base. Clip the corners and press the seams open.

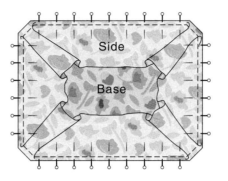

Diagram 2

2. Repeat Step 1 to sew the side lining to the base lining.

FINISHING THE BOX

1. Turn under a ½-inch seam allowance along the top edge to the wrong side of the fabric on both the box and the lining. Finger press, as shown in **Diagram 3.**

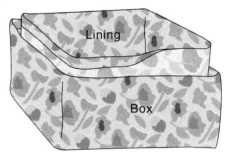

Diagram 3

2. Referring again to **Diagram 3**, with wrong sides together, place the lining inside the box.

3. Sandwich the taped edge of the fringe between the lining and the box. Pin and edge stitch the lining to the box, as shown in **Diagram 4.** For more information, see "Edge Stitching and Topstitching" on page 242.

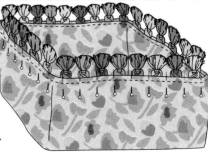

Diagram 4

4. Fill the box with potpourri, lacy handkerchiefs, or scented soaps.

MATERIALS LIST

FABRIC REQUIREMENT
- ½ YARD OF FLORAL PRINT

OTHER SUPPLIES
- 1 YARD OF COORDI-NATING FRINGE
- SEWING THREAD TO MATCH THE FABRIC

FABRIC OPTIONS
- TAPESTRY
- HEAVYWEIGHT WOOL
- PRINTED DENIM

Herbal Sleep Pillow

It's a pleasure to succumb to sleep with the soothing scent of this sleep pillow. This gift is an absolute dream for those who find it difficult to drift off to sleep. You can even make the Herbal Sleep Mix on page 111 and then fill the special pouch with it.

SIZE: The finished size of the sleep pillow is 15 inches in diameter. The finished size of the pouch is $5 \times 9^{1}/_{2}$ inches.

NOTE: Measurements in the cutting directions include the seam allowances. Sew all seams with $^{1}/_{2}$-inch seam allowances, unless indicated otherwise.

CUTTING THE PILLOW AND POUCH

1. From the pink solid, cut three 13-inch-diameter circles. One will be used for the pillow front, one for the back, and one for the pocket. Cut two 5×42-inch strips for the gathered welting.

2. From the green solid, cut one 11×13-inch rectangle for the pouch. Cut one 3×25-inch strip for the tie.

3. From the batting, cut one 13-inch-diameter circle.

4. From the interfacing, cut one 13-inch-diameter circle.

SEWING THE POCKET TO THE PILLOW FRONT

1. With wrong sides together, fold the circle for the pocket in half and press the fold.

2. Pin and sew the pocket to the pillow front, as shown in **Diagram 1.**

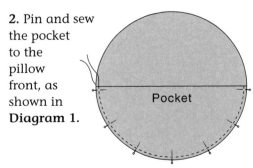

Diagram 1

SEWING THE PILLOW FRONT AND PILLOW BACK

1. With the wrong side of the pillow front facing up, pin and sew the batting to the pillow front, inside the seam allowance, as shown in **Diagram 2.**

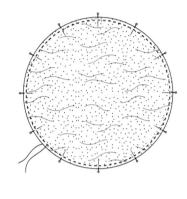

Diagram 2

2. Repeat Step 1 to sew the interfacing to the pillow back.

SEWING THE GATHERED WELTING

1. With right sides together, pin and sew the short ends of the welting strips into a continuous circle, as shown in **Diagram 3.** Be careful not to twist the strips when sewing the last seam together. Press the seams open.

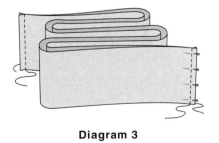

Diagram 3

2. Referring to **Diagram 4** on page 110, with wrong sides together, fold the

MATERIALS LIST
FABRIC REQUIREMENTS

- $1^{1}/_{4}$ YARDS OF PINK SOLID FOR THE GATHERED WELTING AND THE PILLOW FRONT, BACK, AND POCKET
- $^{1}/_{2}$ YARD OF GREEN SOLID FOR THE POUCH AND TIE
- 18-INCH SQUARE OF HIGH LOFT BATTING FOR LINING THE PILLOW FRONT
- $^{1}/_{2}$ YARD OF INTERFACING FOR LINING THE PILLOW BACK

OTHER SUPPLIES

- $1^{1}/_{2}$ YARDS OF 1-INCH JUMBO CORDING
- SEWING THREAD TO MATCH THE FABRICS
- HAND-SEWING NEEDLE
- 1-POUND BAG OF POLYESTER FIBERFILL
- SAFETY PINS

FABRIC OPTIONS

- MOIRÉ
- POLISHED COTTON
- LINEN
- COTTON
- TAFFETA
- SATIN

welting around the cording, matching the raw edges. Using a safety pin, securely fasten the cording to the end of the welting, 4 inches from one end of the cording.

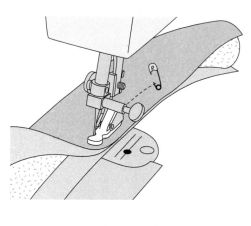

Diagram 4

3. Using a zipper foot, sew the welting ³/₈ inch from the raw edges for about 10 inches and stop sewing, making sure to leave the needle in the fabric, as shown in **Diagram 4.**

4. Carefully gather the welting behind the needle by pulling the cording toward you until the casing is tightly gathered, as shown in **Diagram 5.**

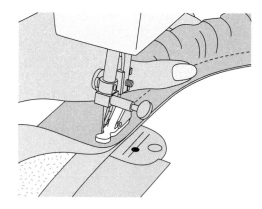

Diagram 5

5. Continue to sew and gather the welting in the same manner, stopping 4 inches from the end of the welting. Fasten this end of the cording to the welting with a safety pin.

SEWING THE WELTING TO THE PILLOW FRONT

1. With the right side of the pillow front facing up, pin the welting to the front, making sure the raw edges are even.

2. Referring to **Diagram 6,** turn the welting out into the finished position. Adjust the cording around the pillow so that the welting lies smoothly. Match the ends of the cording together and cut off the excess cording. Wrap transparent tape around each end of the cording to prevent unraveling and hand sew the ends together.

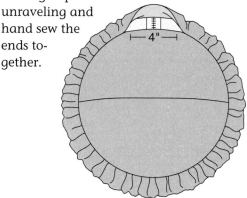

Diagram 6

3. Encase the cording within the 4-inch length of fabric yet to be sewn and gathered. Using a long stitch length, sew a row of gathering stitches along the 4 inches of fabric. Pull up the bobbin thread to gather the remaining welting, as shown in **Diagram 7.** Return the welting to the original position as described in Step 1 and pin the remaining welting to the pillow front, making sure the raw edges are even.

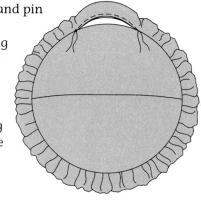

Diagram 7

4. Sew the welting to the pillow front, as shown in **Diagram 8.**

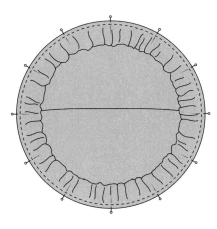

Diagram 8

SEWING THE PILLOW TOGETHER

1. With right sides together, pin and sew the pillow back to the pillow front, leaving a 5-inch opening. Trim the seam allowance to ¼ inch and clip several V-shaped notches, as shown in **Diagram 9.**

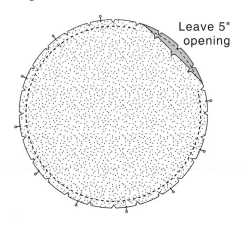

Leave 5" opening

Diagram 9

2. Trim the batting close to the seam allowance. Turn the pillow right side out and stuff with polyester fiberfill. Turn under the seam allowance along the opening and blindstitch it closed. For information on blindstitching, see "Embroidery and Hand-Sewing Stitches" on page 244.

SEWING THE POUCH

1. With right sides together, fold and pin the rectangle for the pouch in half crosswise, matching the raw edges. Sew the edges together, as shown in **Diagram 10.**

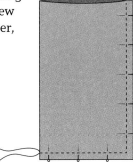

Diagram 10

2. Turn down and press a ½-inch hem along the top edge of the pouch. Turn down and press 3 inches more along the top of the pouch. Turn the pouch right side out and press.

3. With right sides together, fold and pin the strip for the tie in half lengthwise, matching the raw edges. Sew the edges together, leaving one end open for turning, as shown in **Diagram 11.** Turn the tie right side out and press. Turn under the seam allowance along the open end and blindstitch it closed.

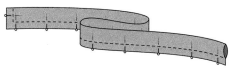

Diagram 11

FINISHING THE PILLOW

1. Fill the pouch with your favorite potpourri or the Herbal Sleep Mix on the right. Be sure the recipient of the pillow is not allergic to the floral materials in the recipe before using it in the pouch.

2. Close the pouch with the tie and insert it into the pocket on the front of the pillow.

Know&Sew

INSTEAD OF THE TWO-STEP METHOD OF NOTCHING AND TRIMMING THE SEAM ALLOWANCE AFTER SEWING THE PILLOW BACK AND FRONT TOGETHER, SAVE TIME AND DO IT ALL IN ONE STEP. USE PINKING SHEARS TO TRIM THE SEAM ALLOWANCE AND THERE WILL BE NO NEED TO CLIP ANY NOTCHES. THE PINKED EDGE HELPS TO RELEASE THE SEAM ALLOWANCES ON THE CURVE.

HERBAL SLEEP MIX

1 cup of dried mint
1 cup of dried rosebuds
½ cup of dried chamomile
½ tablespoon of ground cloves
½ tablespoon of pinhead orris root

Mix all the ingredients together in a bowl.

Bow Picture Decoration

Transform any wall into an elegant picture gallery with this decorative bow. A breeze to sew in no time at all, it will draw instant attention to your favorite picture or painting.

SIZE: The finished size is approximately 10 inches wide and 32 inches long.

NOTE: Measurements in the cutting directions include the seam allowances. Sew all the seams with ¹/₂-inch seam allowances.

CUTTING THE DECORATION

From the floral print, cut the following:
- 2 strips, each 8 × 45 inches, for the large bow
- 1 strip, 8 × 45 inches, for the small bow
- 1 rectangle, 2 × 5 inches, for the center strip

SEWING THE LARGE BOW

1. With right sides together, pin and sew the strips for the large bow together along one short side. Trim the seam allowance to ¹/₄ inch and press the seam open. The strip is now 89 inches long. Open the strip.

2. With right sides together, fold the strip in half lengthwise and pin. Sew the lengthwise edges together, leaving a 3-inch opening at the short center seam, as shown in **Diagram 1.**

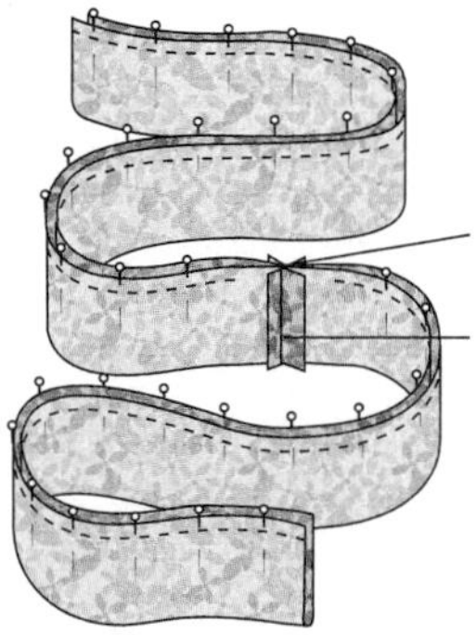

Leave 3" opening

Short center seam

Diagram 1

3. Center the seam between the two folded edges and press the seam open, as shown in **Diagram 2.** Turn the strip over.

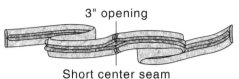

3" opening

Short center seam

Diagram 2

4. Referring to **Diagram 3**, measure 42 inches on either side of the short center seam and mark each point with a straight pin.

Short center seam

Diagram 3

5. Referring to **Diagram 4**, use a chalk pencil to mark a 45-degree angle at each marker pin. Sew along these angles.

45°

Short center seam

Diagram 4

6. Clip off the corners on either end and trim the seam allowances to ¹/₄ inch, as shown in **Diagram 5.**

Diagram 5

7. Turn the strip right side out and press. Slip stitch the opening closed. For information on slip stitching, see

MATERIALS LIST

FABRIC REQUIREMENT
- ³/₄ YARD OF 45-INCH-WIDE FLORAL PRINT

OTHER SUPPLIES
- SEWING THREAD TO MATCH THE FABRIC
- ¹/₂-INCH-DIAMETER PLASTIC OR METAL RING
- HAND-SEWING NEEDLE
- CHALK PENCIL

FABRIC OPTIONS
- POLISHED COTTON
- COTTON JACQUARD
- VELVET
- SATIN
- MOIRÉ
- LINEN

"Embroidery and Hand-Sewing Stitches" on page 244.

8. With the seam side facing up, and the points of the strip ends toward you, measure 5$\frac{1}{2}$ inches on either side of the short center seam. Mark each point with a straight pin, as shown in **Diagram 6.**

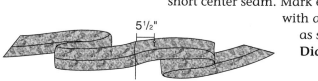

Short center seam

Diagram 6

9. Fold the left side of the strip until the pin matches the short center seam, as shown in **Diagram 7.** Repin through all the layers of fabric. Repeat with the right side of the strip. Pin the right side of the strip on top of the left side of the strip at the short center seam to complete the bow.

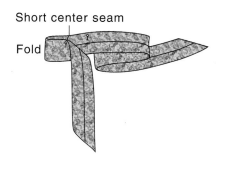

Short center seam

Fold

Diagram 7

10. To make a crimp in the bow, fold the bow in half lengthwise. Place a straight pin along the short center seam, 1 inch up from this bottom fold. Using a wide zigzag stitch, tack all thicknesses of the fabric together only at this point, as shown in **Diagram 8.** Unfold the bow.

Tack at this point only

Short center seam

Diagram 8

SEWING THE SMALL BOW

1. With right sides together, fold and pin the strip for the small bow in half lengthwise. Sew the lengthwise edges together, leaving a 3-inch opening at the center. Then repeat Step 3 under "Sewing the Large Bow."

2. Fold the strip in half crosswise and press. Open the strip up and mark the center fold with a pin.

3. Measure 20 inches on either side of the center pin and mark each point with a straight pin.

4. Referring to **Diagram 4** on page 113, use a chalk pencil to mark a 45-degree angle at each marker pin. Sew along these angles.

5. Repeat Steps 6 and 7 under "Sewing the Large Bow."

6. With the seam side facing up, and the points of the strip ends toward you, measure 4$\frac{1}{2}$ inches on either side of the center pin. Mark each point with a straight pin, as shown in **Diagram 6.**

7. Repeat Steps 9 and 10 under "Sewing the Large Bow," substituting the center pin for the short center seam.

SEWING THE CENTER STRIP

1. With right sides together, fold and pin the center-strip rectangle in half lengthwise. Sew the edges together, leaving one short side open. Clip the corner and trim the seam allowance to $\frac{1}{4}$ inch, as shown in **Diagram 9.**

Diagram 9

2. Turn the strip right side out. Set the machine for a narrow stitch width and a short stitch length. Zigzag along the remaining short side to prevent fraying.

ASSEMBLING THE DECORATION

1. Center the zigzagged end of the center strip on the center back of the large bow. Thread a hand-sewing needle with matching thread and sew this end of the strip to the bow.

2. With the angled ends hanging down, lay the small bow on top of the large bow. Wrap the center strip up and over the small bow, as shown in **Diagram 10,** and then back around to the large bow.

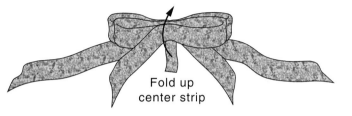

Fold up
center strip

Diagram 10

3. Pull the center strip tightly enough to hold the bows in place and pin. Securely hand tack the ends of the center strip in place.

FINISHING THE DECORATION

With the back of the large bow facing up, place the plastic or metal ring in the middle of the center strip. Hand tack the ring in three places, as shown in **Diagram 11.**

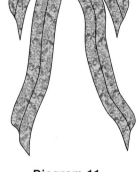

Diagram 11

Pillow Sachet

This sweetly scented pillow is meant to be pleasingly plump when filled with your favorite potpourri. The clever design of the pillow back allows you to change the potpourri as often as you wish. Slip into spring with a mixture of garden fragrances. Or warm up to winter with cinnamon and cloves.

SIZE: The finished size is 21 inches long and 14$\frac{1}{2}$ inches high.

NOTE: Measurements in the cutting directions include the seam allowances. Sew all the seams with $\frac{1}{2}$-inch seam allowances.

CUTTING THE PILLOW SACHET

1. Trace the pattern pieces on pages 119–121 onto tracing paper, making sure to match the two sections of the pillow front and the two sections of the pillow back before cutting. Cut out the pattern pieces and open up the pillow front pattern.

2. From the blue-and-white print, with the right side of the fabric facing up, cut one pillow front, one pillow back, and one pillow back reverse. Cut two 6 × 41-inch bias strips for the ruffle.

3. From the eyelet, cut one 81-inch-length for trimming the ruffle.

SEWING THE RUFFLE

1. With right sides together, pin and sew the ruffle strips together along the short ends, as shown in **Diagram 1**. Press the seams open.

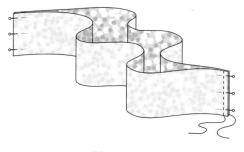

Diagram 1

2. With wrong sides together, fold the ruffle in half lengthwise, maintaining the circular shape, and press.

3. With right sides together, fold the eyelet in half crosswise. Pin and sew the short ends together.

4. Finish the raw edges of the eyelet with a medium-width zigzag stitch, as shown in **Diagram 2**.

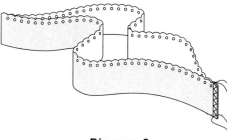

Diagram 2

5. Referring to **Diagram 3**, pin the eyelet inside the ruffle, matching the raw edges. The right side of the eyelet should be facing the right side of the ruffle.

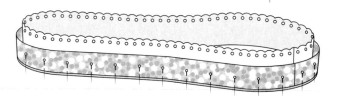

Diagram 3

6. To make two rows of gathering stitches, use the longest machine stitch and sew $\frac{1}{4}$ inch from the raw edges.

7. Sew another line of stitches $\frac{1}{4}$ inch away from the first row of stitching, as shown in **Diagram 4** on page 118. Pull up the bobbin threads and evenly gather the ruffle to fit around the pillow front. Secure the ends of the threads with a knot.

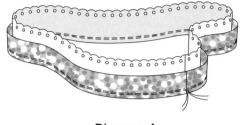

Diagram 4

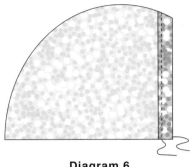

Diagram 6

Know & Sew

FOR A MORE LUXURIOUS-LOOKING PILLOW, ADD COORDINATING PIPING TO THE PILLOW BEFORE ATTACHING THE RUFFLE. STARTING AT THE BOTTOM EDGE, PIN AND SEW THE PIPING TO THE PILLOW FRONT, MAKING SURE TO OVERLAP THE EDGES OF THE PIPING. THEN TRIM THE EXCESS PIPING. TO CONTINUE SEWING THE PILLOW, TRY USING A JEANS NEEDLE TO HELP SEW THROUGH THE MANY LAYERS OF FABRIC.

SEWING THE RUFFLE TO THE PILLOW FRONT

1. Pin the ruffle to the right side of the pillow front, making sure that the raw edges are even and that the eyelet is sandwiched between the pillow front and the ruffle.

2. Sew the ruffle to the pillow front between the two rows of gathering stitches, as shown in **Diagram 5**. Remove the second row of gathering stitches.

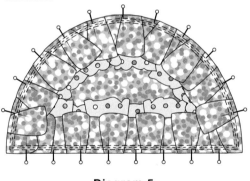

Diagram 5

HEMMING THE PILLOW BACKS

1. To make a hem on the pillow back, turn under $1/2$ inch along the short straight edge of the pillow back and press.

2. Turn under 1 inch more and press the hem again.

3. Edge stitch the hem in place along the inner edge, as shown in **Diagram 6**. For more information, see "Edge Stitching and Topstitching" on page 242.

4. Repeat Steps 1 through 3 to hem the short straight edge of the pillow back reverse.

ASSEMBLING THE PILLOW

1. With the right side of the pillow front facing up, fold the ruffle toward the center of the pillow front.

2. With right sides together, pin the pillow back to the pillow front. Then pin the pillow back reverse to the pillow front. The pillow back and back reverse should overlap, as shown in **Diagram 7**.

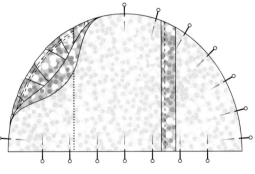

Diagram 7

3. Sew the pillow back to the pillow front. Clip several V-shaped notches in the curves and turn the pillow right side out.

FINISHING THE PILLOW SACHET

Fill the pillow sachet with your favorite potpourri.

Pillow Front
(section 2 of 2)

Match to section 1

Pillow Front
(section 1 of 2)
Cut 1

Match to section 2

Place on fold of tracing paper

Pillow Back and Pillow Back Reverse
(section 1 of 2)
Cut 1 of each

Match to section 2

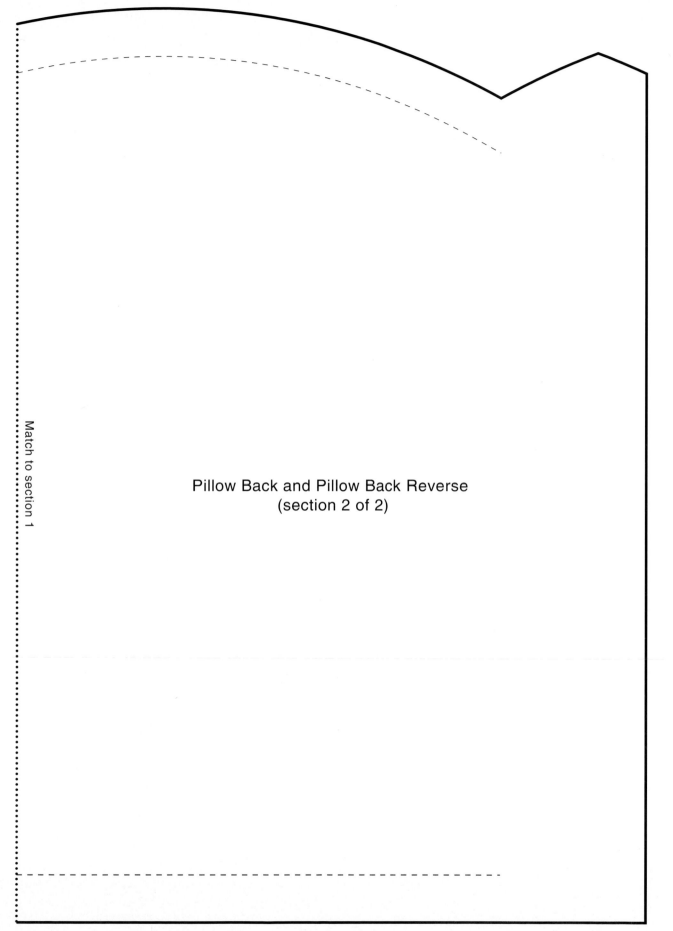

Match to section 1

Pillow Back and Pillow Back Reverse
(section 2 of 2)

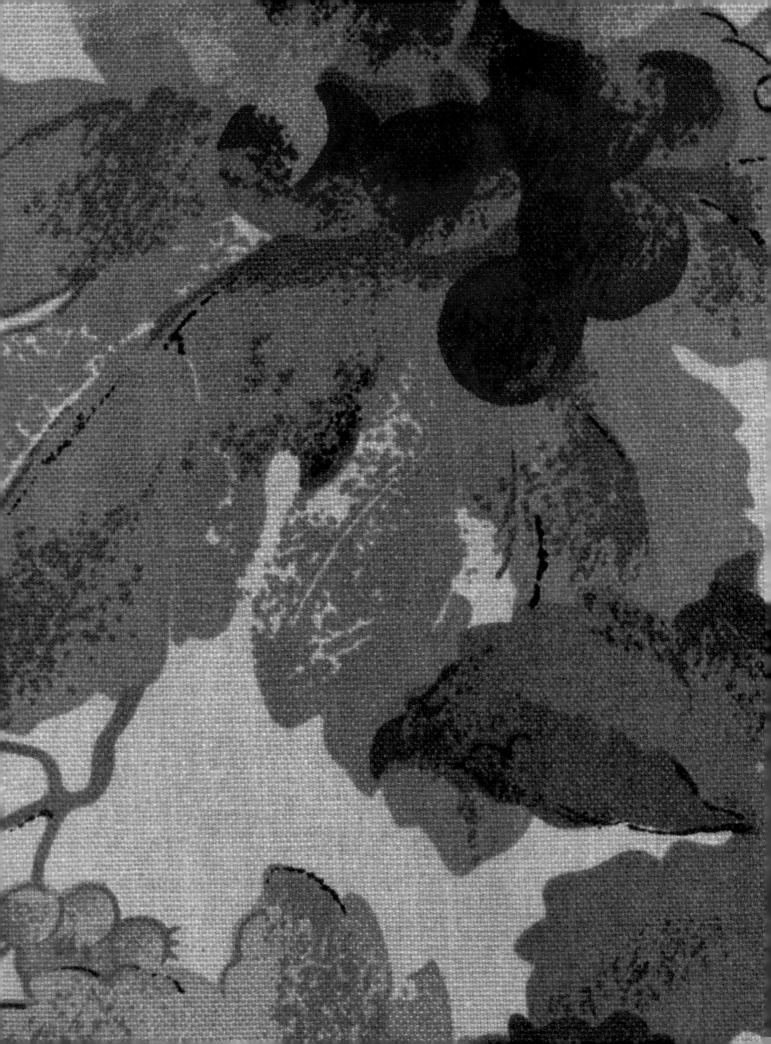

BAG IT – FOR PEOPLE ON THE GO

Drawstring Evening Bag

For an evening of sophisticated fun, tote this little drawstring bag along to the theater, ballet, or formal affair. Though petite, there's plenty of room in it for all of the evening's essentials. To complete a weekend wardrobe, make one bag embellished with satin stitching and another with rhinestones.

SIZE: The finished size is 12$\frac{1}{2}$ inches wide and 8$\frac{1}{2}$ inches high.

NOTE: Measurements in the cutting directions include the seam allowances. Sew all seams with $\frac{1}{4}$ inch seam allowances. There are two options for decorating the front of the evening bag. Follow the appropriate section on embellishing according to your choice.

CUTTING THE EVENING BAG

1. To make the complete evening bag pattern, fold a sheet of tracing paper in half and trace the pattern piece on page 128 onto the paper, transferring all markings. Cut out the pattern and open it up.

2. From the black solid, cut two evening bags. One will be used for the bag front and one will be used for the bag back. Using a chalk pencil, transfer all markings to the right side of the bag front and bag back.

3. From the black lining, cut two evening bags. One will be used for the lining front and one will be used for the lining back.

4. Cut the black cording into two lengths.

EMBELLISHING THE BAG WITH RHINESTONES

1. Trace the rhinestone spiral pattern on page 129 onto tracing paper. Center and transfer the pattern to the right side of the bag front.

2. Following the manufacturer's directions, attach the rhinestones to the right side of the bag front at the indicated placements dots, as shown in **Diagram 1**.

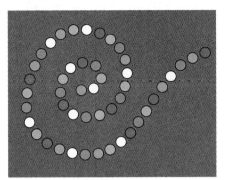

Rhinestones

Diagram 1

EMBELLISHING THE BAG WITH SATIN STITCHING

1. Trace the satin stitch spiral pattern on page 129 onto tracing paper. Center and transfer the pattern to the right side of the bag front.

2. Set the sewing machine for a narrow zigzag stitch and a short stitch length. With metallic thread, zigzag each pattern line in a different color, tapering the satin stitch as you near the end, as shown in **Diagram 2**. Clip the threads close to the stitching.

Tapered satin stitch

Diagram 2

MATERIALS LIST
FABRIC REQUIREMENTS
- $\frac{3}{8}$ YARD OF BLACK SOLID FOR THE BAG
- $\frac{3}{8}$ YARD OF BLACK SOLID FOR THE LINING

OTHER SUPPLIES
- $\frac{3}{4}$ YARD OF $\frac{1}{8}$-INCH BLACK PIPING
- 2 YARDS OF $\frac{1}{4}$-INCH BLACK CORDING
- SEWING THREAD TO MATCH THE FABRIC
- HAND-SEWING NEEDLE
- 2 BLACK TASSELS, EACH 2 INCHES LONG
- 12 METAL RINGS, EACH $\frac{5}{8}$ INCH DIAMETER
- TRACING PAPER
- CHALK PENCIL

OPTIONAL SUPPLIES FOR EMBELLISHMENT
- METALLIC SEWING THREAD IN RED, GOLD, PURPLE, AND BLUE
- PACKAGE OF ASSORTED GLUE-ON RHINESTONES OR RHINESTONE STUDS

FABRIC OPTIONS
FOR THE EVENING BAG
- VELVET
- VELVETEEN
- POLISHED COTTON
- LINEN
FOR THE LINING
- POLYESTER
- SATEEN
- MOIRÉ

SEWING THE PIPING TO THE BAG FRONT

1. With the right side of the bag front facing up, pin the piping around the sides and bottom of the bag front, matching the raw edges.

2. Using a zipper foot, sew the piping to the bag front, as shown in **Diagram 3**.

Diagram 3

SEWING THE FRONT AND BACK TOGETHER

1. With right sides together, pin the bag front and the bag back together, making sure the piping is sandwiched between the layers, as shown in **Diagram 4**. Do not turn right side out at this time.

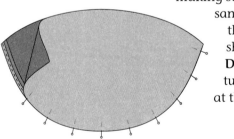

Diagram 4

2. Using a zipper foot, sew the bag front and bag back together directly over the line of stitching for the piping, making sure to leave the top open.

SEWING THE LINING

1. With right sides together, pin and sew the lining front and lining back together, leaving a 3-inch opening at the bottom for turning, as shown in **Diagram 5**. Turn the lining right side out.

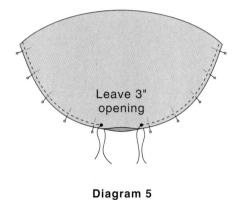

Leave 3" opening

Diagram 5

2. With the right sides of the lining and the bag facing each other, insert the lining into the bag, as shown in **Diagram 6**.

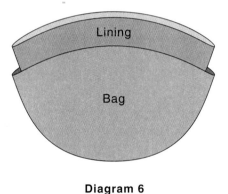

Lining

Bag

Diagram 6

3. Pin and sew the lining to the bag along the top edge, as shown in **Diagram 7**.

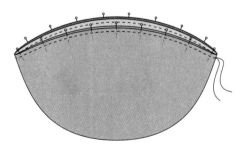

Diagram 7

4. Turn the bag right side out through the 3-inch opening in the lining. Turn under the seam allowance along the opening and slip stitch it closed. For information on slip stitching, see "Embroidery and Hand-Sewing Stitches" on page 244.

ATTACHING THE RINGS

Referring to the ring placement marks on the right side of the bag, securely hand tack each ring with a few stitches, as shown in **Diagram 8**.

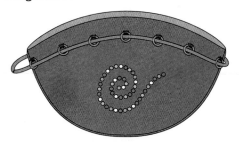

Diagram 8

FINISHING THE EVENING BAG

1. Beginning and ending at one side seam, insert one length of cording through all of the rings, as shown in **Diagram 9**.

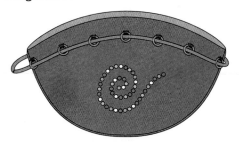

Diagram 9

2. Hand tack the ends of the cording together with a few stitches.

3. Referring to **Diagram 10**, insert the remaining length of cording through all of the rings, beginning and ending at the other side seam.

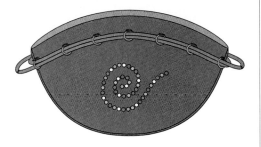

Diagram 10

4. Hand tack the ends of this length of cording together with a few stitches.

5. Hand tack one tassel to the joined end of each length of cording, as shown in **Diagram 11**.

Diagram 11

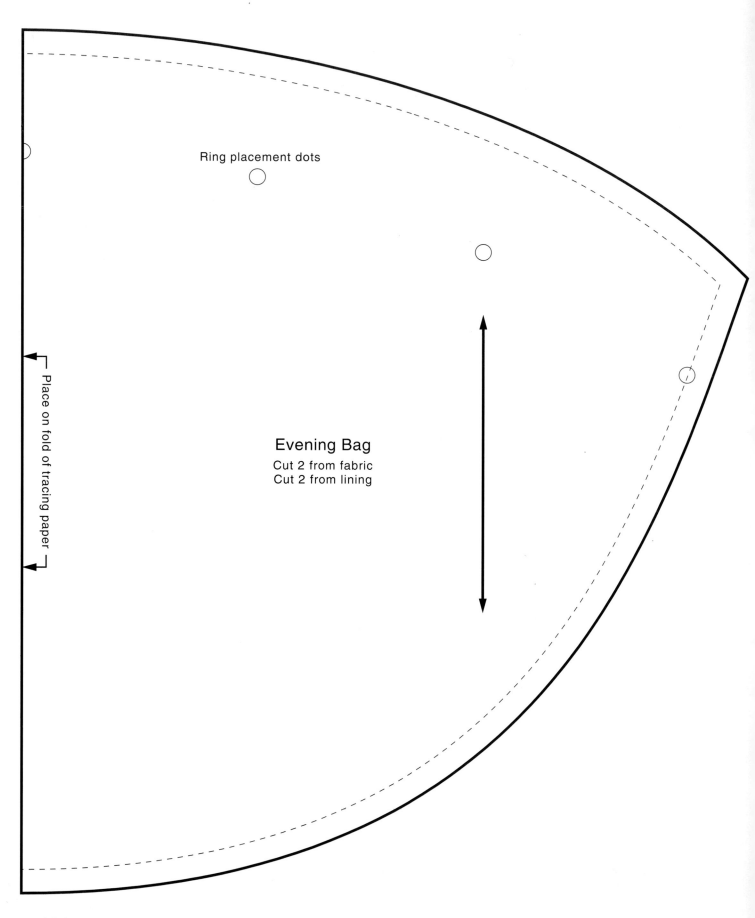

Ring placement dots

Place on fold of tracing paper

Evening Bag

Cut 2 from fabric
Cut 2 from lining

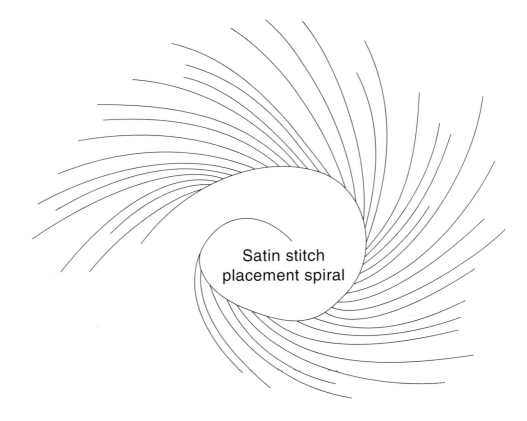

Satin stitch
placement spiral

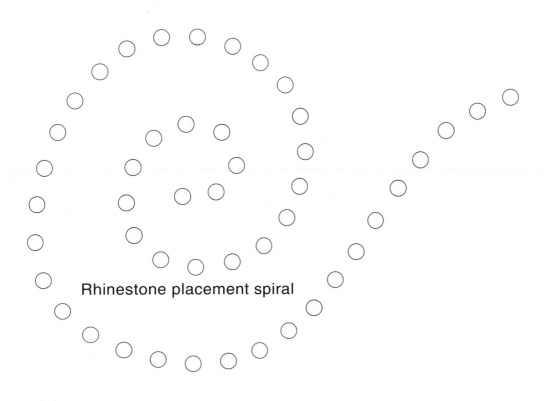

Rhinestone placement spiral

Business Portfolio

This fully lined portfolio is a practical carryall for today's businesswoman. The inside and outside pockets make it easy to locate important paperwork, files, appointment books, and more. Special pockets hold pens, pencils, and business cards. This stylish accessory is one that every professional woman should have.

SIZE: The finished size is approximately 18 inches wide and 13 inches high.

NOTE: Measurements in the cutting directions include the seam allowances. Sew all seams with ¼-inch seam allowances, unless otherwise indicated.

CUTTING THE PORTFOLIO

1. Trace the pattern pieces on pages 135–143 onto tracing paper, transferring all markings. Cut out the pattern pieces.

2. To make the complete pattern, align all of the pieces along the indicated lines and tape them together, as shown in **Diagram 1**. Using a chalk pencil, transfer all of the markings onto the right side of the fabric.

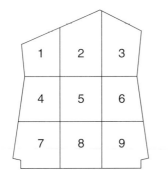

Diagram 1

Note: In the following cutting instructions, cut all the pieces with the pattern right side up on the right side of the fabric unless otherwise indicated.

3. From the print, cut one front, one back pocket, and one front pocket. Cut one full-size portfolio with the pattern wrong side up and placed on the right side of the fabric.

4. From the lining, cut one full-size portfolio, one front, one back pocket lining, and one front pocket lining.

5. From the webbing, cut one front, one back pocket lining, and one front pocket lining. Cut one full-size portfolio with the wrong side of the pattern facing up on the right side of the webbing.

6. From the interfacing, cut one front. Cut one full-size portfolio with the wrong side of the pattern facing up.

7. From the fusible knit interfacing, cut one full-size portfolio and one front.

8. From the suede, cut one 5 × 7-inch rectangle for the business card pocket.

9. From the plastic, cut one $2\frac{1}{2} \times 3\frac{1}{2}$-inch piece for the business card pocket.

FUSING THE PORTFOLIO

1. Remove the paper from the webbing for the full-size portfolio. Place it between the wrong side of the print full-size portfolio and the interfacing for the full-size portfolio, as shown in **Diagram 2**. Repeat this step for the front pieces of webbing, print, and interfacing.

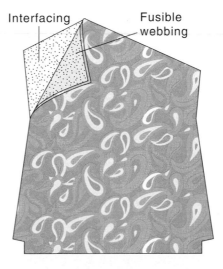

Interfacing   Fusible webbing

Diagram 2

MATERIALS LIST

FABRIC REQUIREMENTS
- $1\frac{1}{8}$ YARDS OF PRINT FOR THE PORTFOLIO
- $1\frac{1}{8}$ YARDS OF COORDINATING FABRIC FOR THE LINING
- 2 YARDS OF FUSIBLE WEBBING
- $1\frac{1}{8}$ YARDS OF 22-INCH-WIDE INTERFACING
- $\frac{3}{4}$ YARD OF 60-INCH-WIDE FUSIBLE KNIT INTERFACING
- 5 × 7-INCH RECTANGLE OF SYNTHETIC SUEDE

OTHER SUPPLIES
- SEWING THREAD TO MATCH THE FABRICS
- HAND-SEWING NEEDLE
- 3 × 5-INCH RECTANGLE OF LIGHTWEIGHT PLASTIC
- MAGNETIC SNAP
- TRACING PAPER
- CHALK PENCIL
- CRAFT GLUE

FABRIC OPTIONS

FOR THE PORTFOLIO
- TAPESTRY
- BROCADE
- DENIM
- SYNTHETIC SUEDE
- SYNTHETIC LEATHER

FOR THE LINING
- POLISHED COTTON
- COTTON

Know&Sew

HERE ARE A FEW
POINTERS FOR TROUBLE-
SHOOTING WHEN USING
FUSIBLE INTERFACING.
ALWAYS REMEMBER TO
TEST THE INTERFACING
WITH A SCRAP OF FABRIC
BEFORE USING IT ON ALL
OF THE FABRIC. IF THE
INTERFACING BUBBLES
AFTER YOU HAVE FUSED
IT TO THE FABRIC, THE
IRON WAS PROBABLY
TOO HOT. LOWER THE
TEMPERATURE OF THE
IRON AND TEST AGAIN.
IF THE INTERFACING
READILY PEELS AWAY
FROM THE FABRIC AFTER
FUSING, THE IRON WAS
PROBABLY TOO COOL.
SET THE IRON FOR A
HIGHER TEMPERATURE
AND TEST AGAIN.

2. Following the manufacturer's directions, fuse the full-size portfolio pieces together. Repeat this step for the front pieces.

3. Following the manufacturer's directions, iron the fusible knit interfacing for the full-size portfolio to the wrong side of the full-size portfolio lining. Repeat this step for the front pieces of fusible knit interfacing and lining.

FUSING THE FRONT AND BACK POCKETS

1. With right sides together, pin and sew the print front pocket to the front pocket lining along the top edge, as shown in **Diagram 3**.

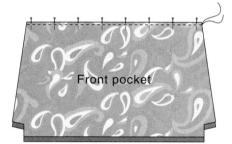

Front pocket lining

Diagram 3

2. Following the manufacturer's directions, iron the fusible webbing for the front pocket lining to the wrong side of the front pocket lining.

3. Remove the paper backing from the fusible webbing and turn the pieces to the right side. The fusible webbing will be sandwiched between the wrong sides of the print and the lining.

4. Pull the bottom edge of the front pocket down to the bottom edge of the front pocket lining, matching the raw edges and allowing ¼ inch of the lining to show along the top edge, as shown in **Diagram 4**. Fuse the pieces together.

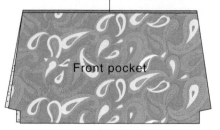

Front pocket lining

Diagram 4

5. Repeat Steps 1 through 4 to fuse the print back pocket to the back pocket lining.

SEWING THE BUSINESS CARD POCKET

1. Fold the synthetic suede in half crosswise, finger press and unfold. Cut one $2\frac{1}{4} \times 3\frac{1}{4}$-inch window out of the center of one side, as shown in **Diagram 5**.

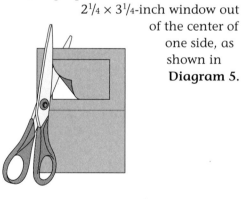

Diagram 5

2. With the wrong side of the fabric facing up, glue the plastic piece to the window and let dry. Stitch the plastic in place, as shown in **Diagram 6**.

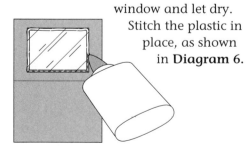

Diagram 6

3. With wrong sides together, fold the synthetic suede in half along the previous fold and sew it along three sides, leaving the top edge open, as shown in **Diagram 7**. Trim the seam allowance close to the stitching line with pinking shears.

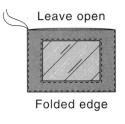

Leave open

Folded edge

Diagram 7

4. Pin the business card pocket to the right side of the front pocket, 1 inch from the top edge and 1 inch from the side edge at the right, as shown in **Diagram 8**. Sew the business card pocket to the front pocket on top of the previous stitching lines, making sure to leave the top edge open.

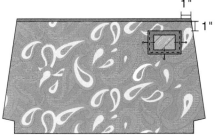

1"

1"

Diagram 8

INSERTING THE MAGNETIC SNAP

1. Following the manufacturer's directions, attach half of the snap to the print side of the front pocket, at the indicated placement mark.

2. Attach the other half of the snap to the flap of the full-size portfolio lining, at the indicated placement mark, so that the two halves of the snap align when closed.

SEWING THE POCKET COMPARTMENTS

1. With right sides facing up, pin and sew the front pocket to the front inside the seam allowance, making sure the raw edges are even along the sides and bottom and the top edge of the pocket is left open, as shown in **Diagram 9**.

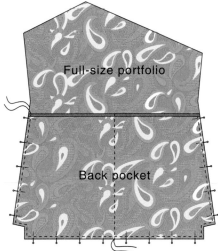

Front

Front pocket

Snap

Diagram 9

2. Sew the front pocket and front together along the pencil-holder stitching lines to form a pen-and-pencil compartment, as shown in **Diagram 9**.

3. With right sides facing up, pin and sew the back pocket to the full-size portfolio inside the seam allowance, making sure the raw edges are even along the sides and bottom and the top edge of the pocket is left open, as shown in **Diagram 10**.

Full-size portfolio

Back pocket

Diagram 10

4. Beginning at the upper edge of the back pocket, sew the back pocket to the full-size portfolio down the center to form two pockets, as shown in **Diagram 10**.

SEWING THE PORTFOLIO TOGETHER

1. With right sides together, pin and sew the back pocket–full-size portfolio unit to the front pocket–front unit along the side and bottom seams, making sure to leave an opening between the dots at each corner, as shown in **Diagram 11.** Do not turn right side out.

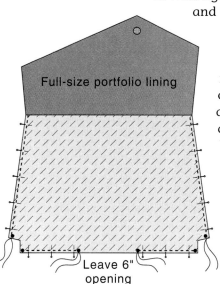

Diagram 11

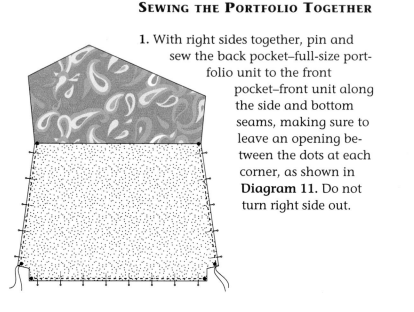

Side edge

Bottom edge

Diagram 13

2. With right sides together, pin and sew the full-size portfolio lining to the front lining along the side and bottom seams, making sure to leave an opening between the dots at each corner and a 6-inch opening at the bottom, as shown in **Diagram 12.** Do not turn right side out. Set this unit aside.

Full-size portfolio lining

Leave 6" opening

Diagram 12

3. Turn the bottom edge of the portfolio up to align with one side edge, making sure the edges are even. Miter the corner by stitching along the edge of the corner, as shown in **Diagram 13.** Repeat for the remaining side edge and corner of the portfolio. Turn the portfolio right side out.

4. Repeat Step 3 to miter the corners of the portfolio lining. Do not turn the lining right side out.

FINISHING THE PORTFOLIO

1. With right sides together, insert the portfolio into the lining. Referring to **Diagram 14,** sew around the flap from one dot to the other. Then sew from one dot to the other along each side.

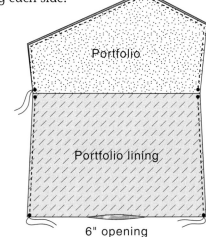

Portfolio

Portfolio lining

6" opening

Diagram 14

2. Finally, sew across the top of the front, making sure to sew through only one layer of print and one layer of lining.

3. Turn the portfolio right side out through the opening in the lining. Turn under the seam allowance along the opening in the lining and slip stitch it closed. For information on slip stitching, see "Embroidery and Hand-Sewing Stitches" on page 244. Insert the lining into the portfolio.

Portfolio
(section 1 of 9)

Match to section 2

Match to section 4

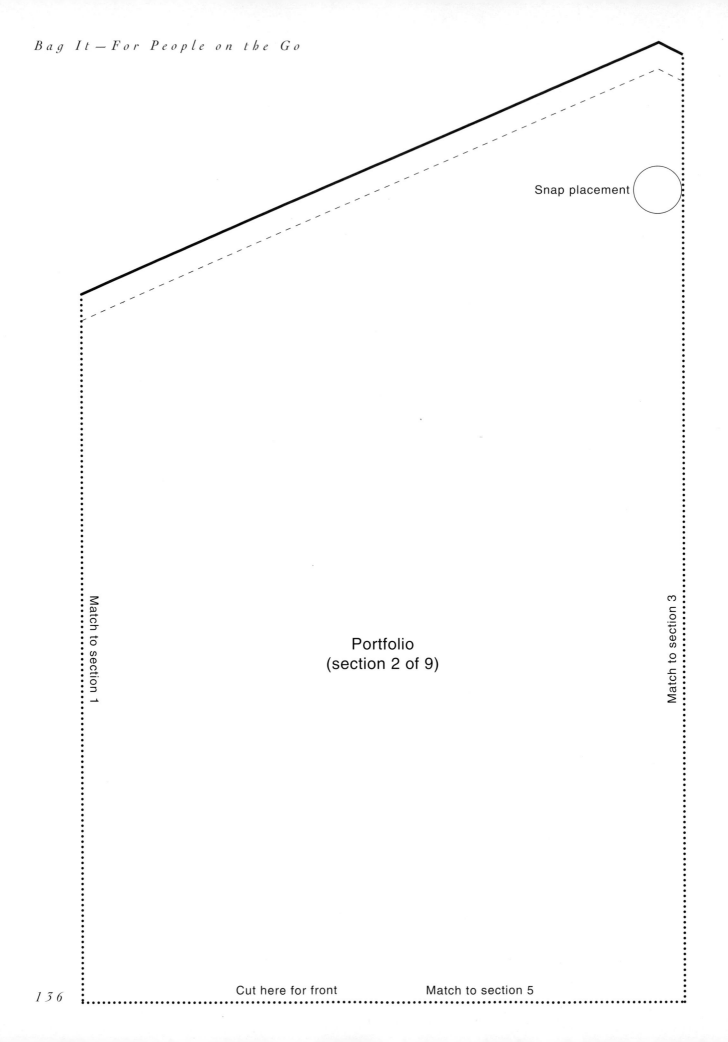

Snap placement

Match to section 1

Match to section 3

Portfolio
(section 2 of 9)

Cut here for front

Match to section 5

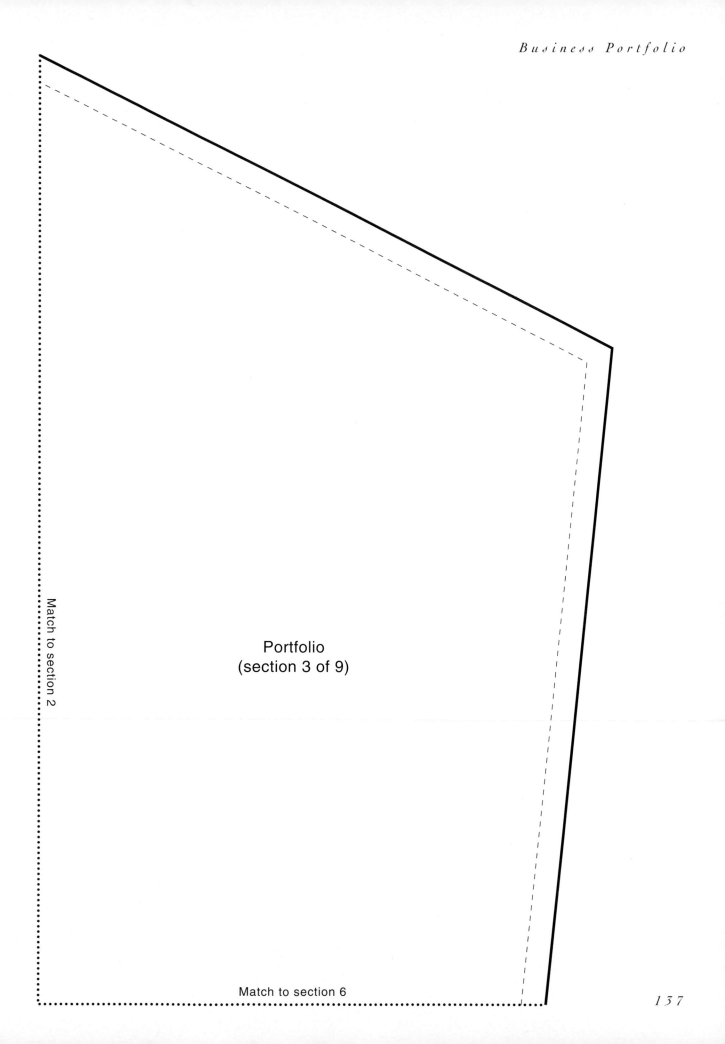

Portfolio
(section 3 of 9)

Match to section 2

Match to section 6

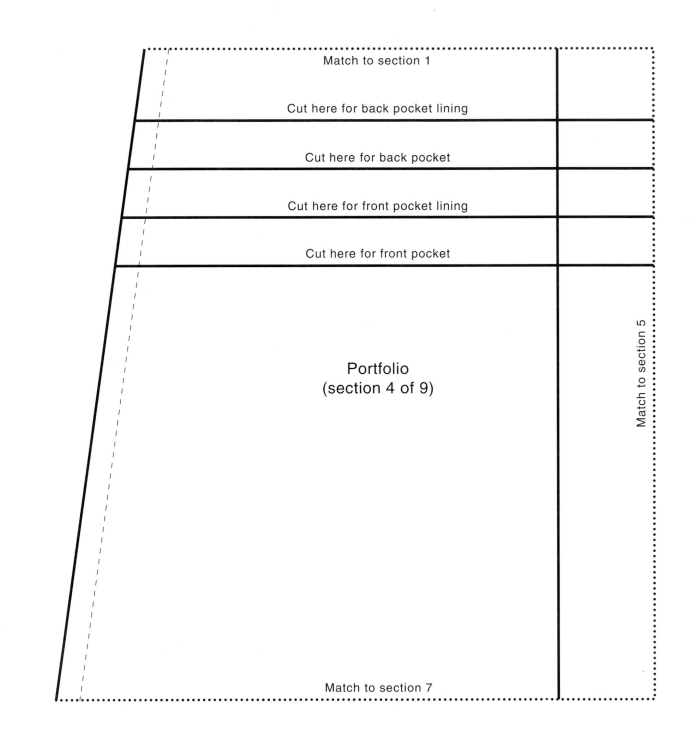

Match to section 1

Cut here for back pocket lining

Cut here for back pocket

Cut here for front pocket lining

Cut here for front pocket

Portfolio
(section 4 of 9)

Match to section 5

Match to section 7

Match to section 2

Match to section 4

Portfolio
(section 5 of 9)

Match to section 6

Match to section 8

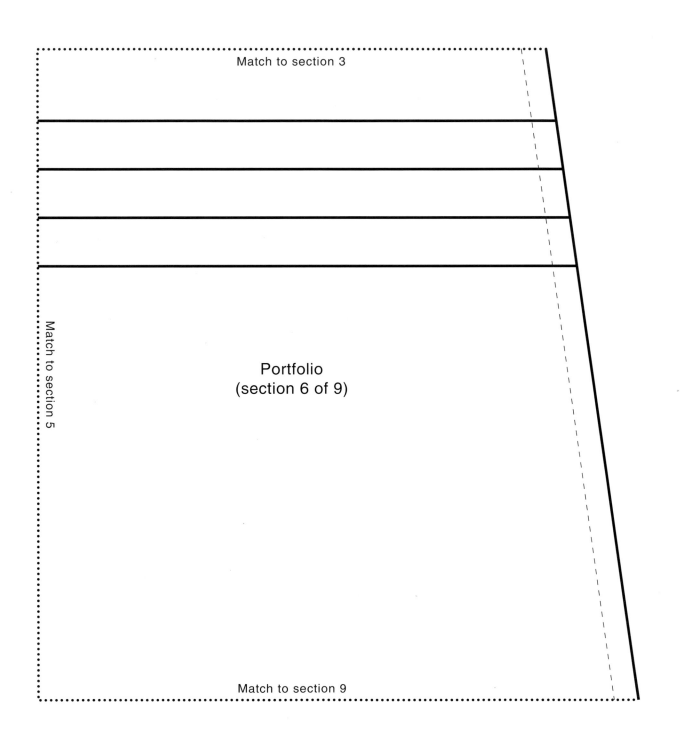

Match to section 3

Match to section 5

Portfolio
(section 6 of 9)

Match to section 9

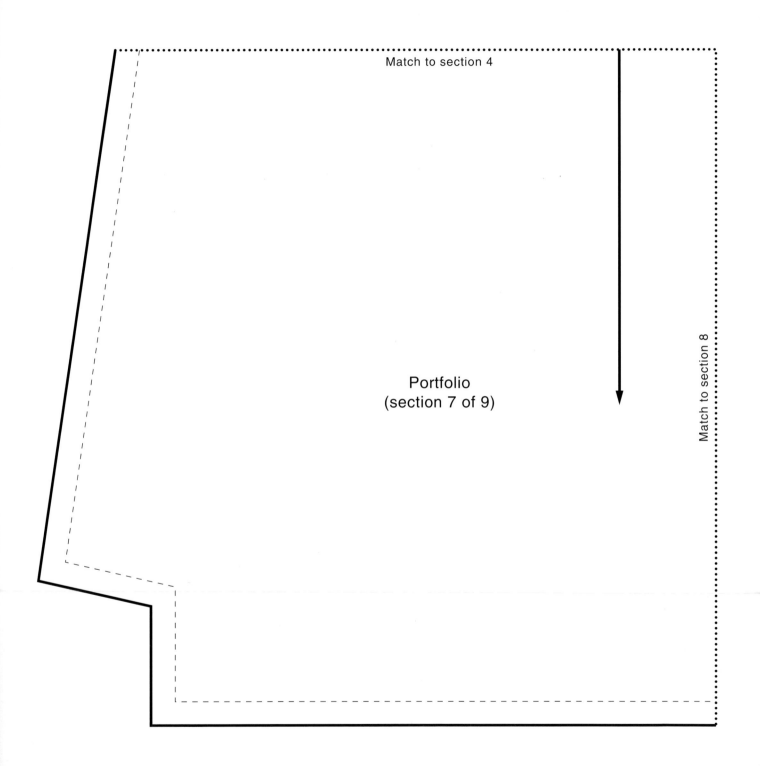

Match to section 4

Match to section 8

Portfolio
(section 7 of 9)

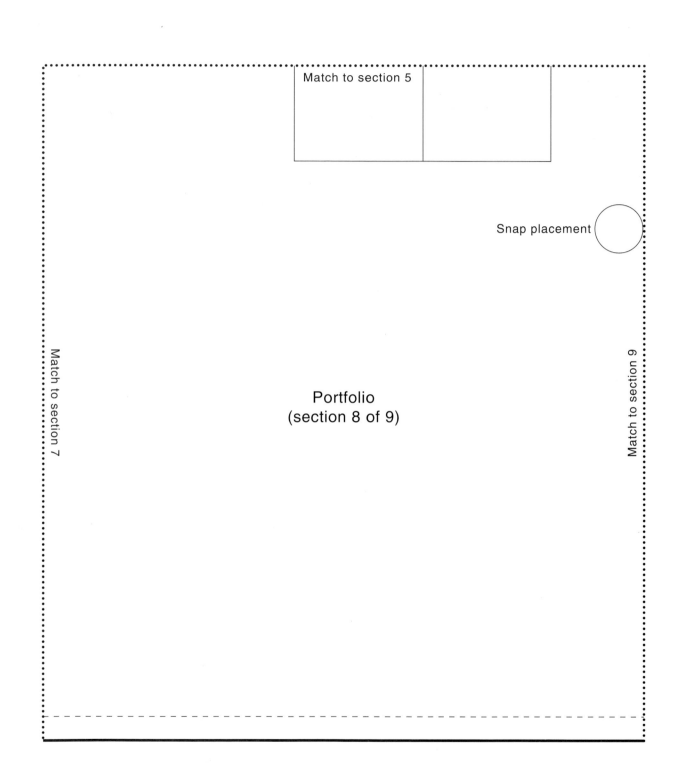

Match to section 5

Snap placement

Match to section 7

Match to section 9

Portfolio
(section 8 of 9)

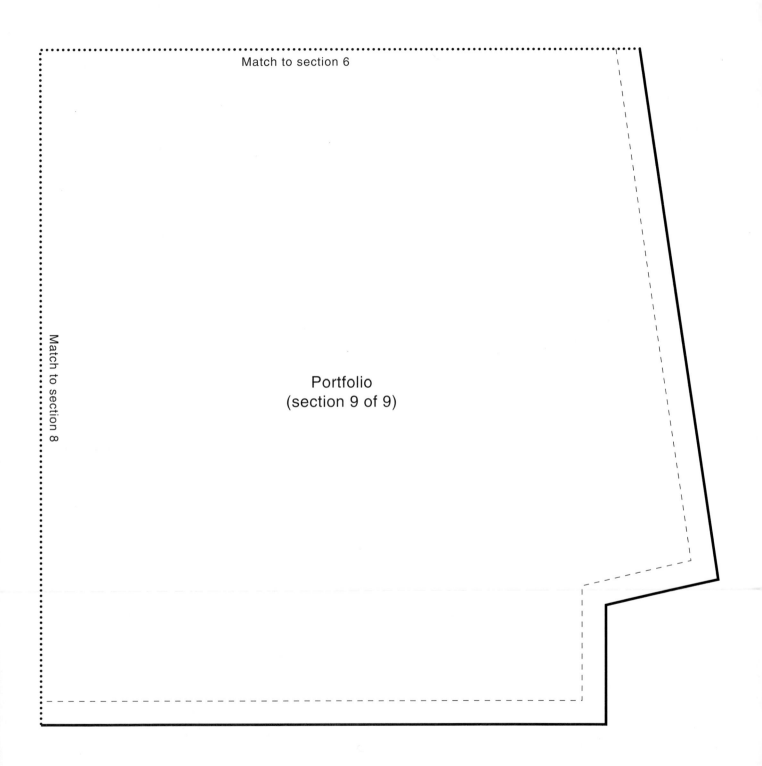

Match to section 6

Match to section 8

Portfolio
(section 9 of 9)

Jewelry Roll

Precious pearls, pins, and earrings are hard to lose when stored in this elegant jewelry roll. A traveling companion no woman should be without, this plush pouch has six pockets and is small enough to fit inside a purse.

SIZE: The finished size is $4\frac{1}{2}$ inches wide and $8\frac{1}{2}$ inches long.

NOTE: Measurements in the cutting directions include the seam allowances. Sew all the seams with $\frac{5}{8}$-inch seam allowances.

CUTTING THE JEWELRY ROLL

1. Trace the pattern pieces on pages 149–151 onto tracing paper, transferring all markings. Cut out the patterns.

2. From the peach solid, cut two end pockets, one center pocket, and one flap. Cut two jewelry rolls. One will be used for the roll and one will be used for the lining.

3. Using a chalk pencil, transfer all of the snap placement marks and the stitching lines to the right side of the fabric.

4. From the remaining peach solid, cut nine $2\frac{1}{4} \times 7\frac{3}{8}$-inch bias strips for the binding.

5. From the fusible fleece, cut three jewelry rolls.

SEWING THE END POCKETS TO THE LINING

1. With wrong sides together, fold one end pocket in half lengthwise and press.

2. Pin the pocket to the right side of the lining along the lower edge, making sure all of the curves and the raw edges are even.

3. Baste the pocket in place $\frac{1}{2}$ inch from the raw edges, as shown in **Diagram 1**.

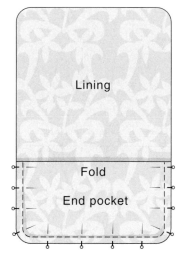

Diagram 1

4. Repeat Steps 1 through 3 to sew the remaining end pocket to the opposite end of the lining.

5. Beginning at the folded edge, topstitch down the center of one end pocket to create two smaller pockets, as shown in **Diagram 2**. For information, see "Edge Stitching and Topstitching" on page 242.

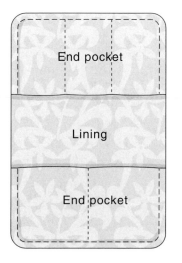

Diagram 2

6. Referring again to **Diagram 2**, and beginning at the folded edge, topstitch

the remaining end pocket to create three smaller pockets.

FUSING THE FLEECE TO THE ROLL

1. Following the manufacturer's directions, iron one fusible-fleece jewelry roll to the wrong side of the peach jewelry roll.

2. Remove the paper backing from the fleece and iron a second piece of fleece onto the previous one.

3. Remove the paper backing from the second piece of fusible fleece and iron the last piece of fleece on top of the previous two.

4. With wrong sides together, pin and baste the lining to the jewelry roll 1/2 inch from the raw edges, as shown in **Diagram 3**.

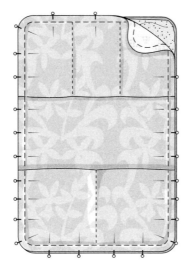

Diagram 3

SEWING THE CENTER POCKET

1. With right sides facing, fold the center pocket in half crosswise, making sure the raw edges are even, and press.

2. Beginning at the dot along one side seam, sew around the unfolded edge of the pocket, back tacking several times

just before the center dot, as shown in **Diagram 4**.

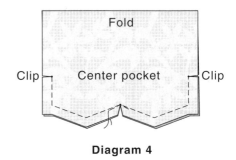

Diagram 4

3. Beginning at the center dot, back tack several times before sewing to the other side-seam dot. Back tack several times at the side-seam dot.

4. Referring to **Diagram 4**, carefully clip into the seam allowance at each side-seam dot, making sure not to cut through the stitching. Clip one V-shaped notch into the seam allowance at the center dot.

5. Trim the seam allowance along the sewn edge to 1/4 inch. Turn the pocket right side out and press.

6. Referring to **Diagram 5**, pin the center pocket to the lining, making sure the raw edges along the sides are even. The sewn, lower edge of the pocket forms the flap for one end pocket. The sides of the flap will not extend into the seam allowance.

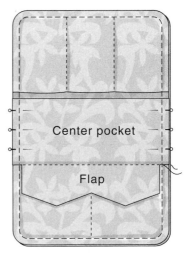

Diagram 5

7. Machine baste the center pocket to the lining ¹/₂ inch from the raw edges, as shown in **Diagram 5.**

8. Topstitch the center pocket along the indicated stitching line at the bottom edge of the pocket, as shown in **Diagram 5.**

SEWING THE FLAP

1. With right sides together, fold the flap in half lengthwise, making sure the raw edges are even. Press the fold of the flap.

2. Pin the long side and one short side together, making sure the raw edges are even.

3. Referring to **Diagram 6**, and beginning at the fold, sew along one short side and the long side. Do not sew the remaining short side.

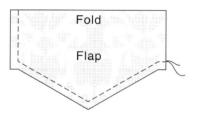

Diagram 6

4. Clip the corners and trim the seam allowance to ¹/₄ inch. Do not trim the seam allowance along the remaining short side. Turn the flap right side out and press.

5. Turn under the seam allowance along the open edge and blindstitch it closed. For more information on blindstitching, see "Embroidery and Hand-Sewing Stitches" on page 244.

6. Pin and topstitch the flap to the lining along the indicated stitching line, making sure the folded edge overlaps the end pocket to form a flap, and the pointed edge overlaps the center pocket to form a flap, as shown in **Diagram 7.**

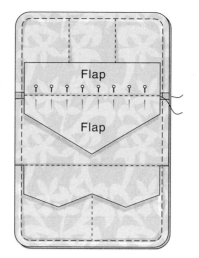

Diagram 7

SEWING THE BINDING

1. To make the binding, with right sides together, lay the end of one bias strip on top of the end of another to form a right angle. Sew the strips together on the diagonal and trim the seam allowance to ¹/₄ inch, as shown in **Diagram 8.** Repeat this step until the binding is 42 inches long.

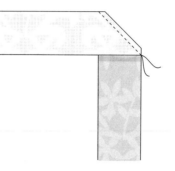

Diagram 8

2. With the wrong side facing up, turn up a ⁵/₈-inch hem along one long and one short side of the binding, as shown in **Diagram 9.**

Diagram 9

Know & Sew

TO LINE UP THE TWO HALVES OF THE SNAP SO THEY MEET PRECISELY FOR CLOSURE, TRY THIS QUICK TIP. FIRST SEW THE BALL HALF OF THE SNAP IN PLACE. THEN RUB THE TIP OF THE BALL WITH TAILOR'S CHALK. CLOSE THE POCKET FLAP AND PRESS WITH YOUR FINGER. THE CHALK WILL LEAVE A MARK ON THE FLAP. THIS AUTOMATICALLY BECOMES THE PLACEMENT AREA FOR THE OTHER HALF OF THE SNAP.

3. Position the roll so the pockets and lining are facing down and the outside of the roll is facing up. With right sides together, pin the short, hemmed edge of the binding to the center, bottom edge of the two-sectioned end pocket. Continue pinning the binding to the roll, matching the raw edges and making sure to ease the fullness of the binding at each corner. To finish, overlap the remaining short end of the binding onto the hemmed, short end. Sew the binding to the roll, as shown in **Diagram 10.**

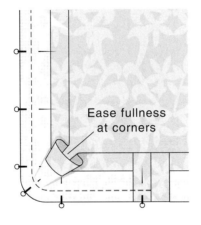

Ease fullness at corners

Diagram 10

4. Turn the long, hemmed edge of the binding to the lining side of the roll.

Thread a hand-sewing needle with matching thread and blindstitch the binding to the lining.

FINISHING THE JEWELRY ROLL

1. Cut enough floral motifs from the lace to trim the flap over the center pocket and the outside flap of the closed jewelry roll.

2. Referring to the photograph on page 144, arrange the motifs on the flap of the center pocket. Using thread to match the lace, hand sew the motifs in place. With a beading needle, randomly sew the pearls on top of the floral motifs.

3. Close the jewelry roll by folding it into thirds. Repeat Step 2 and sew floral motifs and pearls to the outside flap of the jewelry roll.

4. At the indicated placement marks, sew two size 2/0 snaps to each end pocket and their corresponding flaps. Sew one size 2/0 snap to the center pocket and its corresponding flap.

5. Fold the jewelry roll into thirds. Sew one size 2 snap to the outside and the inside of the roll so that it will close.

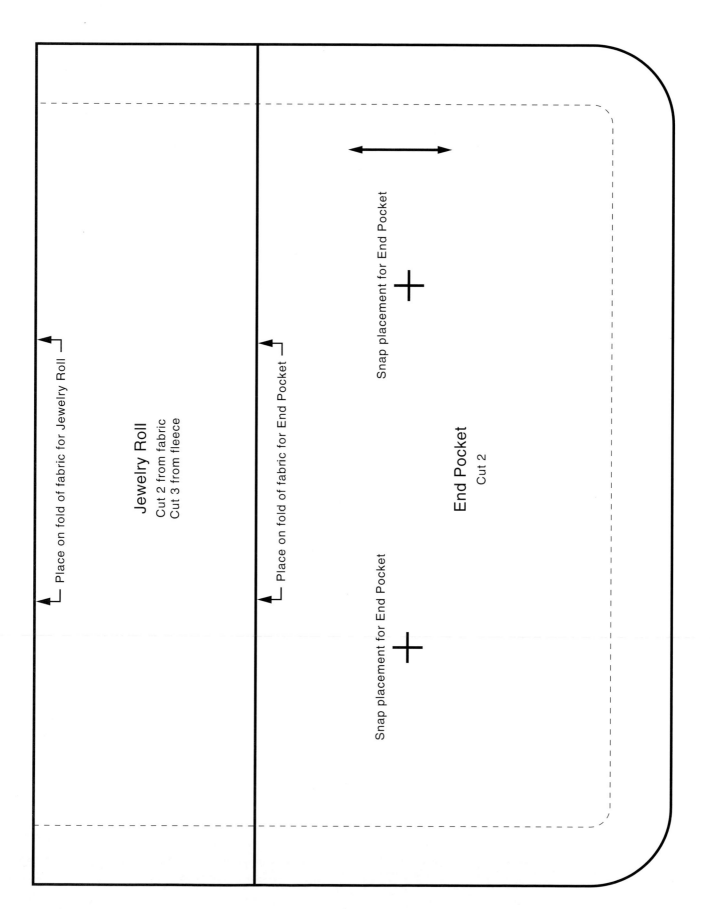

Place on fold of fabric for Jewelry Roll

Jewelry Roll

Cut 2 from fabric
Cut 3 from fleece

Place on fold of fabric for End Pocket

Snap placement for End Pocket

Snap placement for End Pocket

End Pocket

Cut 2

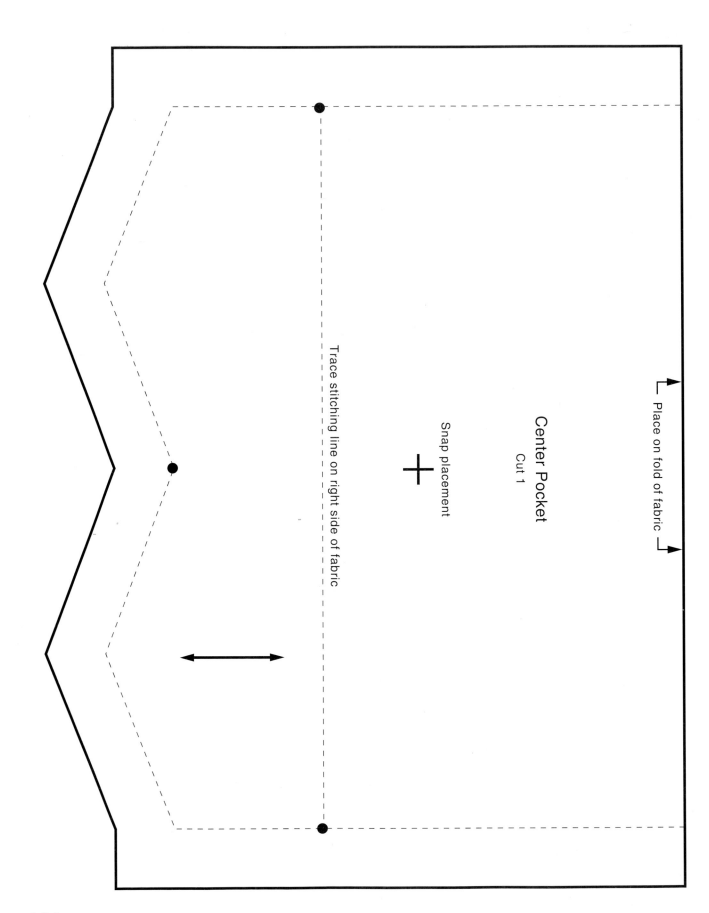

Trace stitching line on right side of fabric

Snap placement

Center Pocket
Cut 1

Place on fold of fabric

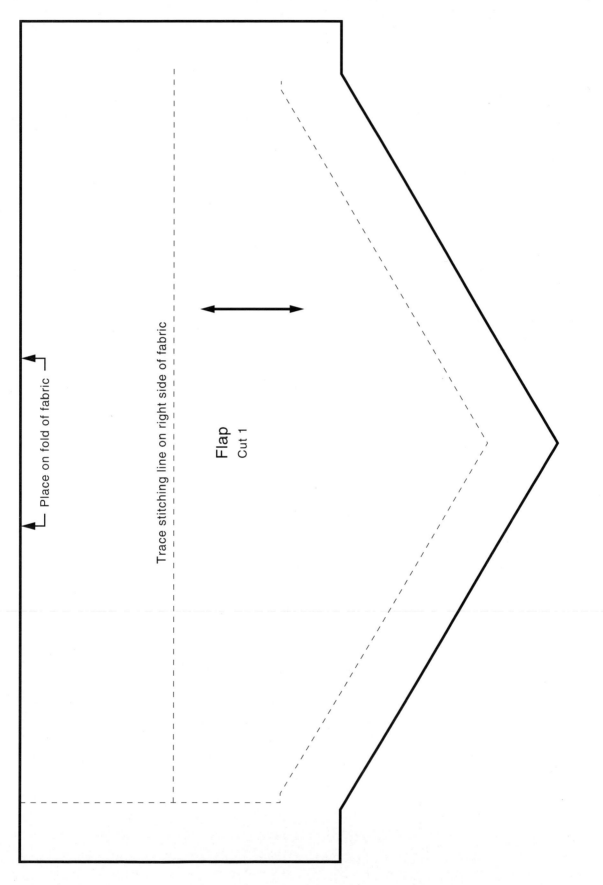

Place on fold of fabric

Trace stitching line on right side of fabric

Flap
Cut 1

Lingerie Bag

*Soft and frilly garments deserve a luxurious travel bag of their own.
A stylish way to protect delicates from pulls and tears, this lingerie bag is a
sensationally sensible addition to any traveler's wardrobe.*

SIZE: The finished size is 12½ inches wide and 15½ inches long.

NOTE: Measurements in the cutting directions include the seam allowances. Sew all the seams with ½-inch seam allowances.

CUTTING THE LINGERIE BAG

1. To make the complete lingerie bag pattern, fold a 9 × 15-inch piece of tracing paper in half and trace the entire pattern piece on page 155 onto the paper. Cut out the pattern and open it up.

2. To make the complete pocket pattern, fold a 9 × 15-inch piece of tracing paper in half and trace the pocket portion of the pattern piece on page 155 onto the paper. Cut out the pattern and open it up.

3. From the purple print, cut one lingerie bag for the bag front. Cut four pockets. Two of the pieces will be used for the pocket fronts and two will be used for the pocket linings.

4. From the purple solid, cut one lingerie bag for the bag lining.

5. From the interfacing, cut one lingerie bag and two pockets.

6. Cut the satin ribbon in half.

SEWING THE INTERFACING

1. With the wrong side of the fabric facing up, pin the bag interfacing to the bag front inside the ½-inch seam allowance.

2. Sew the bag interfacing to the bag front, as shown in **Diagram 1.**

Diagram 1

3. Repeat Steps 1 and 2 to sew the pocket interfacing pieces to the two pocket linings.

SEWING THE POCKETS

1. With right sides together, pin one pocket lining to one pocket front. Sew the pieces together along the straight edge only, as shown in **Diagram 2.**

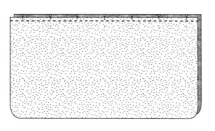

Diagram 2

2. Trim the seam allowance to ¼ inch. Turn the pocket to the right side and press.

3. Repeat Steps 1 and 2 to sew the remaining pocket front and pocket lining together.

MATERIALS LIST

FABRIC REQUIREMENTS

• 1 YARD OF PURPLE PRINT FOR THE FRONT AND POCKETS

• ½ YARD OF PURPLE SOLID FOR THE LINING

• ½ YARD OF MEDIUM-WEIGHT NON-WOVEN INTERFACING

OTHER SUPPLIES

• ¾ YARD OF ¼-INCH-WIDE PURPLE SATIN RIBBON

• SEWING THREAD TO MATCH THE FABRICS

• HAND-SEWING NEEDLE

• TRACING PAPER

FABRIC OPTIONS

FOR THE FRONT AND POCKETS

• PRINTED JACQUARD

• COTTON

• POLISHED COTTON

• LINEN

• SATIN

FOR THE LINING

• CREPE-BACKED SATIN

• COTTON

• POLISHED COTTON

• LINEN

• SATIN

4. With right sides together, pin and sew each pocket to the bag lining, as shown in **Diagram 3.**

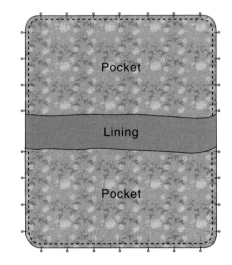

Diagram 3

Know&Sew

TO SEW A PERFECTLY STRAIGHT LINE OF TOP STITCHING FOR THE POCKET, USE A SHEET OF PAPER AS YOUR GUIDE. TAPE A PLAIN SHEET OF PAPER TO THE FABRIC SO THAT THE EDGE OF THE PAPER IS TO THE LEFT OF THE NEEDLE. MAKE SURE THE PAPER'S EDGE IS UNDER THE LEFT TOE OF THE FOOT CLOSE TO THE NEEDLE BUT NOT UNDER IT. SLOWLY STITCH NEXT TO THE EDGE OF THE PAPER.

5. With the right side facing up, topstitch down the center of one pocket to make two pockets, as shown in **Diagram 4.** For more information, see "Edge Stitching and Topstitching" on page 242.

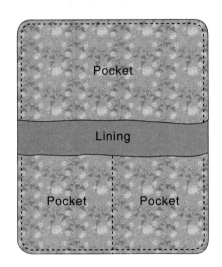

Diagram 4

FINISHING THE LINGERIE BAG

1. Pin one length of satin ribbon to the center of each pocket, matching the raw edges, as shown in **Diagram 5.**

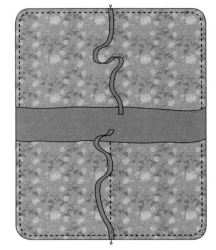

Diagram 5

2. Referring to **Diagram 6,** with right sides together, pin and sew the bag front to the bag lining, sandwiching the pockets between the layers and leaving a 3-inch opening for turning. Trim the seam allowance and clip several V-shaped notches in the curves so the bag lies flat when turned right side out.

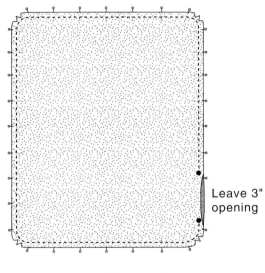

Leave 3" opening

Diagram 6

3. Turn the lingerie bag right side out and press.

4. Turn under the seam allowance along the opening and blindstitch it closed. For information on blind-stitching, see "Embroidery and Hand-Sewing Stitches" on page 244.

Place on fold of fabric for the Lingerie Bag

Cut here for the Pocket

Place on fold of tracing paper for the Lingerie Bag and Pocket

Lingerie Bag

Cut 1 from print fabric
Cut 1 from lining fabric
Cut 1 from interfacing

Pocket

Cut 4 from print fabric
Cut 2 from interfacing

Shoe Bag

Protect shoes from scuffs and scrapes whether they're in the closet or in a suitcase. You can easily sew several of these fully lined bags in one evening and use them for a trip the next day.

SIZE: The finished size is 11½ inches wide and 17 inches long.

NOTE: Measurements in the cutting directions include the seam allowances. Sew all the seams with ⅝-inch seam allowances.

CUTTING THE SHOE BAG

From the print, cut two 18½ × 24-inch rectangles. One will be used for the outer bag and one will be used for the lining.

SEWING THE OUTER BAG

1. With right sides together, fold the outer bag in half crosswise and pin.

2. Referring to **Diagram 1**, sew the side seam to within 1½ inches of the top. Backstitch and stop.

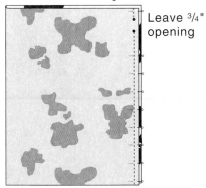

Leave ¾" opening

Diagram 1

3. Referring to **Diagram 1**, finish the side seam by sewing ¾ inch down from the top, leaving a ¾-inch opening along the side. Backstitch and stop. Press the side seam open.

4. To form the drawstring casing, fold down ¾ inch from the top, as shown in **Diagram 2**. Press the casing and turn the bag right side out.

Diagram 2

SEWING THE LINING

1. With right sides together, fold the lining in half crosswise and pin. Sew the side seam and press it open.

2. Fold down ¾ inch from the top of the lining and press. Do not turn the lining right side out.

SEWING THE LINING TO THE OUTER BAG

1. Referring to **Diagram 3**, with right sides together, place the outer bag inside the lining, making sure the side seams and the top and bottom edges are evenly aligned.

Outer bag

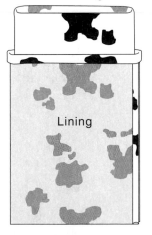

Lining

Diagram 3

MATERIALS LIST

FABRIC REQUIREMENT

• ¾ YARD OF BLACK-AND-WHITE PRINT

OTHER SUPPLIES

• 30 INCH-LONG SHOE LACE

• SEWING THREAD TO MATCH THE FABRIC

• SMALL SAFETY PIN

FABRIC OPTIONS

• FLANNEL

• SHEETING

• POLISHED COTTON

• LINEN

• PINWALE CORDUROY

• VELVETEEN

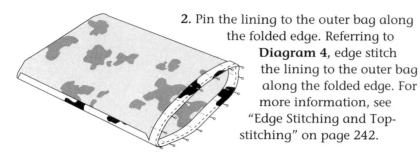

2. Pin the lining to the outer bag along the folded edge. Referring to **Diagram 4**, edge stitch the lining to the outer bag along the folded edge. For more information, see "Edge Stitching and Top-stitching" on page 242.

Diagram 4

3. Pull the outer bag out of the lining, as shown in **Diagram 5**.

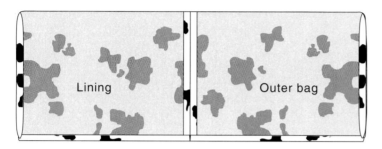

Lining   Outer bag

Diagram 5

4. Gently fold the lining over the outer bag so that the right side of the lining is on the outside of the outer bag, as shown in **Diagram 6**. The right side of the outer bag will be on the inside. Adjust the lining and the outer bag so that the side seams and bottom edges are even.

Lining

Outer bag

Diagram 6

5. Referring to **Diagram 7**, pin and sew the lining and the outer bag together along the bottom edge. Turn the bag right side out.

Diagram 7

6. To finish the casing, topstitch around the open end of the bag $\frac{5}{8}$ inch from the edge, as shown in **Diagram 8**, making sure not to sew the drawstring opening closed. For more information, see "Edge Stitching and Topstitching" on page 242.

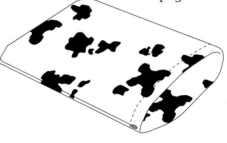

Diagram 8

FINISHING THE SHOE BAG

Insert a small safety pin through one end of the shoe lace and weave it through the casing, as shown in **Diagram 9**. Remove the safety pin. Pull the shoe lace tight and tie a bow to close the bag.

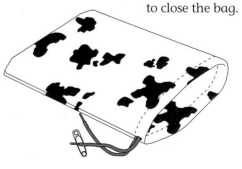

Diagram 9

Duffel Bag

This fully lined duffel bag is compact and convenient for trips to the gym or the office or even for travel. One large inner compartment and four outside pockets help keep large and small items handy. Why not buy extra fabric and make a matched set that can be used over and over again?

Duffel Bag

❖

MATERIALS LIST

FABRIC REQUIREMENTS

- 1½ YARDS OF 54-INCH-WIDE PRINT FOR THE BAG
- 2 YARDS OF 54-INCH-WIDE COORDINATING FABRIC FOR THE LINING
- 1¾ YARDS OF 60-INCH-WIDE FUSIBLE KNIT INTERFACING
- 1 YARD OF FUSIBLE WEBBING

OTHER SUPPLIES

- 2¼ YARDS OF PIPING TO MATCH THE FABRIC
- SEWING THREAD TO MATCH THE FABRIC
- 22-INCH SPORT ZIPPER WITH 2 ZIPPER PULLS FOR THE TOP OF THE BAG
- 2 SPORT ZIPPERS, 12 INCHES EACH, FOR THE END POCKETS
- TRACING PAPER
- CHALK PENCIL

FABRIC OPTIONS

- POLISHED COTTON
- TAPESTRY
- DENIM
- SYNTHETIC SUEDE
- SYNTHETIC LEATHER

SKILL LEVEL: *ADVANCED*

SIZE: The finished size is approximately 22 inches long and 12 inches high.

NOTE: Measurements in the cutting directions include the seam allowances. Sew all the seams with ¼-inch seam allowances.

CUTTING THE DUFFEL BAG

1. Trace the pattern pieces on pages 164–165 onto tracing paper, transferring all markings and making sure to match the two sections before cutting out the pattern pieces.

2. To save time, follow the manufacturer's directions and fuse the knit interfacing to the wrong side of the print before cutting any pieces from the fabric.

3. From the print-and-interfacing unit, cut two 19 × 23-inch rectangles for the bag sides. Cut two 12 × 15-inch rectangles for the side pockets. Cut four end pockets. Using a chalk pencil, transfer all pocket markings to the right side of the fabric.

4. From the lining, cut one 23 × 37½-inch rectangle for the bag lining. Cut two 12 × 15½-inch rectangles for the side pocket lining. Cut four end pockets for the end pocket lining. Cut two 4 × 70-inch strips for the straps.

5. From the fusible webbing, cut two 12 × 15½-inch pieces.

6. Cut the piping into two pieces.

SEWING THE SIDE POCKETS

1. With right sides together, pin and sew one side pocket–interfacing unit to one side pocket lining along one short end, as shown in **Diagram 1.**

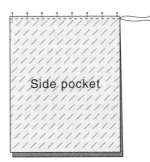

Side pocket lining

Diagram 1

2. Following the manufacturer's directions, iron one piece of fusible webbing to the wrong side of the side pocket lining.

3. Remove the paper backing from the fusible webbing and turn the pieces to the right side. The fusible webbing will be sandwiched between the wrong sides of the side pocket–interfacing unit and the side pocket lining.

4. Pull the bottom edge of the side pocket down to the bottom edge of the side pocket lining, matching the raw edges and allowing ¼ inch of the lining to show along the top edge. Fuse the pieces together, as shown in **Diagram 2.**

Side pocket lining

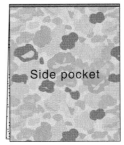

Side pocket

Diagram 2

5. Repeat Steps 1 through 4 for the remaining side pocket and side pocket lining.

SEWING THE SIDE POCKETS TO THE BAG SIDES

1. With right sides facing up, center and pin one side pocket onto one bag side, making sure to match the bottom raw edges. Move and angle the upper edges of the side pocket ¼ inch in at the top corners and pin them in place. There should be a slight gap between the upper edge of the pocket and the bag side. The bottom edge of the pocket should be flat against the bag side, as shown in **Diagram 3**. Machine baste the side pocket in place inside the seam allowance.

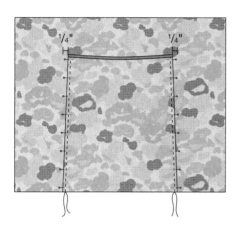

Diagram 3

2. Repeat Step 1 for the remaining side pocket and bag side.

SEWING THE STRAPS

1. With the wrong side facing up, fold the long sides of one 4 × 70-inch strip toward the center and press, as shown in **Diagram 4**.

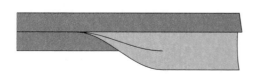

Diagram 4

2. Fold the strip in half lengthwise and press the fold. Edge stitch the length of the strip along both sides, as shown in **Diagram 5**. For more information, see "Edge Stitching and Topstitching" on page 242.

Diagram 5

3. Repeat Steps 1 and 2 to make the remaining strap.

SEWING THE STRAPS TO THE BAG SIDES

1. Beginning at the lower edge of one bag side, pin a strap up one side of the pocket and down the other side, making sure to cover the raw edges of the pocket. This is the time to shorten the straps if necessary. To shorten, extend each end of the strap below the bottom edge of the bag side and trim away the excess strap.

2. Edge stitch each side of the strap from the bottom of the bag to ¼ inch beyond the top of the pocket. Double stitch across the width of the strap at the top of the pocket for durability, as shown in **Diagram 6**.

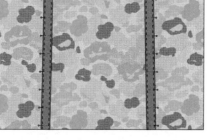

Diagram 6

3. Repeat Steps 1 and 2 for the remaining strap and bag side.

SEWING THE ZIPPER

1. With right sides together, pin and hand baste the 22-inch zipper along the upper edge of one bag side, matching the raw edges, as shown in **Diagram 7**.

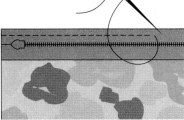

Diagram 7

2. Pin the right side of the bag lining to the wrong side of the zipper along the upper edge, making sure the raw edges are even. Hand baste the lining in place over the previous line of stitching, as shown in **Diagram 8**.

Diagram 8

3. Turn the bag side and the bag lining to the right side so the right side of the zipper faces up and press. Edge stitch close to the zipper along the right side of the bag, as shown in **Diagram 9**.

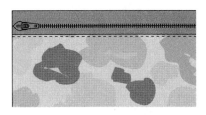

Diagram 9

4. Repeat Steps 1 through 3 to sew the remaining bag side, bag lining, and the other side of the zipper together in order to create a tube with the bag lining, as shown in **Diagram 10**.

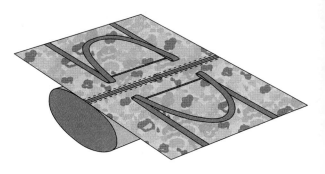

Diagram 10

5. With the right sides facing, pin and sew the two bag sides together along the bottom edge, making sure that the pocket and strap edges match up, as shown in **Diagram 11**.

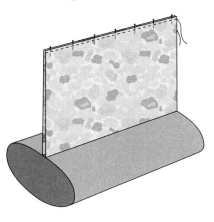

Diagram 11

6. Carefully turn the bag lining right side out and the bag sides will automatically be inserted into the lining in the process. The bag lining and the bag sides will form a tube with the lining on the outside.

7. Machine baste the lining and the sides together along the raw edges at each end of the bag, as shown in **Diagram 12**.

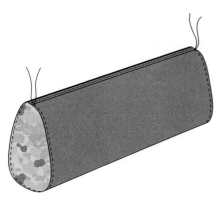

Diagram 12

the second end pocket. Machine baste the four layers together along the raw edges, as shown in **Diagram 14.**

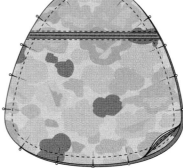

Diagram 14

SEWING THE END POCKETS

1. Cut one end pocket and one end pocket lining along the zipper insertion line. Follow Steps 1 through 3 under "Sewing the Zipper" and insert one 12-inch zipper.

2. With wrong sides together, pin and machine baste the end pocket and end pocket lining inside the seam allowance, making sure the raw edges are even and making sure to catch the end tabs of the zipper in the seam allowance, as shown in **Diagram 13.**

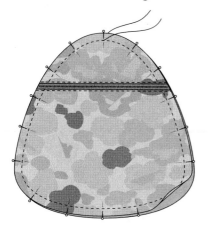

Diagram 13

3. With wrong sides together, place a second end pocket on top of a second end pocket lining. On top of these layers, place the zippered end pocket unit, making sure the right side of the zippered lining faces the right side of

4. Repeat Steps 1 through 3 to complete the other end pocket.

SEWING THE PIPING TO THE END POCKETS

1. With the right side of the zippered end pocket facing up, and beginning at the center of the bottom edge, pin one length of piping to the pocket along the raw edges, making sure the ends overlap, as shown in **Diagram 15.**

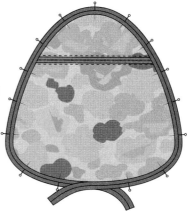

Diagram 15

2. Use a zipper foot to machine baste the piping in place, stitching as close to the piping as possible. Trim away the excess piping.

3. Repeat Steps 1 and 2 for the remaining end pocket and piping.

FINISHING THE DUFFEL BAG

1. With the right sides of the bag and one end pocket together, match and pin the notch on the bottom of the

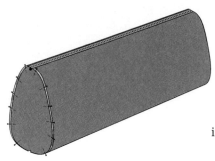

Diagram 16

end pocket to the lower seam of the bag. Match and pin the center dot at the top of the end pocket to the end of the bag zipper. Ease and pin the remaining edges of the end pocket and the bag together, as shown in **Diagram 16.**

2. Sew the end pocket to the bag as close to the piping as possible.

3. To finish, zigzag around the entire pocket inside the seam allowance.

4. Repeat Steps 1 and 2 for the remaining end of the bag. Turn the bag right side out.

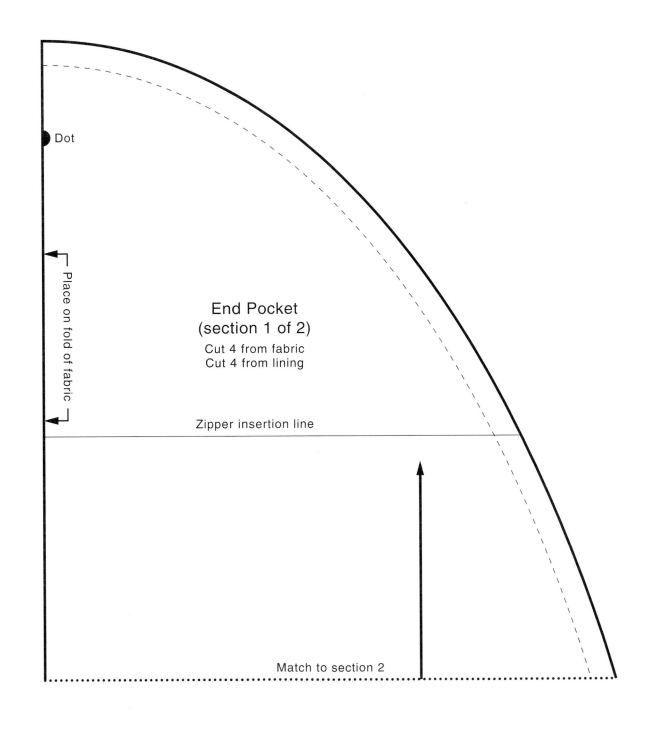

Dot

Place on fold of fabric

**End Pocket
(section 1 of 2)**

Cut 4 from fabric
Cut 4 from lining

Zipper insertion line

Match to section 2

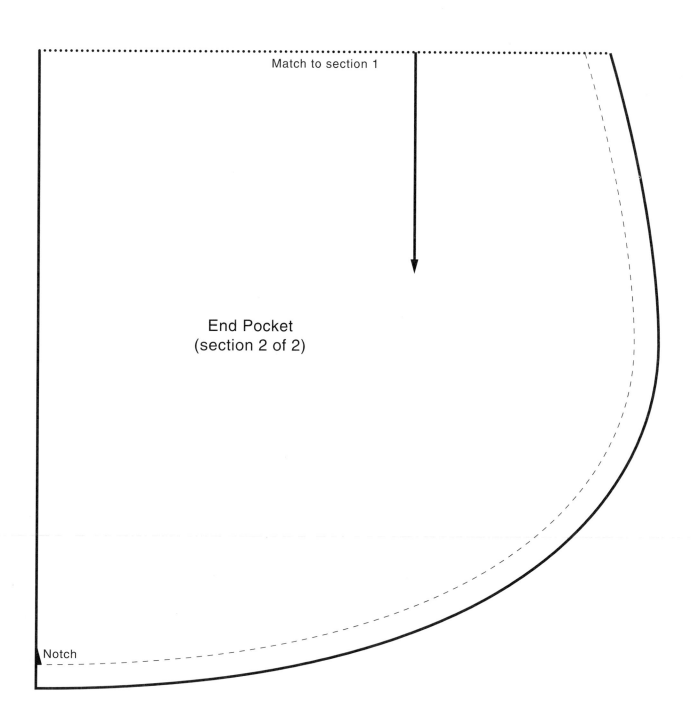

Match to section 1

End Pocket
(section 2 of 2)

Notch

Lunch Bags

Lunches and snacks will never be forgotten at home when they're packed in these reusable lunch bags. Mix and match your own appliqué designs and create a set for a family picnic in the park.

Plaid Lunch Bag

SKILL LEVEL: *ADVANCED*

SIZE: The finished size is $6^1/2$ inches × $4^1/2$ inches × $10^1/2$ inches. A child-size thermos will fit into this bag.

NOTE: Measurements in the cutting directions include the seam allowances. Sew all the seams with $^1/2$-inch seam allowances.

CUTTING THE LUNCH BAG

1. From the teal solid, cut one $12^3/4 \times 23$-inch rectangle for the teal body. Cut two $5^1/2 \times 7^1/2$-inch rectangles for the base pieces.

2. From the plaid, cut one 6×23-inch rectangle for the plaid body.

3. From the belt webbing, cut two 15-inch lengths for the handles.

SEWING THE BODY

1. Pin and sew the right side of the plaid body onto the wrong side of the teal body, making sure the raw edges are even, as shown in **Diagram 1**.

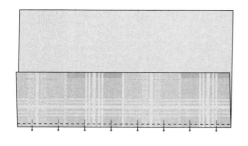

Diagram 1

2. Open the fabric and press the seam toward the teal.

3. Turn under $^1/2$ inch along the remaining long edge of the plaid body and press toward the wrong side.

4. Fold the plaid body up over the right side of the teal body and press the bottom seam flat. Pin the upper edge of the plaid body to the teal body, as shown in **Diagram 2**.

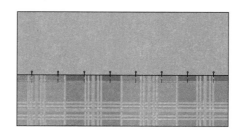

Diagram 2

5. Referring to **Diagram 3**, use tailor's chalk to mark the placement lines for the four side edges of the body using the following measurements. On the right side of the plaid body, and beginning at the left short side, draw one placement line $^1/2$ inch from the raw edge.

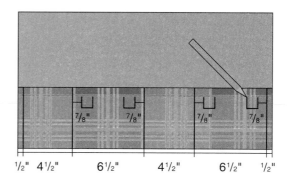

Diagram 3

6. Draw the second placement line $4^1/2$ inches from the first line.

7. Draw the third placement line $6^1/2$ inches from the second line.

8. Draw the fourth placement line $4^1/2$ inches from the third line.

9. Draw the fifth placement line 6¹/₂ inches from the fourth line.

10. Referring to **Diagram 3** on page 167, draw the placement lines for the handles along the upper edge of the plaid body, ⁷/₈ inch from either side of the placement lines for the side edges.

INSERTING THE HANDLES

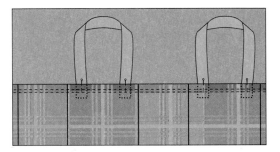

Diagram 4

1. Referring to **Diagram 4**, insert and pin 1 inch of the handles between the plaid body and the teal body at the placement lines, making sure both handles align.

Know&Sew

IF YOU FIND IT DIFFICULT TO SEW THROUGH DENIM FABRIC, HERE ARE TWO WAYS OF OVERCOMING THIS PROBLEM. YOU CAN USE A JEANS NEEDLE THAT HAS A THICK SHAFT AND A SHARP POINT THAT WILL PENETRATE THE FABRIC. YOU CAN ALSO RUB THE SEAMS WITH SOAP TO LUBRI-CATE THE NEEDLE AS IT MOVES IN AND OUT OF THE FABRIC.

2. Referring to **Diagram 4**, edge stitch through all the layers of fabric along the upper edge of the plaid body. Stitch again ¹/₄ inch below the previous line of edge stitching. For more informa-tion, see "Edge Stitching and Topstitching" on page 242.

FORMING THE SIDE EDGES

1. With the right side of the body facing up, fold the left edge over to the right edge and pin. Sew the edges together, making sure to leave the bottom open. There are now four layers in the seam allowance: a teal layer, two plaid layers, and another teal layer.

2. Carefully trim the seam allowance of the top teal layer to ¹/₄ inch. Trim the seam allowance of the top plaid layer to ¹/₈ inch. Trim the seam allowance of the second plaid layer to ¹/₄ inch. Do not trim the bottom teal layer.

3. Referring to **Diagram 5**, fold the seam allowance of the bottom teal

layer over the other three seam al-lowances and machine zigzag it in place. Press this four-layered seam al-lowance to one side.

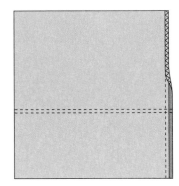

Diagram 5

4. Turn the body right side out. To form the four side edges of the body, press along the placement lines to make four creases, as shown in **Diagram 6**.

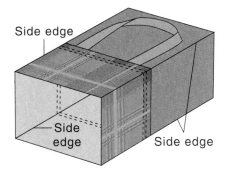

Side edge
Side edge
Side edge
Side edge

Diagram 6

SEWING THE BASE

1. With right sides together, pin and sew the teal base pieces together around all four sides, leaving a 2-inch opening for turning. Clip the corners and trim the seam allowance to ¹/₄ inch. Turn the base right side out.

2. Turn under the seam allowance along the opening and press. Topstitch around the entire base ¹/₄ inch from the edge. For more information, see "Edge Stitching and Topstitching" on page 242.

SEWING THE BASE TO THE BODY

1. Place the base inside the bottom of the body. Pin one long side of the base to one long side of the body, making sure the edges are even.

2. Beginning ⅛ inch from the corner, edge stitch through all the layers, ending ⅛ inch from the other corner, as shown in **Diagram 7**.

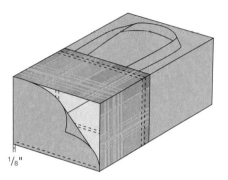

1/8"

Diagram 7

3. To finish sewing the base to the body, repeat Steps 1 and 2 for the opposite long side of the base and then for the short sides of the base. The stitching lines should meet at each corner.

FINISHING THE LUNCH BAG

1. Turn under ¼ inch along the top of the lunch bag and press. Turn under 1 inch more and press. Edge stitch around the upper edge of the bag. Then topstitch ¼ inch from the edge stitching, as shown in **Diagram 8**.

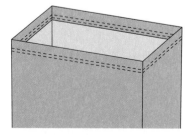

Diagram 8

2. Referring to **Diagram 9**, fold one side edge along the crease line so that the side of the bag and the front of the bag are layered together. Edge stitch through both layers, stopping ⅛ inch from the bottom. Repeat this step for the three remaining side edges.

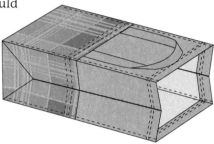

Diagram 9

3. Fold the bag as you would fold a traditional brown bag and press, as shown in **Diagram 10**.

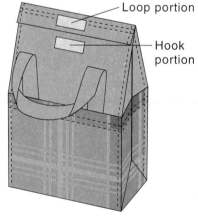

Diagram 10

4. Referring to **Diagram 11**, center and pin the loop portion of the Velcro strip along the outside of one side of the bag opening, ¼ inch from the upper edge. Hand sew the piece in place.

Loop portion

Hook portion

Diagram 11

5. Close the bag and fold down 1 inch and then 1 inch again, as shown in **Diagram 11**. Sew the hook portion of the Velcro to the bag where it would meet the loop portion.

MATERIALS LIST

FABRIC REQUIREMENTS

- ¹/₂ YARD OF KHAKI SOLID FOR THE BODY AND BASE

- ¹/₂ YARD OF AQUAMARINE SOLID FOR THE BODY

- 1 SCRAP EACH OF YELLOW PRINT, PINK PRINT, AND ORANGE PRINT FOR THE FISH

OTHER SUPPLIES

- 3 PIECES OF FUSIBLE WEBBING, EACH 2 INCHES SQUARE

- 1 YARD OF BEIGE BELT WEBBING

- SEWING THREAD TO MATCH THE FABRICS

- SHINY AQUAMARINE, YELLOW, PINK, AND ORANGE TOPSTITCHING THREAD

- 18 WHITE SEED BEADS

- 6 SEED BEADS OF ASSORTED COLORS

- CLEAR MONOFILAMENT THREAD

- SIZE 16 BEADING NEEDLE

- 2-INCH STRIP OF VELCRO

- TEMPLATE PLASTIC

- FINE-POINT, PERMANENT MARKER

- CHALK PENCIL

- TAILOR'S CHALK

FABRIC OPTIONS

FOR THE BODY AND BASE

- CANVAS
- DENIM
- HEAVYWEIGHT TWILL
- DUCK CLOTH

FOR THE FISH

- COTTON
- FELT

Appliquéd Fish Lunch Bag

SKILL LEVEL: *ADVANCED*

SIZE: The finished size is 6¹/₂ inches × 4¹/₂ inches × 10¹/₂ inches. A child-size thermos will fit into this bag.

NOTE: Measurements in the cutting directions include the seam allowances. Sew all the seams with ¹/₂-inch seam allowances.

CUTTING THE LUNCH BAG

1. Trace the wave pattern on page 173 onto template plastic and cut out the pattern.

2. From the khaki solid, cut one 12³/₄ × 23-inch rectangle for the khaki body. Cut two 5¹/₂ × 7¹/₂-inch rectangles for the base pieces.

3. From the aquamarine solid, cut one 6 × 23-inch rectangle for the aquamarine body.

4. From the belt webbing, cut two 15-inch lengths for the handles.

5. Following the manufacturer's directions, iron one square of fusible webbing onto the wrong side of the scrap of yellow print.

6. Cut two oval shapes, each approximately 1¹/₂ inches long, for the fish bodies. Cut two crescent shapes, each approximately ⁵/₈ inch to ³/₄ inch long, for the tails.

7. Repeat Steps 5 and 6 for the pink print and the orange print.

SEWING THE BODY

1. Pin and sew the right side of the aquamarine body onto the wrong side of the khaki body, as shown in **Diagram 12**. Open the fabric and press the seam toward the khaki.

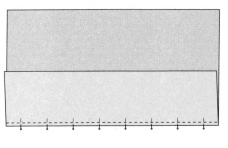

Diagram 12

2. Fold the aquamarine body up over the right side of the khaki body and press the bottom seam flat. Pin the upper edge of the aquamarine body to the khaki body, as shown in **Diagram 13**.

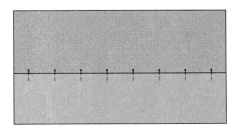

Diagram 13

3. Using a chalk pencil, trace the wave pattern along the length of the upper edge of the aquamarine body, ¹/₂ inch from the edge of the aquamarine, as shown in **Diagram 14**.

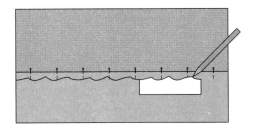

Diagram 14

4. Referring to **Diagram 15**, use tailor's chalk to mark the placement lines for the four side edges of the body using the following measurements. On the right side of the aquamarine body, and beginning at the left short side, draw a placement line ¹/₂ inch from the raw edge.

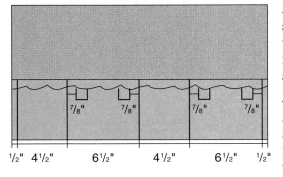

Diagram 15

5. Draw the second placement line 4½ inches from the first line.

6. Draw the third placement line 6½ inches from the second line.

7. Draw the fourth placement line 4½ inches from the third line.

8. Draw the fifth placement line 6½ inches from the fourth line.

9. Referring to **Diagram 15**, draw the placement lines for the ends of the handles along the upper edge of the aquamarine body, ⅞ inch from either side of the placement lines for the side edges.

INSERTING THE HANDLES AND SEWING THE WAVES

1. Referring to **Diagram 16**, insert and pin 1 inch of the handles between the layers of fabric at the placement lines.

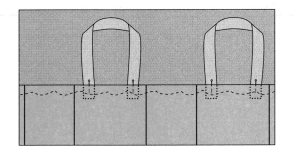

Diagram 16

2. Change only the thread in the top of the sewing machine to shiny aquamarine thread.

3. Referring to **Diagram 16**, straight stitch along the wave line through all the layers of fabric. Trim the aquamarine seam allowance close to the stitching line.

4. Set the sewing machine for a wide zigzag stitch and a short stitch length. Satin stitch over the previous stitching line to create the wave effect, as shown in **Diagram 17**. For more information, see "Machine Appliqué" on page 242.

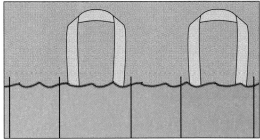

Diagram 17

SEWING THE FISH

1. Remove the paper backing from the fusible webbing on the fish bodies and tails. Referring to the photograph on page 166 for placement, iron one yellow, one pink, and one orange fish body and tail onto the aquamarine fabric below one of the handles. Repeat this step to iron the remaining fish below the other handle.

2. Change only the thread in the top of the sewing machine to shiny yellow thread. With a medium zigzag stitch and a short stitch length, satin stitch around the yellow fish. Repeat this step using shiny pink and shiny orange thread to satin stitch around the pink and orange fish.

3. Thread a size 16 beading needle with one strand of clear monofilament thread. Referring to **Diagram 18**, sew three white seed beads above each fish for the air bubbles. Sew one of the colored seed beads on each fish for the eye.

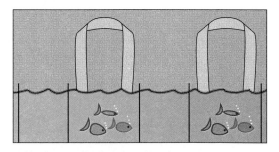

Diagram 18

FORMING THE SIDE EDGES

1. Change the thread in the top of the sewing machine to khaki. With the right side of the body facing up, fold the left edge over to the right edge and pin the layers together. Sew the edges together, making sure to leave the bottom edge open. There are now four layers of fabric in the seam allowance: a khaki layer, two aquamarine layers, and another khaki layer.

2. Carefully trim the seam allowance of the top khaki layer to $1/4$ inch. Trim the seam allowance of the top aquamarine layer to $1/8$ inch. Trim the seam allowance of the second aquamarine layer to $1/4$ inch. Do not trim the seam allowance of the bottom khaki layer.

3. Referring to **Diagram 19**, fold the seam allowance of the bottom khaki layer over the other three seam allowances, and zigzag it in place. Press this four-layered seam allowance to one side.

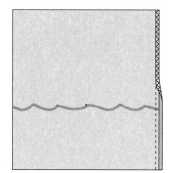

Diagram 19

4. Turn the body right side out. To form the four side edges of the body, press along the placement lines to make four creases, as shown in **Diagram 20**.

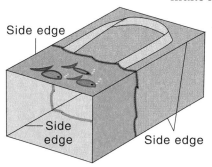

Side edge

Side edge

Side edge

Diagram 20

SEWING THE BASE

1. With right sides together, pin and sew the two khaki base pieces around all four sides, leaving a 2-inch opening for turning. Clip the corners and trim the seam allowance to $1/4$ inch. Turn the base right side out.

2. Turn under the seam allowance along the opening and press. Topstitch the base $1/4$ inch from the edge. For more information, see "Edge Stitching and Topstitching" on page 242.

SEWING THE BASE TO THE BODY

1. Place the base inside the bottom of the body. Pin one long side of the base to one long side of the bag, making sure the edges are even.

2. Beginning $1/8$ inch from the corner, edge stitch through all the layers, ending $1/8$ inch from the other corner, as shown in **Diagram 21**. For more information, see "Edge Stitching and Topstitching" on page 242.

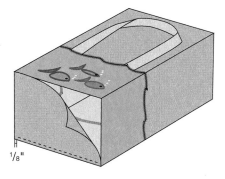

$1/8$"

Diagram 21

3. Repeat Steps 1 and 2 for the opposite long side of the base and then for the short sides of the base. The stitching lines should meet at each corner.

FINISHING THE LUNCH BAG

1. Turn under $1/4$ inch along the top of the lunch bag and press. Turn under 1 inch more and press. Edge stitch around the upper edge of the bag. Then topstitch $1/4$ inch from the edge stitching, as shown in **Diagram 22**.

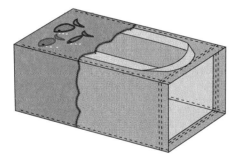

Diagram 22

2. Referring to **Diagram 23**, fold one side edge along the crease line so that the side of the bag and the front of the bag are layered together. Edge stitch through both layers, stopping $1/8$ inch from the bottom. Repeat this step for the three remaining side edges.

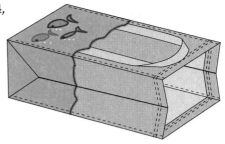

Diagram 23

3. Referring to **Diagram 24**, fold the bag the way you would fold a traditional brown bag and press.

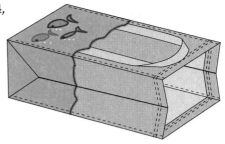

Diagram 24

4. Referring to **Diagram 25**, center and pin the loop portion of the Velcro strip along one side of the bag opening, $1/4$ inch from the upper edge. Hand sew the piece in place.

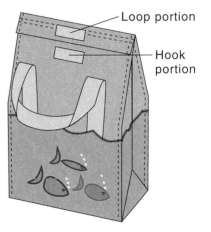

Loop portion

Hook portion

Diagram 25

5. To mark the placement of the hook portion of the Velcro strip, close the bag. Fold down 1 inch and then 1 inch again, as shown in **Diagram 25**. Pin the hook portion of Velcro to the bag where it would meet the loop. Hand sew the piece in place.

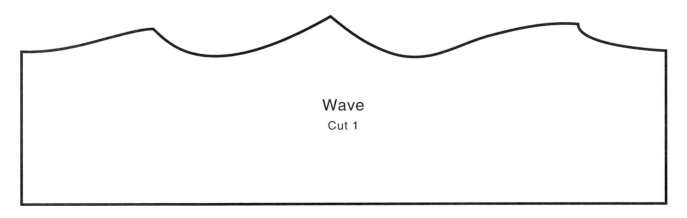

Wave

Cut 1

IT'S OH SEW CHRISTMAS

Advent Calendar

Count down to Christmas with this colorful calendar and capture the holiday spirit. Children, both young and old, will delight in delving into each pocket to discover the hidden gifts that signal Santa is on his way.

SIZE: The finished size is approximately 14 inches wide and 31 inches long.

CUTTING THE ADVENT CALENDAR

1. Trace the pattern pieces on page 180 onto tracing paper, making sure to match the two sections before cutting. Cut out the pattern pieces.

2. From the green felt, cut one tree. Cut one $14^{1}/_{2} \times 32$-inch rectangle for the calendar back.

3. From the red felt, cut one $14^{1}/_{2} \times 32$-inch rectangle for the calendar front.

4. From the tan felt, cut one star. Cut one $1^{1}/_{2} \times 2$-inch rectangle for the trunk.

5. From the green, yellow, orange, white, royal blue, and light blue felt, cut four 2-inch squares from each color for the pockets.

6. From the satin ribbon, cut 48 strips of ribbon, each 7 inches long, for the bows on each pocket.

SEWING THE TREE TO THE CALENDAR FRONT

1. Center the trunk along the base of the tree. Place the tree over the trunk so that it overlaps $1/_{4}$ inch of the trunk and pin it in place.

2. Center the tree along one short end of the calendar front, making sure it is $1/_{2}$ inch from the edge. Pin it to the calendar front.

3. Edge stitch the tree and tree trunk to the calendar front, as shown in **Diagram 1**. For more information, see "Edge Stitching and Topstitching" on page 242.

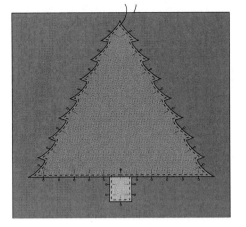

Diagram 1

4. Using pinking shears and the tree as a guide, pink the calendar front $1/_{4}$ inch away from each branch of the tree, as shown in **Diagram 2**.

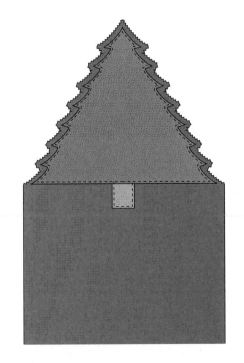

Diagram 2

5. Change to straight shears and trim $1/_{2}$ inch around the remaining three sides of the calendar front.

SEWING THE POCKETS

1. To space the multicolored pockets evenly on the calendar front, begin with the bottom, left-hand corner. Select any color pocket and pin it $1\frac{1}{4}$ inches from the side edge and $\frac{3}{4}$ inch from the bottom edge.

2. Edge stitch the pocket along three sides, leaving the top open, as shown in **Diagram 3**.

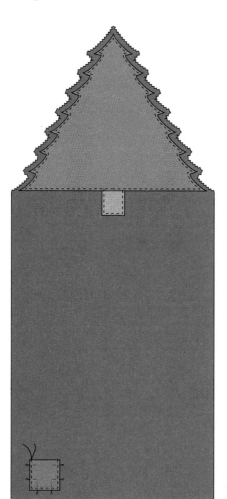

Diagram 3

3. Select another color pocket and pin it 1 inch to the right of the first pocket and $\frac{3}{4}$ inch from the bottom edge. Edge stitch the pocket in place as for the first pocket.

4. Referring to **Diagram 4**, continue pinning and sewing the pockets to the calendar front so that they are 1 inch apart from each other, and there is 1 inch between the bottom of one pocket and the top of the next. When you are finished, you will have six rows with four pockets in each row on the calendar front.

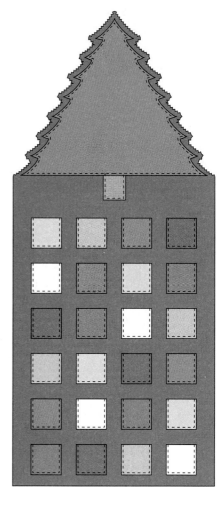

Diagram 4

SEWING THE CALENDAR BACK

1. Center the calendar front on top of the calendar back and pin the two layers together.

2. Edge stitch completely around the tree and the three remaining sides

directly on top of the previous line of edge stitching.

3. With pinking shears, pink the calendar back ¹/₄ inch away from the sides of the calendar front and the pinked edges around the tree, as shown in **Diagram 5.**

Diagram 5

DECORATING THE TREE

1. Using two ribbons at a time, tie 24 double bows and set them aside.

2. Using the Tulip Treasures paint, place a dot of paint approximately the size of the base of a stone anywhere on the tree. Gently push the stone into the paint,

forcing the paint up and around the edges of the stone. Add as many stone ornaments to the tree as you desire.

3. Referring to the photograph on page 176, use the gold glitter dimensional paint to draw several diagonal garlands on the tree.

4. Referring again to the photograph, glue the tan star to the top of the tree with extra thick tacky glue. Outline the tan star with a thick line of gold glitter dimensional paint.

5. Referring again to the photograph, paint the numbers 1 through 24 onto the pockets with gold glitter dimensional paint.

6. Glue one bow to the top of each pocket using extra thick tacky glue.

7. Let the paint and glue dry for two hours before finishing the calendar.

FINISHING THE ADVENT CALENDAR

1. Turn the calendar to the back. Referring to **Diagram 6**, hand tack the metal or plastic ring to the back of the tree, making sure the stitches go only through the green layer of felt.

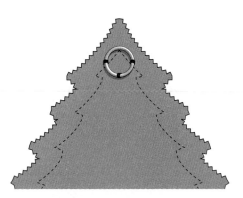

Diagram 6

2. Hang the calendar on a small nail.

3. Fill each pocket with Christmas candy or small gifts.

Know&Sew

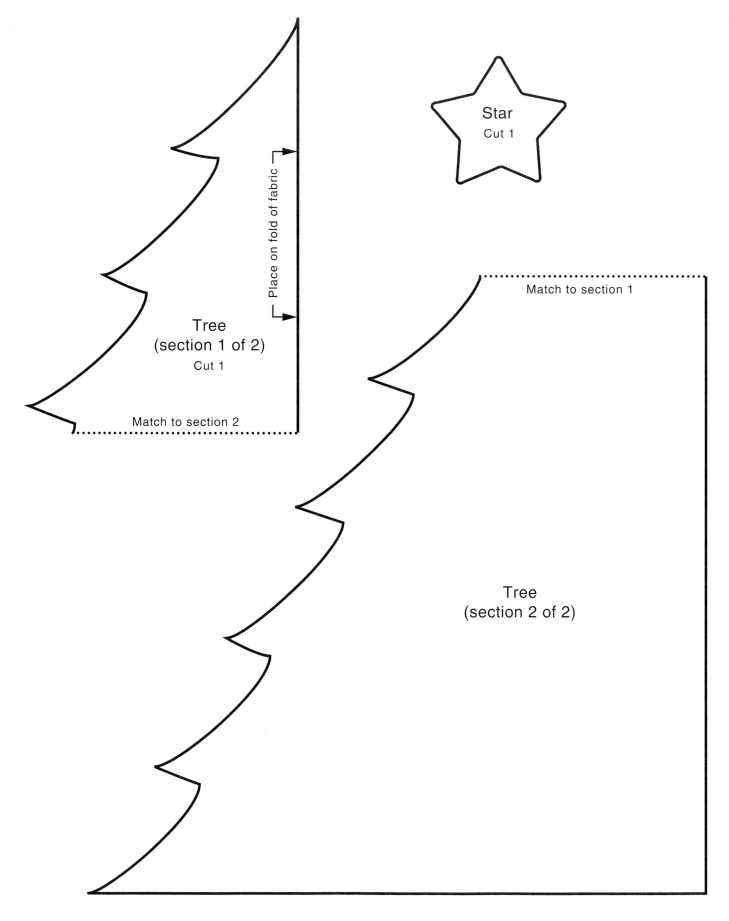

Star
Cut 1

Place on fold of fabric

Tree
(section 1 of 2)
Cut 1

Match to section 2

Match to section 1

Tree
(section 2 of 2)

Christmas Tablecloth

*For a yuletide celebration, set a table topped with tasty treats on
a gift-wrapped Christmas cloth. Trimming the tablecloth is as much fun
as trimming the tree.*

Christmas Tablecloth

❖

MATERIALS LIST

FABRIC REQUIREMENTS

• 70-INCH-ROUND WHITE
TABLECLOTH

• ³/₄ YARD OF RED SOLID
FOR THE PACKAGES

• ³/₄ YARD OF GREEN SOLID
FOR THE PACKAGES

OTHER SUPPLIES

• SEWING THREAD TO
MATCH THE FABRICS

• 8¹/₂ YARDS OF 1¹/₄-INCH-
WIDE RED VELVET RIBBON

• 8¹/₂ YARDS OF 1¹/₄-INCH-
WIDE GREEN VELVET RIBBON

FABRIC OPTIONS

• FELT

• COTTON

• CHINTZ

• FLANNEL

SKILL LEVEL: EASY

SIZE: The finished size of the round tablecloth shown in the photograph on page 181 is 70 inches.

NOTE: If you are not using felt, cut 10¹/₂ inch squares for each package. Turn under ¹/₂ inch along the sides of each package and press before sewing them to the tablecloth.

CUTTING THE PACKAGES

1. From the red solid, cut six 9¹/₂-inch squares for the packages.

2. From the green solid, cut six 9¹/₂-inch squares for the packages.

3. From the red velvet ribbon, cut 12 strips, each 10¹/₂ inches long, for trimming the green packages. Cut 6 strips, each 25 inches long, for the bows.

4. From the green velvet ribbon, cut 12 strips, each 10¹/₂ inches long, for trimming the red packages. Cut 6 strips, each 25 inches long, for the bows.

SEWING THE PACKAGES

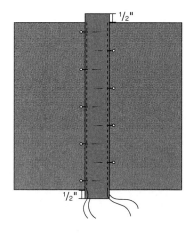

Diagram 1

1. Thread the sewing machine with red thread. Pin and sew one 10¹/₂-inch strip of red ribbon to the center of one green package, extending ¹/₂ inch of the ribbon beyond the top and bottom edges of the package, as shown in **Diagram 1**.

2. Repeat Step 1 to sew one strip of red ribbon to each of the remaining green packages.

3. Rotate each package so that the sewn ribbon is in a horizontal position.

4. Pin and sew a second 10¹/₂-inch strip of red ribbon to the center of each green package, extending ¹/₂ inch of the ribbon beyond the top and bottom edges, as shown in **Diagram 2**.

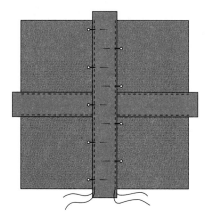

Diagram 2

5. Repeat Step 4 to sew the remaining strips of red ribbon to each of the remaining green packages.

6. Thread the sewing machine with green thread. Repeat Steps 1 through 5 with the red packages and green ribbon.

SEWING THE PACKAGES TO THE TABLECLOTH

1. Pin the green and the red packages around the bottom of the tablecloth so they are 2¹/₂ inches from the edge of the cloth and evenly spaced from each other. Be sure to alternate the colors and turn under the ¹/₂-inch piece of ribbon along each edge, as shown in **Diagram 3**.

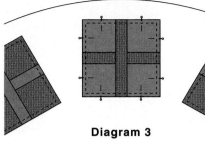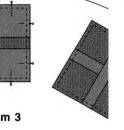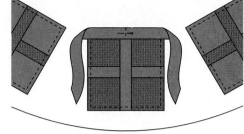

Diagram 3

Diagram 4

2. Sew the red packages to the tablecloth with red thread and the green packages to the tablecloth with green thread.

SEWING THE BOWS TO THE PACKAGES

1. Pin and sew one 25-inch strip of red ribbon to the top and center of each green package using red thread, as shown in **Diagram 4.**

2. Repeat Step 1 using green thread to sew the strips of green ribbon to the red packages.

FINISHING THE TABLECLOTH

Securely tie each ribbon at the top of the packages into a bow, as shown in the photograph on page 181.

Christmas Show Towels

Why not dress up every room in the house for Christmas? Start with purchased towels and gold trim. In a flash, you will add a touch of holiday luxury to the bath.

SIZE: The towels are made from purchased hand and bath towels.

CUTTING THE TRIM

From the gold trim, cut two 16-inch lengths for the hand towels. Cut two 30-inch lengths for the bath towels.

SEWING THE TRIM TO THE TOWELS

1. Pin the trim onto the woven band along one end of each towel, as shown in **Diagram 1**. If there is no woven band on the towel, pin the trim along one short side of the hand towel, 4 inches from the edge. Pin the trim along one short side of the bath towel, $5^1/2$ inches from the edge.

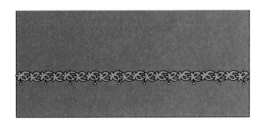

Diagram 1

2. Thread a hand-sewing needle with thread to match the trim. Hand sew the trim to each towel using very small stitches so they do not show on the front of the towels.

SEWING THE APPLIQUÉS TO THE HAND TOWELS

1. To find the midpoint of one hand towel, fold it in half lengthwise and then crosswise. The point at which the two folds meet is the midpoint.

2. Center and pin the appliqué over the midpoint of the towel, making sure the top of the appliqué is 5 inches above the top of the gold trim, as shown in **Diagram 2**.

Diagram 2

3. Thread a hand-sewing needle with thread to match the appliqué and knot both ends of the thread together.

4. With the doubled thread, hand sew the appliqué to the towel, using very small stitches so they do not show on the front of the towel.

5. Repeat Steps 1 through 4 to sew the remaining appliqué onto the other hand towel.

FINISHING THE TOWELS

Fold each show towel in thirds lengthwise and then in half crosswise. Display each hand towel over each bath towel.

Merry Christmas Ornaments

The magic of Christmas is in the air when you deck the halls or trim the tree with merry ornaments. Wonderfully fun to make, these tiny treasures can also be used to top pretty packages and make gift giving thrice as nice.

Ballerina Slipper Ornament

SKILL LEVEL: *INTERMEDIATE*

SIZE: The finished size is 2¹/₂ inches wide and 6 inches high.

NOTE: Measurements in the cutting directions include the seam allowances. Sew all the seams with ¹/₄-inch seam allowances.

CUTTING THE SLIPPER ORNAMENT

1. Trace the pattern pieces on page 189 onto template plastic, transferring all markings with a fine-point, permanent marker. Cut out the pattern pieces.

2. From the pink solid, cut one slipper and one slipper reverse.

3. Using a chalk pencil, mark point A on the right side of the fabric.

4. From the light blue floral print, cut one leg and one leg reverse.

5. Using a chalk pencil, mark points B, C, and D on the right side of the fabric.

6. From the pink ribbon, cut two 13-inch lengths for lacing the slipper. Cut one 5-inch length for the hanging loop. Cut two 3-inch lengths for trimming the slipper.

SEWING THE SLIPPER TO THE LEG

1. With the wrong side of the slipper facing up, fold down ¹/₄ inch along the top edge and press it in place. It may be necessary to clip three or four V-shaped notches along the top, as shown in **Diagram 1**, in order for the fold to lie flat when pressed.

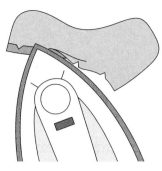

Diagram 1

2. Repeat Step 1 for the slipper reverse.

3. Referring to **Diagram 2**, with right sides together, pin the slipper to the leg, inserting one 13-inch length of ribbon between the slipper and the leg at point A. Make sure the raw edges are even.

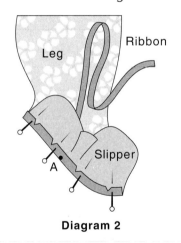

Diagram 2

4. Sew the slipper to the leg, making sure to catch the end of the ribbon in the seam allowance. Press the seam toward the slipper.

5. Repeat Steps 3 and 4 for the slipper reverse and leg reverse.

SEWING THE SLIPPER-AND-LEG UNITS TOGETHER

1. Pin the end of each 13-inch length of ribbon to the right side of the fabric at

MATERIALS LIST

FABRIC REQUIREMENTS

• 8-INCH SQUARE OF PINK SOLID FOR THE SLIPPER

• 8-INCH SQUARE OF LIGHT BLUE FLORAL PRINT FOR THE LEG

OTHER SUPPLIES

• SEWING THREAD TO MATCH THE FABRICS

• 1¹/₈ YARD OF ¹/₈-INCH-WIDE PINK RIBBON

• 12 INCHES OF 1¹/₂-INCH-WIDE PINK-AND-WHITE LACE

• PINK RIBBON ROSE

• TEMPLATE PLASTIC

• FINE-POINT, PERMANENT MARKER

• CHALK PENCIL

FABRIC OPTIONS

FOR THE SLIPPER

• SATIN

• COTTON

• CHINTZ

FOR THE LEG

• COTTON

• CHINTZ

• SATIN

the centers of the leg and leg reverse to prevent the ribbons from getting caught in the seam allowance as you sew.

2. With right sides together, pin and sew the slipper-and-leg unit to the slipper-and-leg reverse unit, leaving the top of the leg open, as shown in **Diagram 3.** Clip several V-shaped notches into the seam allowance along the curves of the slipper and the curves of the leg. Do not turn the ornament right side out.

Diagram 5

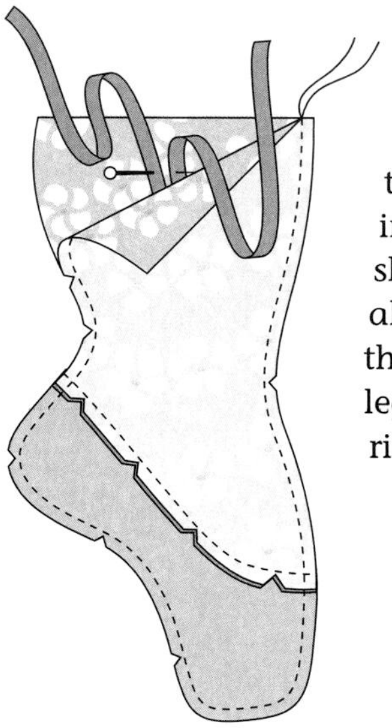

Diagram 3

SEWING THE LACE

1. With right sides together, fold the lace in half crosswise. Pin and sew the ends together, as shown in **Diagram 4.**

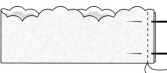

Diagram 4

2. To make one row of gathering stitches, use the longest machine stitch and sew ¼ inch from the raw edges. Pull up the bobbin thread and gather the lace until it measures 6 inches. Secure the ends of the threads with a knot.

SEWING THE LACE TO THE LEG

1. Referring to **Diagram 5,** insert the leg into the lace with the right side of the lace facing the wrong side of the leg. Align the seam of the lace with the seam at the back of the leg and pin.

2. To make the hanging loop, fold the 5-inch length of ribbon in half crosswise. Referring to **Diagram 5,** sandwich and pin the raw ends of the loop between the lace and the leg at the back seam.

3. Referring to **Diagram 5,** sew the lace to the leg, making sure to catch the ends of the loop in the seam allowance. Turn the ornament right side out.

LACING THE SLIPPER

1. Unpin the ribbons from the center of each leg. Referring to **Diagram 6,** crisscross the ribbons at point B, making sure not to twist the ribbon in the process. Hand tack them in place at point B.

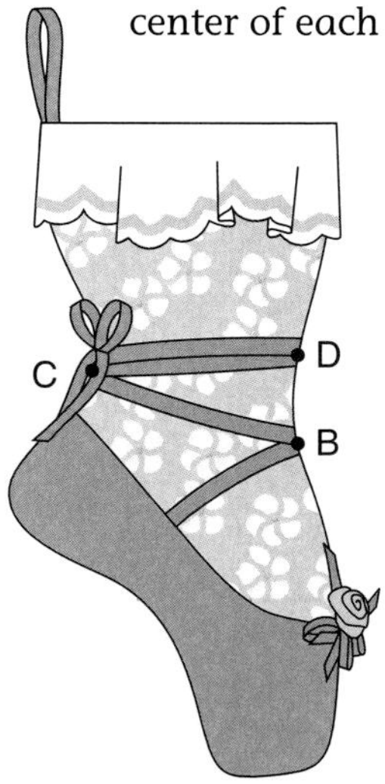

Diagram 6

2. Referring to **Diagram 6,** crisscross the ribbons at point C and hand tack them in place at point C.

3. Referring to **Diagram 6,** crisscross the ribbons at point D and hand tack them in place at point D.

4. Referring to **Diagram 6,** bring the ribbons back to point C and tie them into a bow. Hand tack the bow to the leg of the ornament.

FINISHING THE SLIPPER ORNAMENT

1. Tie the two 3-inch lengths of ribbon into a double bow and hand tack them to the top of the slipper, as shown in **Diagram 6.**

2. Thread a hand-sewing needle with matching thread and hand tack the ribbon rose to the center of the double bow on the slipper.

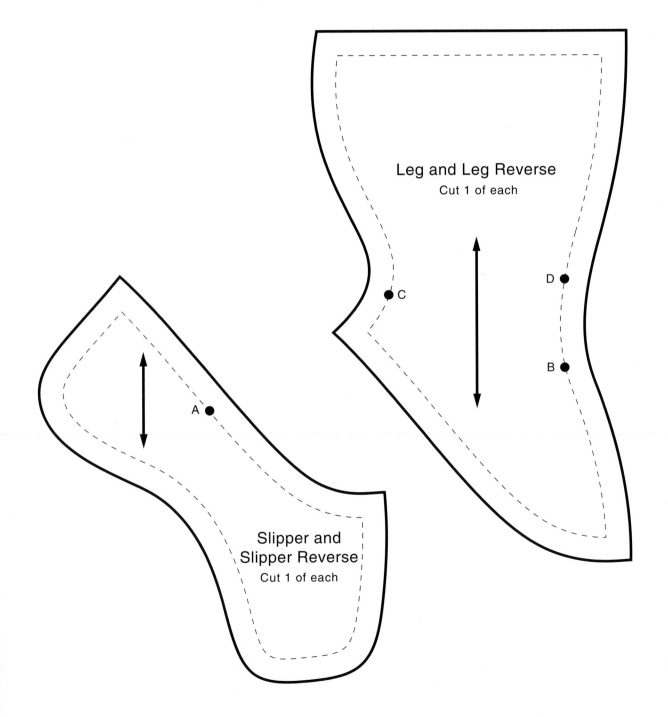

Leg and Leg Reverse
Cut 1 of each

Slipper and
Slipper Reverse
Cut 1 of each

Starry-Eyed Santa Ornament

SKILL LEVEL: *INTERMEDIATE*

SIZE: The finished size is 2 inches wide and 6 inches high.

NOTE: Measurements in the cutting directions include the seam allowances. Sew all the seams with 1/4-inch seam allowances.

CUTTING THE SANTA ORNAMENT

1. Trace the pattern pieces on pages 193–194 onto template plastic tracing paper, transferring all markings with a fine-point, permanent marker. Cut out the patterns pieces.

2. Cut the 8-inch square of fusible interfacing into one 7-inch square and one 1-inch square.

3. Following the manufacturer's directions, iron the 7-inch square of fusible interfacing onto the wrong side of the red solid.

4. Trace the body and the base onto the paper side of the fusible interfacing. Cut out the body and the base.

5. Transfer all markings onto the right side of the fabric with a chalk pencil.

6. From the gold solid, cut one sack and one sack reverse.

7. From the dark green solid, cut four mittens.

8. Following the manufacturer's directions, iron a 1-inch square of fusible interfacing onto the wrong side of the peach solid. Trace the face onto the paper side of the interfacing. Cut out the face.

9. From the white velvet ribbon, cut one 6-inch length for trimming the body. Cut one 3-inch length for trimming the hat. Cut two 1-inch squares for the cuffs.

SEWING THE MITTENS

1. To make one mitten, with right sides together, pin and sew two mitten pieces together, leaving the top edge open. Clip several V-shaped notches into the curves, as shown in **Diagram 7**.

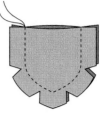

Diagram 7

2. Turn the mitten right side out and lightly stuff with polyester fiberfill. Topstitch the opening closed. For more information, see "Edge Stitching and Topstitching" on page 242.

3. Repeat Steps 1 and 2 with the remaining mitten pieces.

4. Pin the mittens to the right side of the body at points A and B.

5. Using black thread, topstitch along the arm lines, sewing only the tops of the mittens to the body, as shown in **Diagram 8**.

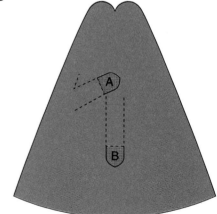

Diagram 8

SEWING THE BELT

1. Cut two 1¾-inch lengths of black satin ribbon. Turn under 1/8 inch along the short ends of both ribbons and press. Place the pearl buckle 3/4 inch from one end of one ribbon.

2. Pin the ribbons to the body along the belt placement lines, making sure the buckle is at the front of the body and below the bent arm. Using black thread, sew the ribbons to the body, as shown in **Diagram 9.**

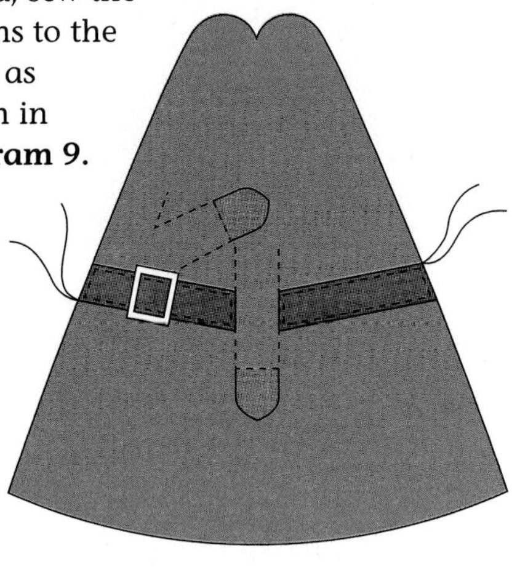

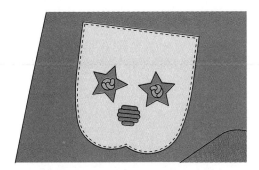

Diagram 9

Embroidering the Face

1. Change the thread to match the face. Pin and sew the face to the body along the indicated placement lines.

2. Using two strands of red floss, embroider the nose with a satin stitch, as shown in **Diagram 10.** For information on satin stitching, see "Embroidery and Hand-Sewing Stitches" on page 244.

Diagram 10

3. Using two strands of blue floss, thread one star sequin onto the floss and embroider one eye with a French knot, as shown in **Diagram 10.** Repeat with the remaining star sequin to make the other eye. For information on French knots, see "Embroidery and Hand-Sewing Stitches" on page 244.

4. Thread a large-eyed embroidery needle with one 12-inch strand of white tapestry wool and two strands of white embroidery floss and knot the end. Insert the needle into the edge of the face at the upper corner and immediately bring it up next to where the needle was inserted, as shown in **Diagram 11.**

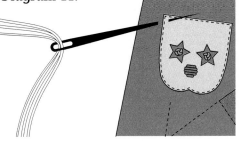

Diagram 11

5. Cut the strands, leaving a 1-inch length on either side of the needle holes. Tie the strands together close to the fabric. Repeat this step to sew the beard around the face and the hair at the back of the head, as shown in **Diagram 12.**

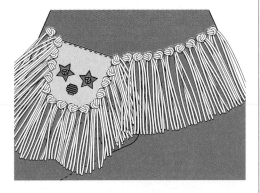

Diagram 12

Stuffing and Trimming the Body

1. With right sides together, fold the body in half lengthwise. Pin and sew

Fabric Options

For the Body
- Velvet
- Velveteen
- Flannel

For the Face and Mittens
- Silk
- Satin
- Cotton

For the Sack
- Lamé
- Chintz
- Cotton

the body together, making sure to catch the belt ribbon in the seam allowance and leaving the bottom edge open for turning. Turn the body right side out and firmly stuff with polyester fiberfill.

2. With right sides together, fold the 3-inch length of white velvet ribbon in half crosswise. Pin and sew the short ends together, as shown in **Diagram 13.** Finger press the seam open.

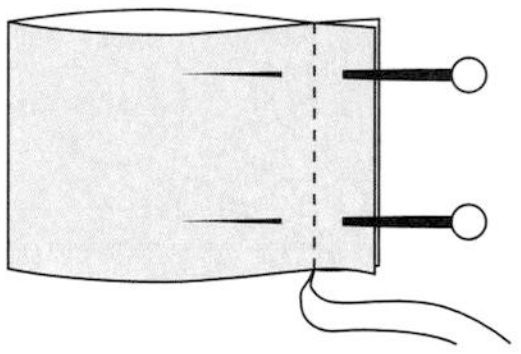

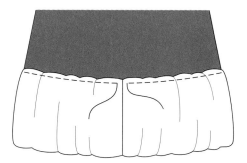

Diagram 13

3. Fold the ribbon in half lengthwise by taking the bottom edge of the ribbon and folding it up to meet the top edge. Make sure to keep the shape circular. The wrong sides of the ribbon will be facing each other and the right sides of the ribbon will be on the outside and inside of the ring. To make one row of gathering stitches, use the longest machine stitch and edge stitch along the raw edges through the layers of ribbon. For more information, see "Edge Stitching and Topstitching" on page 242.

4. With the folded edge of the ribbon even with the knots for the hair, place the velvet ribbon around the bottom edge of the hat, covering the top of the face and the hair knots around the back of the hat, as shown in **Diagram 14.** Pull up the bobbin thread and evenly gather the ribbon around the bottom of the hat. Secure the ends of the threads with a knot. Slip stitch the ribbon in place around the bottom of the hat. For information on slip stitching, see "Embroidery and Hand-Sewing Stitches" on page 244.

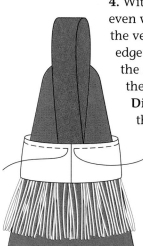

Diagram 14

5. To make the hanging loop, fold the dark green ribbon in half crosswise.

Sandwich and pin the raw ends of the loop between the hat and the white velvet ribbon, as shown in **Diagram 14.**

6. Thread a hand-sewing needle with white thread and slip stitch the top of the white ribbon to the hat, making sure to sew the loop in the seam allowance.

7. With right sides together, fold the 6-inch length of white velvet ribbon in half crosswise.

8. Pin and sew the short ends together.

9. Finger press the seam open and turn the ribbon right side out.

10. To make one row of gathering stitches, use the longest machine stitch and edge stitch along one long edge of the ribbon, keeping the circular shape.

11. With the row of gathering stitches on top, insert the bottom of the body into the ribbon, making sure that the seam of the ribbon is at the back of the body and the bottom raw edges are even.

12. Pull up the bobbin thread and evenly gather the ribbon around the body, as shown in **Diagram 15.** Secure the ends of the threads with a knot.

Diagram 15

13. Slip stitch the top and bottom edges of the ribbon to the body.

14. With the wrong side of one 1-inch square of white velvet ribbon facing up, fold two ends toward the center, as shown in **Diagram 16.** Fold the ribbon in half lengthwise and hand tack the edges together to form one cuff. Repeat this step to make a second cuff with the remaining 1-inch square.

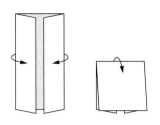

Diagram 16

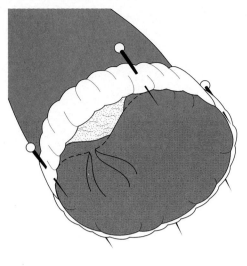

Diagram 17

15. Hand sew the cuffs to the body, making sure to cover the top edge of each mitten.

SEWING THE BASE TO THE BODY

1. To make one row of gathering stitches around the base, use the longest machine stitch and sew ¼ inch from the raw edge. Pull up the bobbin thread and evenly gather the base so that it matches the bottom of the body. Secure the ends of the threads with a knot. Finger press the seam allowance toward the wrong side of the base.

2. Pin the base to the bottom of the body, as shown in **Diagram 17**. Slip stitch the base to the body.

FINISHING THE SANTA ORNAMENT

1. With right sides together, pin and sew the sack and sack reverse together, leaving the top edge open. Turn down a ½-inch hem along the open edge and press. Turn the sack right side out.

2. Lightly stuff the sack with polyester fiberfill. Tie the sack closed with a piece of thread.

3. Referring to the photograph on page 186, hand tack the sack to Santa's shoulder and to one mitten.

Face
Cut 1

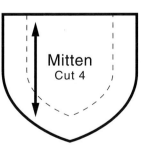

Mitten
Cut 4

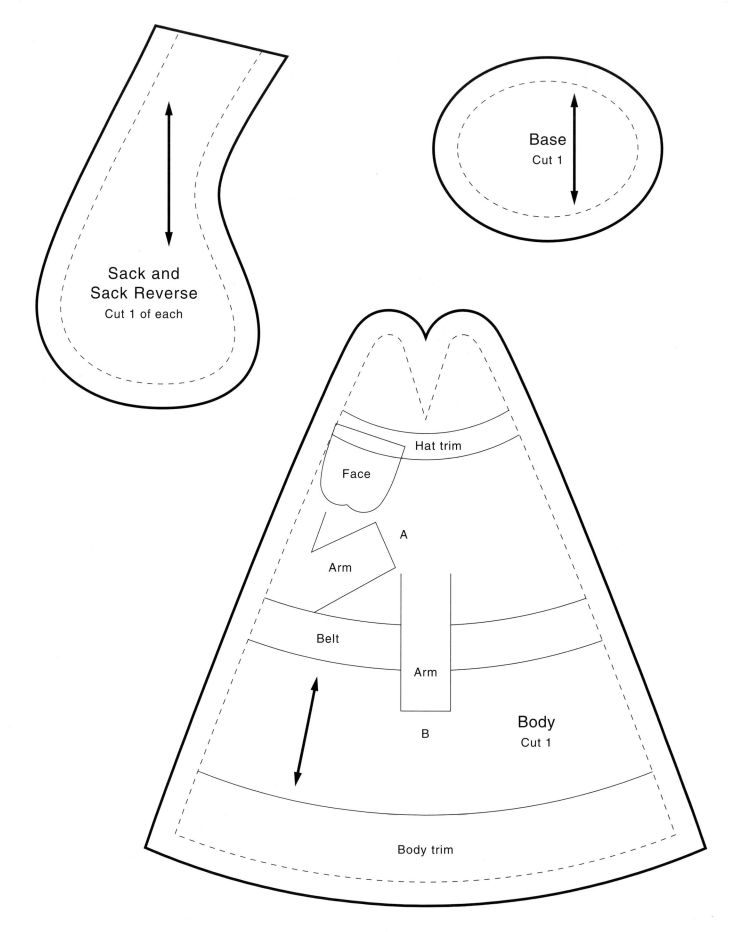

Sack and
Sack Reverse
Cut 1 of each

Base
Cut 1

Hat trim

Face

A

Arm

Belt

Arm

B

Body
Cut 1

Body trim

Toy Soldier Ornament

SKILL LEVEL: *INTERMEDIATE*

SIZE: The finished size is 3 inches wide and 6 inches high.

NOTE: Measurements in the cutting directions include the seam allowances. Sew all the seams with $1/4$-inch seam allowances.

CUTTING THE SOLDIER ORNAMENT

1. Trace the pattern pieces on pages 199–201 onto template plastic, transferring all markings with a fine-point, permanent marker. Cut out the pattern pieces.

2. From the red solid, cut one jacket front, one jacket back, and one jacket back reverse.

3. From the black solid, cut one head back, one head back reverse, one boot front, one boot back, one boot back reverse, and four gloves.

4. From the blue solid, cut one pants, one hat front, one hat back, and one hat back reverse.

5. From the gold solid, cut two keys.

6. From the peach solid, cut one face.

7. From the fusible interfacing, cut one body front, one body back, and one body back reverse. Transfer all markings, using a fine-point, permanent marker.

8. From the yellow satin ribbon, cut two $2^1/2$-inch lengths for the sashes. Cut one 8-inch length for the hanging loop.

9. From the black satin ribbon, cut one 2-inch length for the belt.

PREPARING THE FRONT PIECES

1. Turn under and press $1/4$ inch along the bottom edge of the hat front.

2. Turn under and press $1/4$ inch along the neckline of the jacket front.

3. Clip the seam allowance at the center bottom of the jacket front. Turn under and press $1/4$ inch along each side of the bottom, as shown in **Diagram 18.**

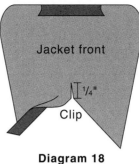

Diagram 18

4. Clip the seam allowance at the center top of the boot front. Turn under and press $1/4$ inch along each side of the top, as shown in **Diagram 19.**

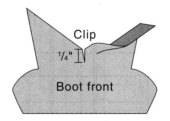

Diagram 19

5. Following the manufacturer's directions and using the placement lines on the pattern piece as a guide, iron the following pieces onto the body front in this order so that the pieces overlap in the proper manner: face, hat front, pants, jacket front, and boot front.

EDGE STITCHING THE BODY FRONT

1. Turn under and press $1/4$ inch along the tops of two gloves. Turn under and press $1/4$ inch along the side of each glove without the seam allowance.

2. Referring to **Diagram 20** on page 196, pin and edge stitch the gloves to

MATERIALS LIST

FABRIC REQUIREMENTS
- 8-INCH SQUARE OF RED SOLID FOR THE JACKET
- 7-INCH SQUARE OF BLACK SOLID FOR THE BOOTS
- 6-INCH SQUARE OF BLUE SOLID FOR THE HAT AND PANTS
- 5-INCH SQUARE OF GOLD SOLID FOR THE KEY
- 3-INCH SQUARE OF PEACH SOLID FOR THE FACE
- 9-INCH SQUARE OF FUSIBLE INTERFACING FOR THE BODY

OTHER SUPPLIES
- $1/2$ YARD OF $1/4$-INCH-WIDE YELLOW SATIN RIBBON
- 4 INCHES OF $3/8$-INCH-WIDE BLACK SATIN RIBBON
- SEWING THREAD TO MATCH THE FABRICS AND RIBBONS
- 1 SKEIN EACH OF BLUE AND BLACK EMBROIDERY FLOSS
- LARGE-EYED EMBROIDERY NEEDLE
- 8-INCH STRAND OF $1/4$-INCH-WIDE BLUE SEQUINS
- 3 RED SEQUINS, EACH $3/4$ INCH DIAMETER
- 3 BLUE FLOWER SEQUINS, EACH $1/2$ INCH
- 12 OUNCE BAG OF POLYESTER FIBERFILL
- TEMPLATE PLASTIC
- FINE-POINT, PERMANENT MARKER
- CRAFT GLUE

the jacket front using black thread. Edge stitch around the boot front. For more information, see "Edge Stitching and Topstitching" on page 242.

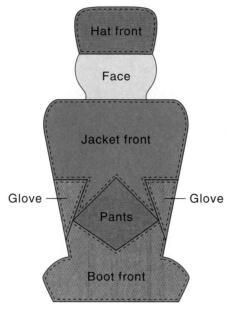

Diagram 20

3. Using red thread, edge stitch completely around the jacket front, as shown in **Diagram 20**.

4. Using blue thread, edge stitch completely around the hat front, as shown in **Diagram 20**.

TRIMMING THE JACKET FRONT

1. Turn under and press ¹/₄ inch along the short ends of the 2-inch ribbon cut for the belt. Using black thread, edge stitch the belt to the jacket front, as shown in **Diagram 21**.

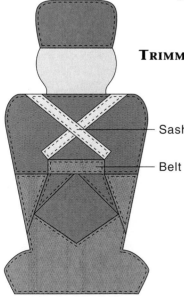

Diagram 21

2. Turn under and press ¹/₄ inch along the short ends of both 2¹/₂-inch ribbons cut for the sashes. Using yellow thread, edge stitch the sashes to the jacket front, as shown in **Diagram 21**.

EMBROIDERING THE FACE

1. Using two strands of blue floss, satin stitch the eyes. For information on satin stitching, see "Embroidery and Hand-Sewing Stitches" on page 244.

2. Using two strands of black floss, embroider the nose with a French knot and the mustache with an outline stitch, as shown in **Diagram 22**. For information on French knots and outline stitching, see "Embroidery and Hand-Sewing Stitches" on page 244.

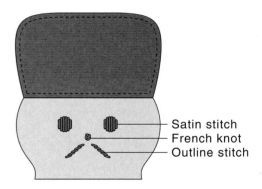

Diagram 22

PREPARING THE BACK PIECES

1. Turn under and press ¹/₄ inch along the bottom edge of the hat back and hat back reverse.

2. Turn under and press ¹/₄ inch along the neckline of the jacket back and jacket back reverse.

3. Turn under and press ¹/₄ inch along the top edge of the boot back and boot back reverse.

4. Following the manufacturer's directions and using the placement lines on the pattern piece as a guide, iron the following pieces onto the body back in this order so that all of the pieces overlap in the proper manner: the head back, the hat back, the jacket back, and the boot back. Repeat this step for the body back reverse and the corresponding reverse pieces.

EDGE STITCHING THE BODY BACK

1. Turn under and press ¼ inch along the tops of the two remaining gloves. Turn under and press ¼ inch along the side of each glove without the seam allowance.

2. Referring to **Diagram 23,** pin and edge stitch one glove to the jacket back and one glove to the jacket back reverse using black thread. Edge stitch around the boot back and boot back reverse.

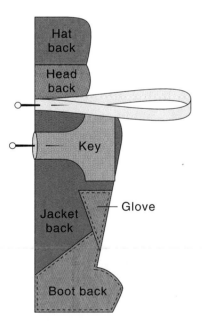

Diagram 23

SEWING THE KEY

1. With right sides together, pin and sew the keys together, leaving the short end open for turning.

2. Turn the key right side out and firmly stuff with polyester fiberfill.

SEWING THE SOLDIER TOGETHER

1. With right sides together, pin the open edge of the key onto the right side of the body back, matching the raw edges, as shown in **Diagram 23.**

2. Fold the 8-inch length of ribbon in half to form the hanging loop.

3. Pin the hanging loop to the base of the head back, making sure the raw edges are even, as shown in **Diagram 23.**

4. With right sides together, pin the body back reverse to the body back along the straight side, making sure to catch the open edge of the key and the raw ends of the loop in the seam allowance.

5. Sew the body back reverse to the body back along the straight side. Make sure that the pieces of the body back reverse align with the body back, as shown in **Diagram 24.** Press the seam open.

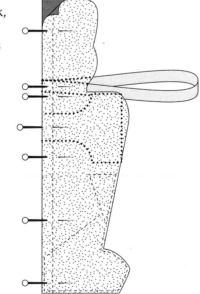

Diagram 24

6. With right sides together, pin and sew the body back to the body front, leaving the bottom edge open, as shown in **Diagram 25** on page 198.

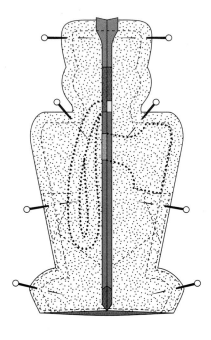

Diagram 25

Diagram 26

7. Turn the soldier right side out and firmly stuff with polyester fiberfill. Turn under the seam allowance along the bottom and blindstitch it closed. For information on blindstitching, see "Embroidery and Hand-Sewing Stitches" on page 244.

FINISHING THE SOLDIER ORNAMENT

1. Referring to **Diagram 26**, hand tack one blue flower sequin to the top of each glove on the front. Hand tack three blue sequins to each shoulder for the epaulets and the strand of blue sequins around the bottom of the hat.

2. Referring to the top of **Diagram 26**, overlap two red sequins and glue them together. Fold the third red sequin in half and glue the straight edge to the center of the overlapped sequins. Glue the sequins unit to the center front of the hat. Glue one blue flower sequin to the center of the red sequins.

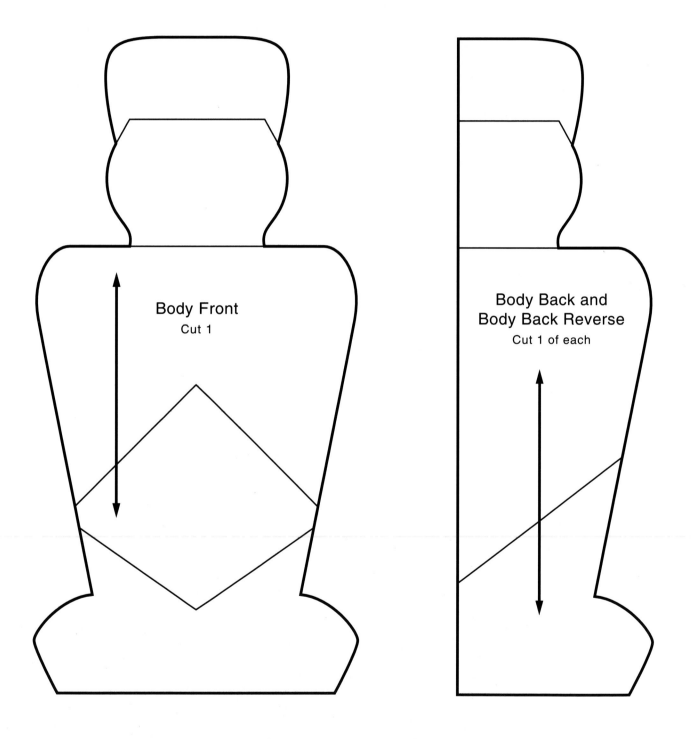

Body Front
Cut 1

Body Back and
Body Back Reverse
Cut 1 of each

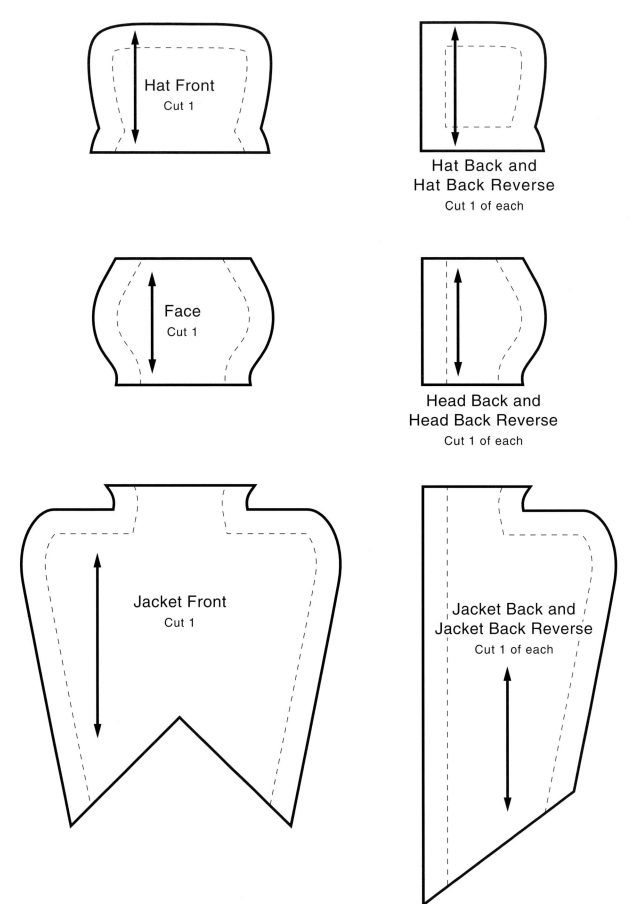

Hat Front
Cut 1

Hat Back and
Hat Back Reverse
Cut 1 of each

Face
Cut 1

Head Back and
Head Back Reverse
Cut 1 of each

Jacket Front
Cut 1

Jacket Back and
Jacket Back Reverse
Cut 1 of each

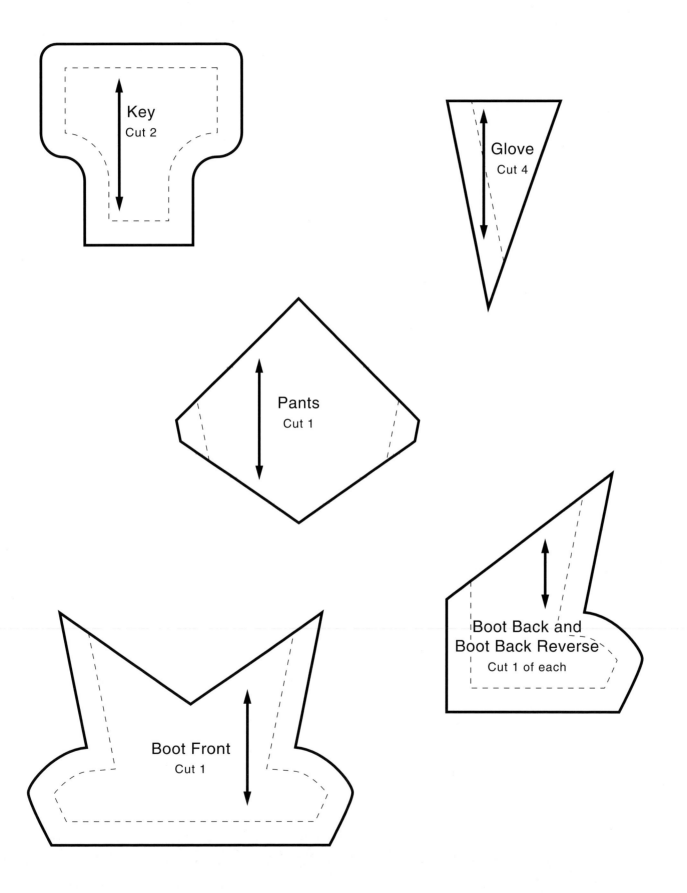

Key
Cut 2

Glove
Cut 4

Pants
Cut 1

Boot Back and
Boot Back Reverse
Cut 1 of each

Boot Front
Cut 1

Nicholas the Bear

*Tuck Nicholas into a holiday basket filled with goodies and glad tidings.
Nestle him into an ivy-and-holly wreath, or let him peer out of a child's
Christmas stocking. When Christmas is over, just change his ribbon,
and Nicholas will be ready to celebrate the next holiday!*

SIZE: Nicholas is an unjointed bear that stands about 8 inches high.

NOTE: Measurements in the cutting directions include the seam allowances. Sew all the seams with ¼-inch seam allowances.

CUTTING THE BEAR

1. Trace the pattern pieces on pages 206–207 onto template plastic with a fine-point, permanent marker, transferring all markings. Cut out the pieces.

2. From the brown solid, with the wrong side facing up, cut one front and one front reverse. Cut one back and one back reverse.

3. With a chalk pencil, transfer all markings onto the wrong side of the fabric.

SEWING THE FRONT AND BACK

1. With right sides together, pin and sew the front and front reverse together between points A and B. Clip into the seam allowance, making sure not to cut through the stitching, as shown in **Diagram 1**. Press the seam open.

Diagram 1

2. With right sides together, pin and sew the back and back reverse together between points C and D and between points E and F, as shown in **Diagram 2.** Press the seam open.

Diagram 2

3. With right sides together and raw edges even, pin the front to the back. Set the sewing machine for a small stitch length and, starting at the side of one leg, sew around the entire body.

4. Clip several notches into the curves, as shown in **Diagram 3.**

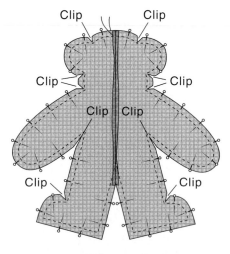

Clip Clip
Clip Clip
Clip Clip
Clip Clip

Diagram 3

MATERIALS LIST

FABRIC REQUIREMENT
• 10 × 24-INCH REC-TANGLE OF BROWN SOLID

OTHER SUPPLIES
• ½ YARD OF 1-INCH-WIDE WIRE-EDGED RED RIBBON
• ½ YARD OF ½-INCH-WIDE WIRE-EDGED GREEN RIBBON
• SEWING THREAD TO MATCH THE FABRIC
• HEAVY-DUTY BLACK THREAD
• SKEIN OF SIZE 3 BROWN PEARL COTTON OR BROWN EMBROIDERY FLOSS
• HAND-SEWING NEEDLE
• 3-INCH DOLL NEEDLE
• LARGE-EYED EMBROIDERY NEEDLE
• 12-OUNCE BAG OF POLY-ESTER FIBERFILL
• CUP OF DRY RICE OR PLASTIC PELLETS
• WOODEN SPOON
• 2 BLACK PLASTIC BEADS, EACH 6MM
• SPRIG OF SILK OR PLASTIC HOLLY WITH BERRIES
• TEMPLATE PLASTIC
• FINE-POINT, PERMANENT MARKER
• CHALK PENCIL

FABRIC OPTIONS
• POLAR FLEECE
• TERRY CLOTH
• VELOUR
• VELVET
• WOOL

Know&Sew

IF YOU DECIDE NOT TO STUFF NICHOLAS WITH RICE AND USE POLYESTER FIBERFILL ONLY, FOLLOW THESE IMPORTANT HINTS. BEGIN BY STUFFING THE HANDS AND FEET. PACK THE STUFFING IN FIRMLY, USING SMALL AMOUNTS OF FIBERFILL. IF YOU'RE HAVING TROUBLE PUSHING THE STUFFING INTO A SMALL AREA WITH YOUR FINGERS, TRY USING THE ERASER END OF A PENCIL. GRADUATE TO LARGER AMOUNTS OF STUFFING AS YOU MOVE TO LARGER AREAS. TO AVOID LUMPING, USE HANDFULS OF STUFFING. PACK THE STUFFING AS YOU ADD IT, CONTINU-ALLY CHECKING FOR LUMPS. PERIODICALLY STEP BACK FROM THE PROJECT TO MAKE SURE YOU'RE SYMMETRICALLY STUFFING THE BEAR. IT MAY TAKE SEVERAL ATTEMPTS BEFORE YOU'RE SATISFIED.

5. Turn the bear right side out and carefully push out the curves with your finger or the handle of a wooden spoon.

STUFFING THE BEAR

Note: If you are making this gift for a small child, it is best to stuff the bear only with polyester fiberfill.

1. Stuff each ear with a small amount of polyester fiberfill.

2. Sew each ear, as shown in **Diagram 4.**

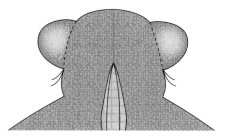

Diagram 4

3. Referring to the photograph on page 202, shape the face and nose by firmly stuffing the head with polyester fiberfill.

4. One at a time, fill each leg with rice or pellets, stopping at the crotch line. Fill each arm with rice or pellets, stop-ping at the body. Use a small amount of polyester fiberfill to hold the rice in place, as shown in **Diagram 5.**

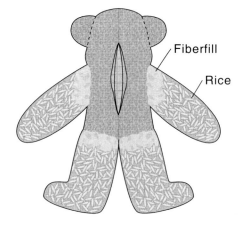

Fiberfill

Rice

Diagram 5

5. Turn the bear onto his tummy and fill the body with rice or pellets. Use a small amount of polyester fiberfill to hold the rice in place.

6. Turn under the seam allowance along the back opening and finger press. Using brown thread, slip stitch the opening closed, making sure to pull the stitches tightly to secure the seam. For information on slip stitching, see "Embroidery and Hand-Sewing Stitches" on page 244.

ATTACHING THE EYES

1. Thread a 3-inch doll needle with heavy-duty black thread and knot both ends of the thread together. Carefully insert the needle at the front of the neck and bring it out approxi-mately $1^1/2$ inches from the nose and $3/4$ inch down from the forehead, as shown in **Diagram 6.**

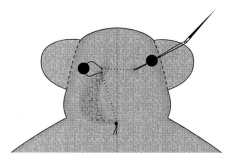

Diagram 6

2. String one black bead onto the thread and push the needle through to the other side of the face. String the other black bead onto the thread. Sew back and forth several times to secure the eyes in place, pulling the thread tightly to slightly indent the eyes into the fabric, as seen in the photograph on page 202.

3. Insert the needle into the head and exit through the neck as close as pos-sible to where the needle was first in-serted. Knot the thread and cut it. The

knot will be covered when the ribbons are tied around the neck.

EMBROIDERING THE NOSE AND MOUTH

1. With a single strand of brown pearl cotton or six strands of brown embroidery floss, thread a large-eyed embroidery needle and knot one end.

2. As close as possible to the place where the needle was inserted for the eyes, insert the needle into the neck and exit at the nose. Embroider the nose with a satin stitch and the mouth with three straight stitches, as shown in **Diagram 7**. When inserting the needle into the face to complete the mouth, exit through the neck as close as possible to the place where the needle was first inserted. Knot the thread and cut it. For information on satin stitching and straight stitching, see "Embroidery and Hand-Sewing Stitches" on page 244.

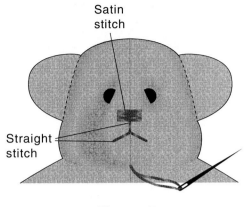

Diagram 7

FINISHING THE BEAR

1. Referring to the photograph on page 202, place the wire-edged red ribbon around the neck and tie it into a bow.

2. Place the wire-edged green ribbon around the neck on top of the red ribbon and tie it into a bow.

3. Tuck a small piece of silk or plastic holly with berries into the bow.

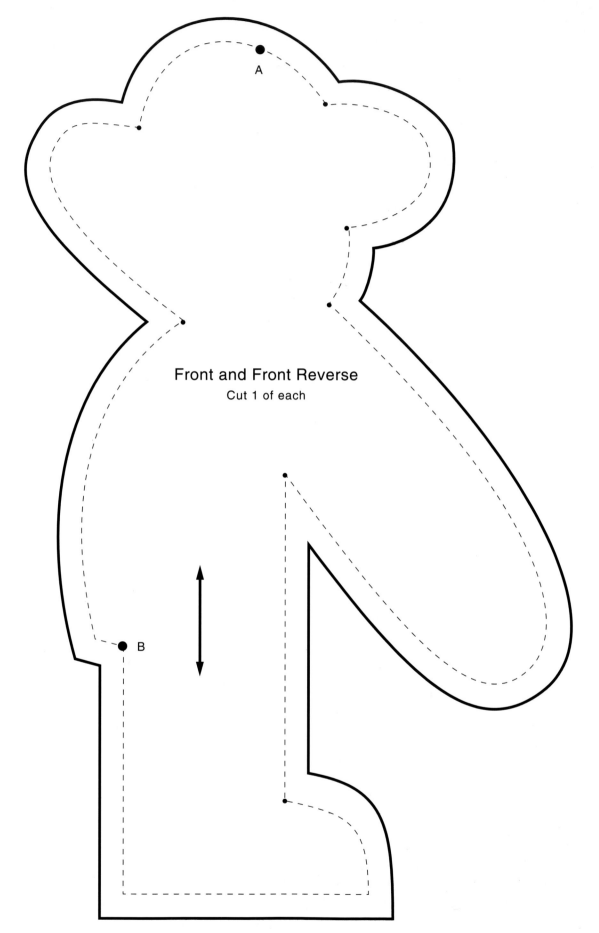

Front and Front Reverse

Cut 1 of each

A

B

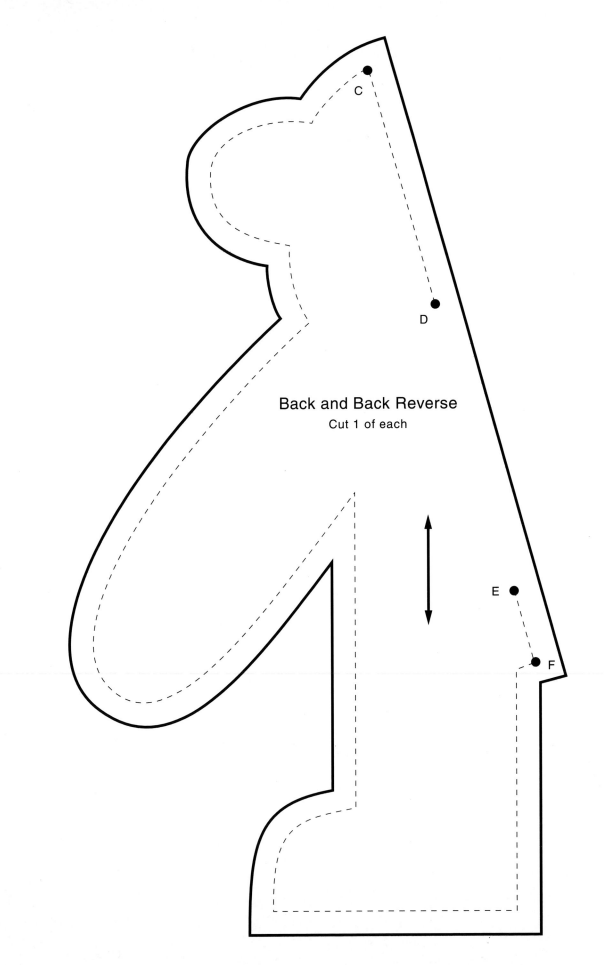

Back and Back Reverse

Cut 1 of each

Christmas Wreath

Usher in the holiday spirit with this magnificent Christmas wreath. You can create this impressive gift while you enjoy an evening listening to carols. The stunning effect of the wreath is dazzling when hung above a fireplace or in a room with a cathedral ceiling.

SIZE: The finished size is 30 inches in diameter.

NOTE: Measurements in the cutting directions include the seam allowances. Sew all the seams with 1/2-inch seam allowances.

CUTTING THE CASINGS

1. From the muslin, cut three 11 × 108-inch strips for the inner casings.

2. From each of the three Christmas prints, cut two 13 × 90-inch strips for the outer casings.

SEWING THE INNER CASINGS

1. With right sides together, fold and pin one muslin strip in half lengthwise, matching the raw edges on all sides of the strip.

2. Sew the strip together along the long side and one short side, as shown in **Diagram 1**.

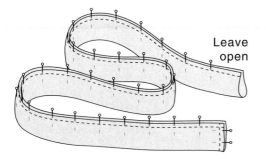

Leave open

Diagram 1

3. Turn the casing right side out through the opening on the short side and press.

4. Repeat Steps 1 through 3 with the remaining muslin strips to make two more inner casings.

5. Lightly stuff each casing with polyester fiberfill to within 3 inches of the end of each casing.

6. Secure the end of each casing by tying a piece of string around the open end.

SEWING THE OUTER CASINGS

1. With right sides together, pin one set of print strips together along one short end, making sure raw edges are even, as shown in **Diagram 2**.

Diagram 2

2. Sew the strips together along the short end. Open up the strip so that it is 179 inches long. Press the seam open.

3. Repeat Steps 1 and 2 for the remaining two sets of print strips.

4. Turn under a 1-inch hem along one short end of the 179-inch strip and press it toward the wrong side of the fabric.

5. With right sides together, fold the strip in half lengthwise, matching the raw edges. Pin and sew the strip along the long side, as shown in **Diagram 3** on page 210. Turn the casing right side out.

MATERIALS LIST

FABRIC REQUIREMENTS
- 3 1/4 YARDS OF MUSLIN FOR THE INNER CASINGS
- 2 3/4 YARDS EACH OF THREE COORDINATING CHRISTMAS PRINTS FOR THE OUTER CASINGS

OTHER SUPPLIES
- DECORATIVE COORDINATING BOW
- SEWING THREAD TO MATCH THE FABRICS
- HAND-SEWING NEEDLE
- 2 BAGS OF POLYESTER FIBERFILL, EACH 2 POUNDS
- STRING
- 3 LARGE SAFETY PINS
- OVER-THE-DOOR HANGER

FABRIC OPTIONS
- COTTON
- POLISHED COTTON
- LIGHTWEIGHT DAMASK
- SHEETING

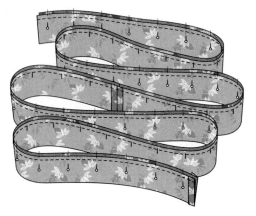

Diagram 3

6. Repeat Steps 4 and 5 with the remaining 179-inch strips to make two more outer casings.

RUCHING THE TUBES

1. Referring to **Diagram 4**, stuff the sewn end of one muslin inner casing into the unhemmed end of one outer casing.

Diagram 4

2. To ruche, gently work the outer casing over the stuffed inner casing, allowing gathers to form along the length of the outer casing.

3. Continue pulling the unhemmed end of the outer casing over the inner casing until only 5 inches of the inner casing is exposed.

4. Repeat Steps 1 through 3 for the remaining inner and outer casings. You will now have three tubes.

BRAIDING THE TUBES

1. Place the tied ends of the three tubes together. Tie a piece of string around these ends to hold the three tubes in place and braid them together, as shown in **Diagram 5**. For more information, see "Braiding" on page 243.

Diagram 5

2. Shape the braid into a circle and remove the string holding the three tubes together. Working with one tube at a time, match and pin the ends of the inner casing together with a safety pin, as shown in **Diagram 6**. Repeat this step for the remaining two tubes.

Diagram 6

whipstitching, see "Embroidery and Hand-Sewing Stitches" on page 244 Repeat this step for the remaining two outer casings.

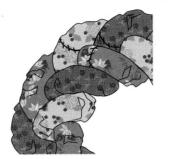

Diagram 7

3. Referring to **Diagram 7**, pull the hemmed end of one outer casing over the other end of the matching outer casing, making sure to conceal the safety pin and the string. Whipstitch the hemmed end to the other end of the outer casing. For information on

FINISHING THE WREATH

1. Tie a decorative bow at the top of the wreath over the place where the ends are joined.

2. Hang the wreath from an over-the-door hanger.

Know & Sew

FOR ADDITIONAL SUPPORT AND EASE WHEN HANGING, TRY MOUNTING THE WREATH ON A METAL RIM FROM A BICYCLE TIRE OR A FLAT WIRE WREATH BASE. USE FLORAL WIRE AND WEAVE IT THROUGH THE BRAID AND AROUND THE TIRE RIM OR WREATH BASE SEVERAL TIMES. THE WREATH WILL KEEP ITS SHAPE FROM YEAR TO YEAR.

EMBELLISH IT!

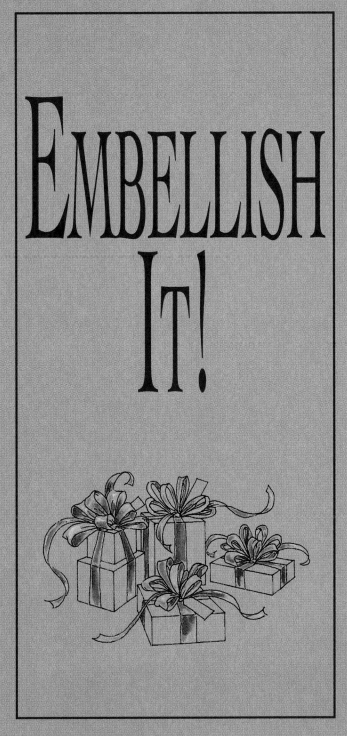

Battenberg Lace Dress

Surprise a special little girl with a pretty party dress embellished with Battenberg lace hearts and gingerbread people. It's such a cinch to sew, you'll probably want to make two or three at the same time.

SIZE: The dress shown in the photograph is a girl's large, but this dress can be made in any size.

SEWING THE LACE TO THE DRESS

1. Referring to **Diagram 1**, pin the heart-shaped appliqués and the gingerbread boy and girl along the neckline on the right side of the dress front.

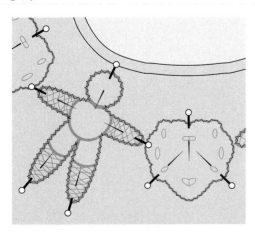

Diagram 1

2. Referring to **Diagram 2**, sew the outer edges of the boy, girl, and hearts to the dress using a very narrow zigzag stitch and a short stitch length. Make sure to use only cotton thread because polyester thread will not absorb the dye.

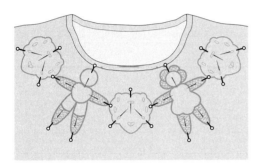

Diagram 2

3. Turn the dress inside out. Carefully trim away the fabric of the dress behind each heart, boy, and girl within the zigzag stitching, leaving a ¹⁄₈-inch seam allowance, as shown in **Diagram 3**.

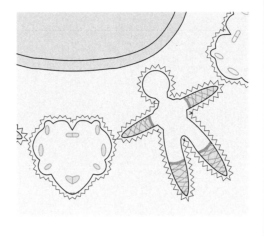

Diagram 3

DYEING THE DRESS

1. Hand or machine wash the dress in warm water with mild detergent and rinse it.

2. Following the manufacturer's directions, dye the dress to the desired color intensity.

FINISHING THE DRESS

1. Press the dress.

2. Cut the blue satin ribbon into three 4-inch lengths. Tie each length into a small bow.

3. With the right side of the dress facing up, hand tack one bow to the top center of each heart.

4. Hand tack a ribbon rose to each bow, as shown in **Diagram 4** on page 216.

MATERIALS LIST
FABRIC REQUIREMENTS
- GIRL'S WHITE DRESS
- 3 WHITE, 2-INCH-DIAMETER, HEART-SHAPED CUTWORK APPLIQUÉS*
- WHITE, 5-INCH BATTENBERG LACE GINGERBREAD BOY*
- WHITE, 5-INCH BATTENBERG LACE GINGERBREAD GIRL*

OTHER SUPPLIES
- ½ YARD OF ¹⁄₁₆-INCH-WIDE BLUE SATIN RIBBON
- WHITE COTTON SEWING THREAD
- HAND-SEWING NEEDLE
- 3 PINK RIBBON ROSES
- DIMENSIONAL FABRIC PAINT IN THE FOLLOWING COLORS: BROWN, PINK, BLUE, GREEN, AND YELLOW
- PACKAGE OF PINK COLD-WATER POWDERED FABRIC DYE

*Note: See the "Buyer's Guide" on page 246 for information.

FABRIC OPTIONS
- COTTON KNIT T-SHIRT DRESS
- WOVEN COTTON DRESS

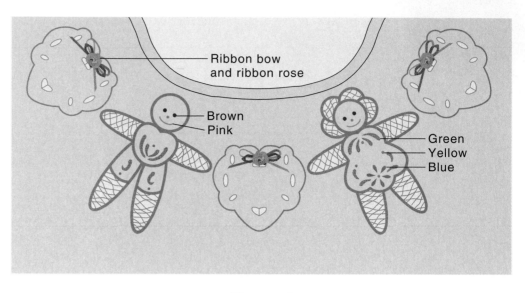

Ribbon bow
and ribbon rose

Brown
Pink

Green
Yellow
Blue

Diagram 4

5. Referring to **Diagram 4**, paint eyes on the boy and girl with brown dimensional paint. Paint noses and mouths with pink dimensional paint. Decorate their garments with blue, green, and yellow dimensional paint.

Farmer-and-Animal Sweatshirt

If Old MacDonald wanted to make a sweatshirt, this would be his choice. With a Velcro barn and fence that goes all the way around the shirt, what better way for him to keep track of his favorite animals?

Farmer-and-Animal Sweatshirt

❖

SKILL LEVEL: *INTERMEDIATE*

SIZE: The sweatshirt shown in the photograph on page 217 is a child's size 6x, but any size can be used.

NOTE: To determine how many yards of Velcro are needed for a larger sweatshirt, measure the circumference of the sweatshirt and add 1 yard.

CUTTING THE FARMER AND ANIMALS

1. Trace the farmer and animal pattern pieces on pages 221–223 onto template plastic and cut out the patterns.

2. Turn the template plastic to the wrong side and trace the pattern pieces onto the paper side of the fusible webbing, making sure not to trace the pieces flush against each other. Record the color of felt that is to be used on the paper side of the fusible webbing. Cut out the pattern pieces $1/4$ inch away from the pattern cutting line.

CUTTING THE BARN AND FENCE

1. To make the complete barn pattern, trace the pattern pieces on pages 221–222 onto tracing paper, making sure to match the two sections before cutting out the pattern. Cut out the pattern. Using a chalk pencil, trace the barn onto the right side of the shirt front.

2. Cut the loop portion of the Velcro in half lengthwise so that it is $3/8$ inch wide. From these two lengths, cut the following:

- 1 barn bottom, $7^3/4$ inches long
- 2 barn sides, each $4^1/2$ inches long
- 2 roof tops, each $3^1/2$ inches long

- 2 roof sides, each 3 inches long
- 1 roof bottom, $7^3/4$ inches long
- 2 beams, each 2 inches long
- 3 loft door pieces, each $2^1/2$ inches long
- 2 loft door pieces, each 2 inches long
- 2 loft door pieces, each 1 inch long
- 2 fence rails, each 21 inches long
- 9 fence posts, each $2^1/2$ inches long

ASSEMBLING THE BARN

1. Pin the Velcro onto the sweatshirt to form the barn, as shown in **Diagram 1**.

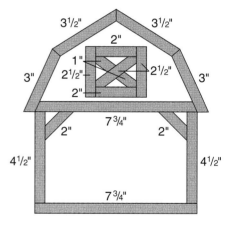

Diagram 1

2. Following the manufacturer's directions, iron the barn onto the sweatshirt. Hand sew around each piece.

ASSEMBLING THE FENCE

1. Referring to **Diagrams 2** and **3**, pin one fence rail to the sweatshirt, starting at the right side of and 1 inch up from the bottom of the barn. Continue to pin the rail around the back of the shirt and finish on the left side of the barn.

MATERIALS LIST

FABRIC REQUIREMENTS

- SWEATSHIRT
- 2 PIECES OF WHITE FELT, EACH 9 INCHES SQUARE
- SCRAPS OF FELT IN PINK, DARK ORANGE, BEIGE, TAN, LIGHT BROWN, DARK BROWN, LIGHT YELLOW, MEDIUM YELLOW, DARK YELLOW, BLUE, GRAY, OLIVE GREEN, AND DARK RED FOR THE FARMER AND THE ANIMALS
- $1/4$ YARD OF FUSIBLE WEBBING

OTHER SUPPLIES

- SEWING THREAD TO MATCH THE FABRICS
- SKEIN OF DARK YELLOW EMBROIDERY FLOSS
- $1^3/4$ YARDS OF TAN $3/4$-INCH-WIDE IRON-ON VELCRO
- 11 MOVABLE EYES, EACH 4MM
- SMALL COWBELL
- TRACING PAPER
- TEMPLATE PLASTIC
- FINE-POINT, PERMANENT MARKER
- CHALK PENCIL
- TWEEZERS
- FABRIC GLUE

Diagram 2

Diagram 3

2. Following the manufacturer's directions, iron the rails onto the sweatshirt.

3. Referring to **Diagrams 2** and **3**, evenly space and iron the posts to the shirt.

4. Hand sew around each fence piece.

ASSEMBLING THE FARMER AND THE ANIMALS

1. Following the manufacturer's directions, carefully iron the fusible webbing pattern pieces onto the corresponding colors of felt.

2. Cut out the pieces along the pattern lines, making sure to trim away the extra $1/4$ inch of webbing.

3. Following the manufacturers's directions, remove the paper backing from the fusible webbing and fuse the larger pieces of the farmer and animals onto the white felt. Make sure you do not fuse them flush against one another.

4. Fuse the smaller pieces onto the corresponding larger figures and the white felt to complete the farmer and animals, as shown in **Diagram 4.** Tweezers may be used to lift the smaller pieces.

Diagram 4

SATIN STITCHING THE FARMER AND THE ANIMALS

1. Set the sewing machine for a ⅛-inch stitch width and a short stitch length. With matching thread, satin stitch around the larger areas to outline the figures, as shown in **Diagram 4** on page 219. For more information, see "Machine Appliqué" on page 242.

2. Cut out the figures, leaving a small edge of white showing all around. Leave the white felt in between the legs of the cow, horse, hen, duck, and pig, as shown in **Diagram 5**.

Diagram 5

FINISHING THE FARMER-AND-ANIMAL SWEATSHIRT

1. Following the manufacturer's directions, center and iron several small pieces of the hook portion of the Velcro onto the back of the farmer and the animals.

2. Thread a hand-sewing needle with matching thread and hand sew around each Velcro piece to secure it in place.

3. Referring to the photograph on page 217, glue two eyes each onto the farmer, the cat, and the dog.

4. Glue one eye each onto the cow, the horse, the duck, the pig, and the hen.

5. Cut three 3½-inch lengths of dark yellow embroidery floss and braid them together. For more information, see "Braiding" on page 243.

6. Thread the braid through the loop of the cow bell and tie it in place around the neck of the cow.

7. Slide the braid so the knot is on the wrong side of the cow and glue it in place. Let the glue dry.

8. Using the fine-point, permanent marker, draw a nose, mouth, and mustache on the farmer's face.

9. Using the marker, draw a nose and mouth on the cat and dog.

10. Using the marker, draw a curved wing on the hen and duck.

11. Place the farmer and animals on the Velcro barn and along the Velcro fence all around the sweatshirt.

12. The sweatshirt is machine washable, but the felt farmer and the animals must be removed before washing and the sweatshirt must be turned inside out.

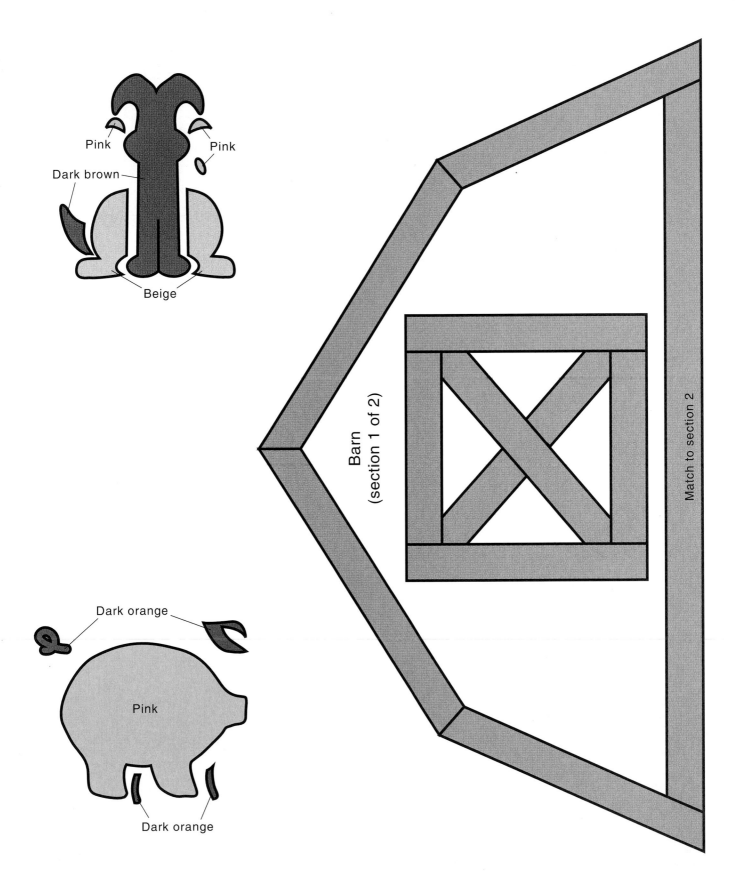

Pink

Pink

Dark brown

Beige

Barn
(section 1 of 2)

Match to section 2

Dark orange

Pink

Dark orange

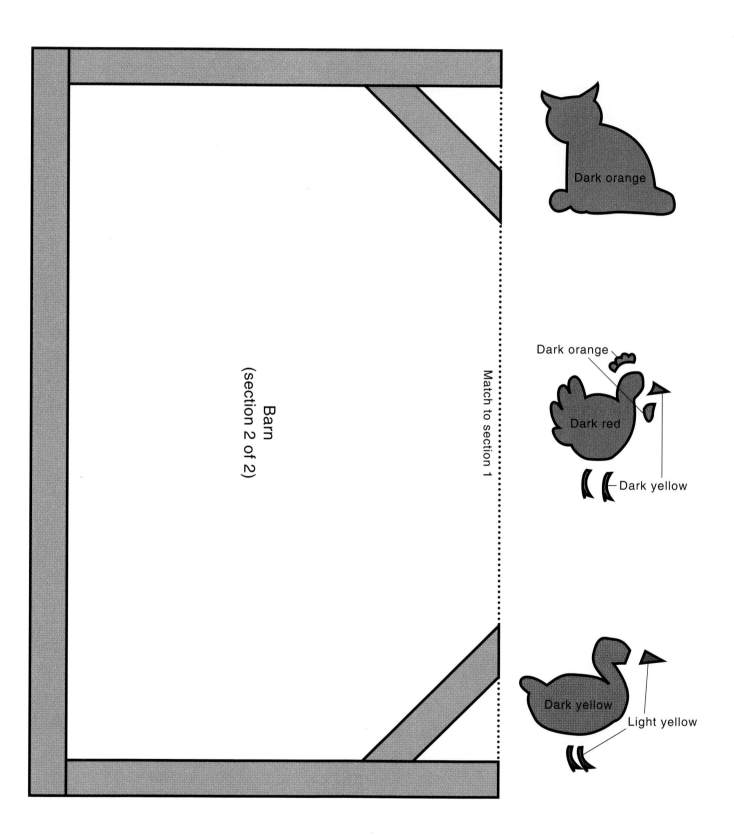

Barn
(section 2 of 2)

Match to section 1

Dark orange

Dark orange

Dark red

Dark yellow

Dark yellow

Light yellow

Clown Sweatshirt

What little girl wouldn't have a carnival of fun at a party, on a picnic, or on a play date when wearing this bright, cheerful sweatshirt? The clown's collar and chenille coils of hair can easily be changed to mix and match with different outfits.

SIZE: The sweatshirt shown in the photograph is a child's size 8, but any size can be used to make this sweatshirt.

NOTE: Sew all the seams with ¼-inch seam allowances.

MAKING THE PATTERN PIECES

Use a 15 × 20-inch sheet of tracing paper to make the following patterns:

1. Cut one 6-inch-diameter circle for the face.

2. Cut one 5 × 7½ × 7½-inch isosceles triangle for the hat.

3. Cut one 1 × 1¼-inch rectangle for the eye. Round off one end of the rectangle to shape the eye, as shown in **Diagram 1.**

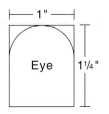

Diagram 1

4. Cut one 1½ × 3½ inch rectangle for the mouth. Curve the sides to shape the mouth, as shown in **Diagram 2.**

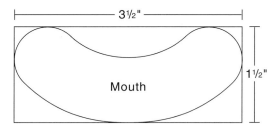

Diagram 2

CUTTING THE BOW, HAIR, AND COLLAR

1. From the rainbow-colored ribbon, cut one 12-inch length for the bow and one 3-inch length for the center of the bow.

2. From the green curly chenille, cut six 7-inch lengths for the hair.

3. From the white solid, cut one 3½ × 20-inch rectangle for the collar.

MAKING THE FACE

1. Using the pattern pieces, trace one face, one hat, one mouth, and two eyes onto the paper side of the fusible webbing with a chalk pencil.

2. Cut out the patterns, leaving ½ inch of webbing around each piece.

3. Following the manufacturer's directions, iron each pattern piece of fusible webbing to the wrong side of the following fabrics:

- the circle to the light orange
- the triangle to the blue
- the eyes to the white
- the mouth to the white

4. Cut out each of the pieces along the pattern lines.

FUSING THE FACE TO THE SWEATSHIRT

1. Following the manufacturer's directions, remove the paper backing from the fusible webbing on each of the shapes.

2. Center and fuse the face onto the lower front of the sweatshirt, as shown in **Diagram 3** on page 226.

MATERIALS LIST
FABRIC REQUIREMENTS

- RED SWEATSHIRT
- 7 × 10-INCH RECTANGLE OF LIGHT ORANGE SOLID FOR THE FACE
- 8-INCH SQUARE OF BLUE SOLID FOR THE HAT
- ⅛ YARD OF WHITE SOLID FOR THE COLLAR, EYES, AND MOUTH
- ¼ YARD OF 22-INCH-WIDE FUSIBLE WEBBING

OTHER SUPPLIES

- 4¾ INCHES OF ¼-INCH-WIDE YELLOW RICKRACK
- 12 INCHES OF ¼-INCH-WIDE DARK BLUE RICKRACK
- ½ YARD OF 1⅝-INCH-WIDE RAINBOW-COLORED RIBBON
- SEWING THREAD TO MATCH THE FABRIC, BUTTONS, AND TRIM
- HAND-SEWING NEEDLE
- 6 RED VELCRO COINS, EACH ½ INCH DIAMETER
- 5 WHITE VELCRO COINS, EACH ½ INCH DIAMETER
- 2 BLACK BUTTONS, EACH ¾ INCH DIAMETER
- 2 RED BUTTONS, EACH ⅞ INCH DIAMETER
- GREEN PIPE CLEANER
- BLACK PIPE CLEANER
- 1½-INCH RED POM POM
- 1 EACH OF ¾-INCH POM POMS IN YELLOW, GREEN, AND RED
- 42 INCHES OF GREEN, WIRED, CURLY CHENILLE
- TRACING PAPER
- CHALK PENCIL
- FABRIC GLUE

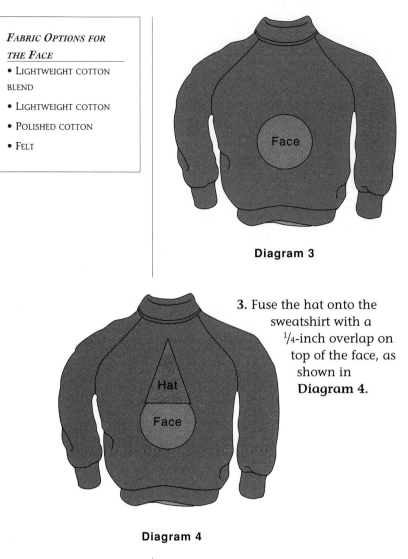

Diagram 3

3. Fuse the hat onto the sweatshirt with a $\frac{1}{4}$-inch overlap on top of the face, as shown in **Diagram 4.**

Diagram 4

4. Fuse the eyes and mouth to the face, as shown in **Diagram 5.**

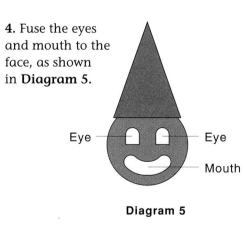

Eye — Eye

Mouth

Diagram 5

SEWING THE COLLAR

1. With the wrong side facing up, turn down and press a $\frac{1}{4}$-inch hem along all the edges of the collar. Pin and sew the hem in place.

2. Glue the length of blue rickrack to the bottom edge of the right side of the collar and trim the excess.

3. To make one row of gathering stitches along the collar top, use the longest machine stitch and sew $\frac{3}{4}$ inch from the edge, as shown in **Diagram 6.**

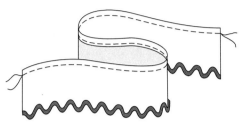

Diagram 6

4. Pull up the bobbin thread and evenly gather the collar until it is 8 inches long. Secure the ends of the threads with a knot.

5. Evenly space and sew the hook portion of five white Velcro coins to the back of the collar along the gathered edge, as shown in **Diagram 7.**

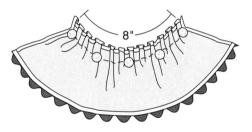

Diagram 7

6. Sew the loop portion of the five white Velcro coins below the clown face, making sure they correspond to the loop portions on the collar.

MAKING THE BOW

1. Fold the ends of the 12-inch length of ribbon toward the center and whipstitch in place. Wrap the 3-inch length of ribbon around the center of the bow and whipstitch the ends together, as shown in **Diagram 8.** For information on whipstitching, see "Embroidery and Hand-Sewing Stitches" on page 244.

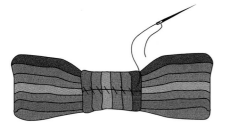

Diagram 8

2. Hand sew the bow onto the gathers at the center of the collar. Attach the collar to the sweatshirt.

MAKING THE HAIR

1. Coil each 7-inch length of chenille around a finger.

2. Hand sew a hook portion of one red Velcro coin to the end of each coil.

3. Machine sew the loop portions of three red Velcro coins to one side of the clown's face and three to the other side, as shown in **Diagram 9.**

Diagram 9

4. Attach the coils of hair to the sweatshirt, as shown in **Diagram 10.**

Diagram 10

FINISHING THE FACE

1. Referring to **Diagram 10,** glue the length of yellow rickrack onto the bottom edge of the hat and trim the excess.

2. Using black thread, sew the black buttons onto the sweatshirt for the eyes. Using red thread, sew the red buttons onto the face for the cheeks, as shown in **Diagram 10.**

3. Cut a 3-inch length of black pipe cleaner for the mouth and use black thread to tack it in place, as shown in **Diagram 10.**

4. Cut two 2½-inch lengths of green pipe cleaner. Bend each one into a V-shape and use green thread to tack one above each eye for the eyebrows, as shown in **Diagram 10.**

5. Hand sew the large, red pom pom to the face for the nose and the three small pom poms to the hat, as shown in **Diagram 10.**

Soutache-Embellished Shirt

Spruce up a denim shirt with a flurry of flowers—all at a fraction of the cost of designer clothes! Once you learn the simple secret of embellishing with soutache, you can design your own jackets and jeans in no time at all.

SIZE: The shirt in the photograph is a woman's small, but any size can be embellished.

CUTTING AND TRACING THE PATTERN

1. Trace the pattern on page 230 onto template plastic with a fine-point, permanent marker and cut out the pattern.

2. Referring to **Diagram 1**, use a chalk pencil and trace four flowers onto the front of the shirt opposite the pocket. Trace one flower onto the front of the shirt above the pocket.

Diagram 1

FINISHING THE SHIRT

1. Beginning at the center of one petal, sew the soutache to the shirt over the chalk pencil line, stopping before the petal is completed. Fold back and overlap the soutache before sewing around the next petal, as shown in **Diagram 2**.

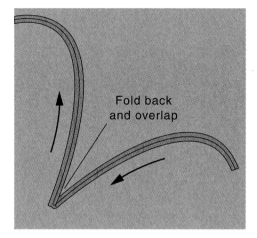

Fold back and overlap

Diagram 2

2. Continue sewing the soutache around each petal in this manner to complete the flower. To finish, cut the soutache, leaving a $3/4$-inch tail. Turn under $1/4$ inch of the tail, as shown in **Diagram 3**. Fold back and overlap it onto the beginning of the first petal. Sew it in place.

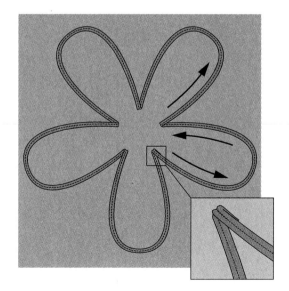

Diagram 3

3. Repeat Steps 1 and 2 to sew the remaining flowers.

MATERIALS LIST

FABRIC REQUIREMENT
• BLUE SOLID SHIRT WITH A POCKET

OTHER SUPPLIES
• 5 YARDS OF BLACK SOUTACHE
• SEWING THREAD TO MATCH THE SOUTACHE
• TEMPLATE PLASTIC
• FINE-POINT, PERMANENT MARKER
• CHALK PENCIL

FABRIC OPTIONS FOR THE SHIRT
• DENIM
• COTTON
• LINEN

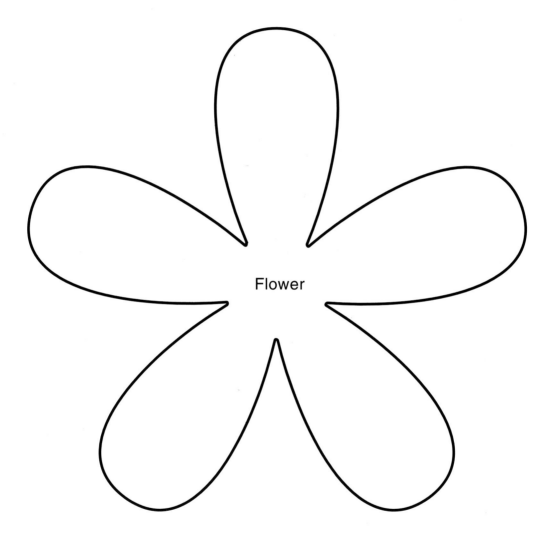

Flower

Lacy Vest

Start with a purchased vest, add a few finely crocheted or Battenberg lace doilies, and in as little as one hour this Victorian-looking vest will be ready to gift wrap!

Lacy Vest

❖

MATERIALS LIST

FABRIC REQUIREMENTS

• BLACK VEST WITHOUT LAPELS

• 6 WHITE, MEDIUM-SIZE CROCHETED DOILIES

• 4 WHITE, MEDIUM-SIZE BATTENBERG LACE DOILIES

• 2 WHITE, SMALL-SIZE CROCHETED DOILIES

OTHER SUPPLIES

• PACKAGE OF BLACK DOUBLE-FOLD BIAS TAPE

• 14 ASSORTED WHITE BUTTONS, EACH $\frac{3}{8}$ INCH DIAMETER

• SEWING THREAD TO MATCH THE VEST

• INVISIBLE THREAD

• HAND-SEWING NEEDLE

• SPRAY STARCH OR SIZING

• SEAM RIPPER

• PERSONALIZED SEWING LABEL (OPTIONAL)

FABRIC OPTIONS

• SATIN

• WOOL

• DENIM

SKILL LEVEL: *INTERMEDIATE*

SIZE: Since you start with a purchased vest, the finished size is a custom fit.

PREPARING THE VEST AND DOILIES

1. With a seam ripper, carefully remove all the pockets, flaps, and buttons from the vest.

2. Following the manufacturer's directions, spray starch both sides of the doilies to medium stiffness. Allow them to dry thoroughly.

3. Lay the vest on a flat surface. Beginning at the top of the vest, symmetrically arrange matching pairs of doilies on either side the vest front. One third of each of the two doilies at the top should extend over the shoulder seams toward the back of the vest, as shown in **Diagram 1**. Continue arranging the remaining doilies along the front and bottom front edges of the vest, making sure that one third of each doily extends over the vest edges.

Diagram 1

4. Fold one third of each doily to the inside of the vest front, as shown in **Diagram 2**.

Diagram 2

5. Unfold the outer two thirds of each doily, leaving the remaining one third inside the front edge. Pin each doily in place, as shown in **Diagram 3**.

Diagram 3

SEWING THE DOILIES TO THE VEST

1. With the right side of the vest facing up, and beginning at the top edge of one side, sew along the vest front using a medium zigzag stitch. Stitch close to the edge of the vest. Make sure to catch the doilies onto the inside of the vest edge. Repeat with the remaining side of the vest front.

2. Turn the vest inside out. Unfold the bias tape. Pin the right side of the unfolded tape edge to the inside of the vest next to the zigzag stitching, as shown in **Diagram 4**. Make sure the rest of the tape lies to the outside of the vest edge. With a straight machine stitch, sew the tape to the vest by stitching in the crease of the tape.

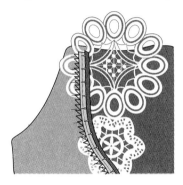

Diagram 4

3. Referring to **Diagram 5**, trim the portion of each doily on the inside of the vest close to the zigzag stitching.

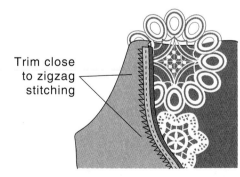

Trim close to zigzag stitching

Diagram 5

4. Referring to **Diagram 6**, refold the bias tape so it is over the raw edges of each trimmed doily and pin in place, mitering the corners at the bottom edges of the vest front. Sew the tape to the vest.

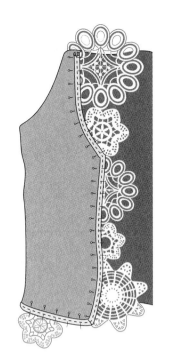

Diagram 6

5. Turn the vest right side out. Fold the remaining part of each doily to the outside of the vest front and press. Pin each doily in place.

6. Thread only the top of the sewing machine with invisible thread. Sew the doilies to the vest by stitching around the outer edge of each doily, as shown in **Diagram 7**.

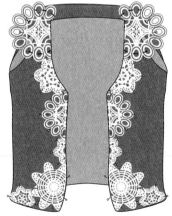

Diagram 7

FINISHING THE VEST

1. Using black thread, randomly hand sew 14 white buttons to the vest, as shown in the photograph on page 231.

2. Sew in your own custom label!

Know & Sew

HERE'S A QUICK-AND-EASY NO-PIN METHOD FOR APPLYING THE BIAS TAPE TO THE VEST. APPLY GLUE STICK TO ONE FOLDED EDGE OF THE TAPE, THEN PRESS IT INTO PLACE NEXT TO THE ZIGZAG STITCHING ON THE VEST. LET THE GLUE DRY. SEW THE TAPE IN PLACE WITH A STRAIGHT STITCH. THIS WILL KEEP THE BINDING FROM SHIFTING AND YOU FROM GETTING STUCK WITH ANY PINS!

Battenberg Lace
Camisole and Tap Pants

Embellished elegance is easy to achieve with a purchased camisole set and Battenberg lace. This romantic ensemble makes an excellent addition to a bride's trousseau.

SIZE: The camisole and pants shown in the photograph are a size medium, but any size can be embellished.

TEA DYEING THE LACE

1. Boil 1¼ cups of water. Place the tea bag in the water for 3 minutes, stirring occasionally until the tea has steeped. Remove the tea bag.

2. Dip the lace triangles into the tea until the lace is a light ivory color. If a darker color is desired, leave the lace in the tea for a longer period of time.

3. Rinse the lace in cool water until the water runs clear. Blot with paper towels to remove the excess water.

4. Machine dry the lace on low heat or lay flat to dry. Press the lace while still slightly damp.

SEWING THE LACE TO THE CAMISOLE

1. With the right side facing up, center the large lace triangle on the front of the camisole and pin it in place with silk pins, as shown in **Diagram 1**.

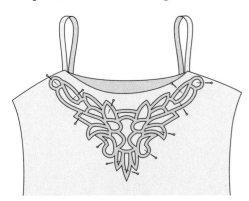

Diagram 1

2. Using a very narrow zigzag stitch and a short stitch length, sew the lace to the camisole, as shown in **Diagram 2**.

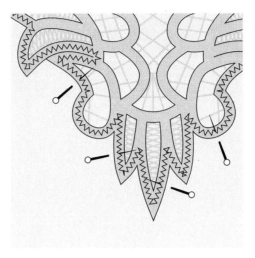

Diagram 2

3. Turn the camisole inside out. Carefully trim away the fabric from behind the lace triangle within the zigzag stitching, leaving a ⅛-inch seam allowance, as shown in **Diagram 3**.

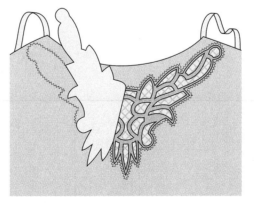

Diagram 3

SEWING THE LACE TO THE PANTS

1. With right sides facing up, place the small lace triangles on the sides of the

MATERIALS LIST

FABRIC REQUIREMENTS
- CAMISOLE WITH MATCHING TAP PANTS
- LARGE BATTENBERG LACE TRIANGLE*
- 2 SMALL BATTENBERG LACE TRIANGLES*

OTHER SUPPLIES
- SEWING THREAD TO MATCH THE DYED LACE
- HAND-SEWING NEEDLE
- ORANGE PEKOE AND CUT BLACK TEA BAG
- PAPER TOWELS
- SILK PINS
- 3 IVORY RIBBON ROSES

*Note: See the "Buyer's Guide" on page 246 for information.

FABRIC OPTIONS
- SILK
- WOVEN COTTON
- WOVEN POLYESTER

pant legs and pin them in place with silk pins, as shown in **Diagram 4.**

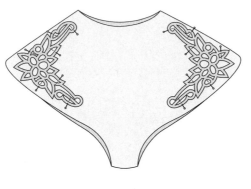

Diagram 4

2. Referring to **Diagram 2** on page 235, use a very narrow zigzag stitch and a

short stitch length to sew the lace triangles to the pant legs.

3. Turn the tap pants inside out. Referring to **Diagram 3** on page 235, carefully trim away the fabric from behind each lace triangle and within the zigzag stitching, leaving a ⅛-inch seam allowance.

FINISHING THE CAMISOLE AND PANTS

Thread a hand-sewing needle with matching thread and referring to the photograph on page 234 for placement, hand tack the ribbon roses to the lace triangle on the camisole front.

Eyelet Sheets and Pillowcases

Sew sensational sheets for less than the cost of a designer set and brighten your bedroom, even in the middle of winter. These lacy linens are also a pleasing present for newlyweds or for an anniversary couple.

Eyelet Sheets and Pillowcases

MATERIALS LIST

FABRIC REQUIREMENTS

- 2 WHITE, STANDARD-SIZE PILLOWCASES

- WHITE, FULL-SIZE FLAT SHEET

OTHER SUPPLIES

- 4³/₄ YARDS OF WHITE, 4¹/₂-INCH-WIDE GATHERED EYELET LACE WITH A BINDING

- SEWING THREAD TO MATCH THE FABRIC

FABRIC OPTIONS FOR THE SHEETS

- COTTON

- POLYESTER/COTTON BLEND

- SATIN

SKILL LEVEL: EASY

SIZE: The sheets in the photograph on page 237 fit a full-size bed. The pillowcases are standard size.

NOTE: Measurements in the cutting directions include the seam allowances. Sew all the seams with ¹/₂-inch seam allowances.

CUTTING THE EYELET

From the eyelet, cut two 41-inch lengths for trimming the pillowcases. Cut one 83-inch length for trimming the flat sheet.

TRIMMING THE PILLOWCASES

1. With right sides together, fold one 41-inch length of the eyelet in half crosswise. Pin the short ends together, matching the raw edges, as shown in **Diagram 1**.

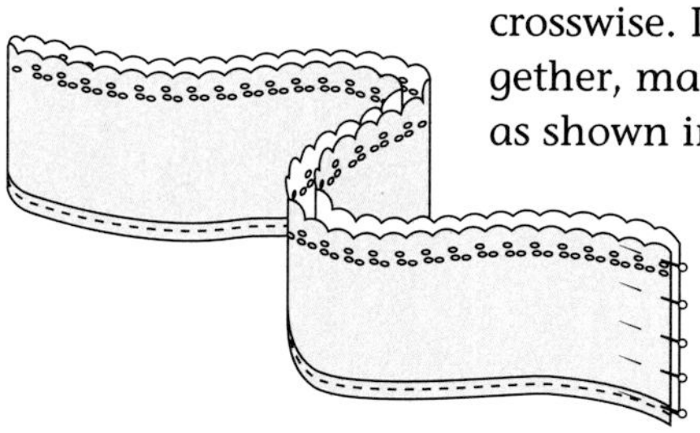

Diagram 1

2. Sew the short ends together. To finish the raw edges, zigzag over the seam allowance, as shown in **Diagram 2**. Press the seam to one side. Turn the eyelet circle right side out.

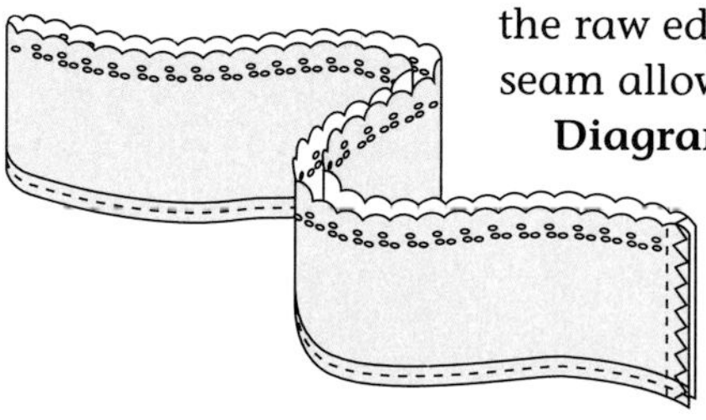

Diagram 2

3. Repeat Steps 1 and 2 for the remaining 41-inch length of eyelet.

4. Referring to **Diagram 3**, with the wrong side of one eyelet circle facing the right side of one pillowcase, match and pin the eyelet binding to the stitching along the top of the wide hem at the opening of the pillowcase. Align the seam of the eyelet with the side seam of the pillowcase. Sew the eyelet to the pillowcase by stitching on top of the eyelet binding.

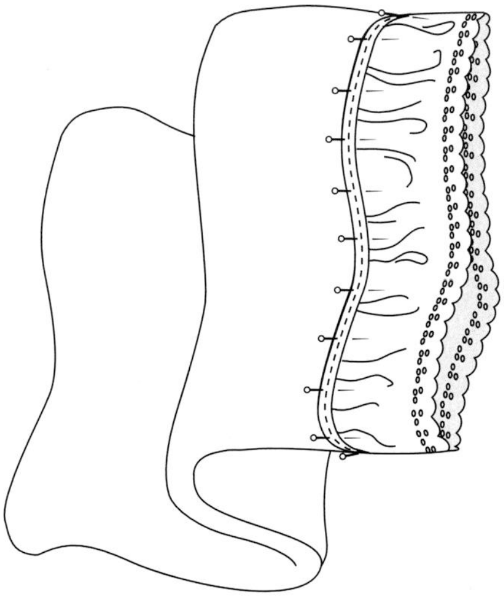

Diagram 3

5. Repeat Step 4 to sew the remaining eyelet circle to the remaining pillowcase.

TRIMMING THE FLAT SHEET

1. Referring to **Diagram 4**, turn ¹/₂ inch along one short end of the 83-inch length of eyelet toward the wrong side and press. Turn ¹/₂ inch more toward the wrong side and pin in place. Edge stitch the hem along the inner edge of the fold. Repeat this step to hem the remaining short end of the eyelet. For information, see "Edge Stitching and Topstitching" on page 242.

2. Referring to **Diagram 5**, with the wrong side of the eyelet facing the right side of the flat sheet, match and pin the eyelet binding to the stitching along the top of the wide hem on one end of the sheet. Sew the eyelet to the sheet by stitching on top of the eyelet binding.

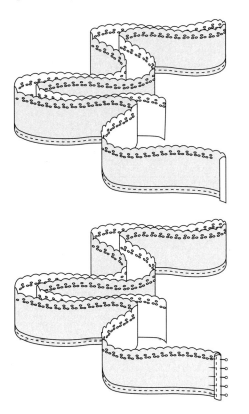

Diagram 4

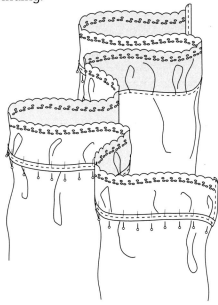

Diagram 5

General Instructions

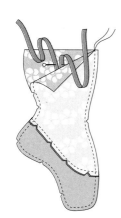

This chapter outlines all of the basic sewing and embroidery techniques you'll need for making each of the projects in *Sew It Tonight, Give It Tomorrow*. If you're a beginner, you'll find these techniques and helpful hints valuable for expanding your growing repertoire of skills. And if you're an experienced sewer, you may enjoy reading through this section to brush up on methods you've already used or to add some new techniques to your list of tried-and-true favorites.

Tools and Supplies

These supplies are staples in a well-stocked sewing room.

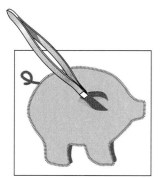

- **Chalk pencil:** This pencil is used to mark darts and dots, transfer appliqué patterns, or copy placement lines to the fabric. It marks well and is easily removed. To remove, use a scrap of the same fabric on which the chalk mark was made and gently rub until the chalk disappears.

- **Interfacing:** Interfacing gives shape, body, and support to fabric. It also adds stability to areas that are likely to be stressed and eventually wear out. Select interfacing that is lighter in weight than the fabric you're using and one that requires similar care.

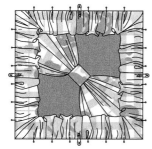

- **Fusible interfacing and fusible webbing:** Fusible interfacing is easy to apply and easy to sew. It is applied to the fabric with an iron that bonds it to the fabric with heat, moisture, and pressure. Take care to avoid blisters in the fabric. Fusible webbing is wonderful for stabilizing appliqué patches and securing them in position on background fabric.

- **Iron and Ironing Board:** Pressing is one of the most important steps in accurate sewing. The most versatile type of iron is a steam iron. You can use it for a variety of pressing needs since it can be set either on dry or on steam.

- **Needles:** Sharps are specifically made for hand sewing. A good rule of thumb is to start with a large-size needle and move to a smaller one as you gain experience in stitching. The larger the number, the smaller and shorter the needle. Experiment with different-size needles to see which are the most comfortable in your hand and which are the easiest to manipulate through the fabric you're using. Embroidery needles have long oval eyes that will accommodate several strands of embroidery floss. Beading needles are long and fine, with small, round eyes that easily go through tiny beads. Soft sculpture or doll needles range from $3^{1}/_{2}$ to 6 inches long and are perfect for making stuffed toys.

- **Scissors:** Use a sharp pair of dressmaker's shears for cutting fabric. They're designed to allow a good grip throughout prolonged use, so you can cut comfortably for long periods of time. A pair of small, sharp embroidery scissors is helpful for trimming threads and seam allowances. And it's a good idea to reserve one pair of scissors for cutting only paper and template plastic.

- *Seam ripper:* This handy, two-pronged tool allows you to remove stitches in a seam without damaging the fibers of the fabric.
- *Straight pins:* Long pins (1½ inches) with glass or plastic heads are easy to use, especially for pinning multiple layers of fabric together. Do not use burred or rusty pins because they might leave marks in the fabric.
- *Template plastic:* Thin, semitransparent plastic, available in sheets at quilt and craft shops, is ideal for making patterns that will be used to mark small shapes on fabric.
- *Thread:* Use high-quality, 100 percent cotton or cotton-covered polyester thread for sewing.
- *Tracing paper:* Large sheets of tracing paper or tissue paper are transparent enough to trace over pattern lines to make master pattern pieces.

Selecting and Purchasing Fabric

COORDINATING COLORS

The "Fabric Requirements" list at the beginning of each project indicates the colors used for that project, making it easy for you to create the same look. You might wish to experiment and use your favorite colors or choose shades to match a specific decor.

FABRIC TYPE AND QUALITY

Since fabric is the most essential element in each project, it's a good idea to buy the best you can afford. You'll be more pleased with the results that come from sewing with high-quality materials. The first fabric listed in each "Fabric Options" list indicates the

fabric used in the project that appears in the photograph. If you wish to use another fabric, look through the other fabric suggestions on this list.

PURCHASING FABRIC

The yardages in this book are based on a 44- to 45-inch fabric width, unless indicated otherwise. They have been double-checked for accuracy and are a bit generous to provide a margin for error. When you purchase fabric, however, remember that the actual width can sometimes be narrower than the size listed on the bolt and that anyone, no matter how experienced, can make a mistake in cutting.

Preparing Patterns and Templates

All of the patterns in this book are full size. Transfer each pattern piece onto tracing paper or template plastic as specified in the instructions. For sewing patterns, tracing paper is recommended, and for very small pattern pieces, template plastic is a better choice.

To make a plastic template, place a piece of template plastic over a page in this book, trace the appropriate pattern pieces using a fine-point, permanent marker. Cut out the patterns from the plastic along the traced lines.

A few of the patterns are too large to present on a single page. These patterns have been split into sections, and they're marked with dotted placement lines and numbers to help match the appropriate sections of each pattern.

To create one of these large pattern pieces, place a sheet of tracing paper over one portion of the pattern and trace that section. Then move the tracing paper to the appropriate page, aligning the placement lines on the pattern. Trace the second section of the pattern. Continue tracing each section of the pattern piece in this manner until the pattern is complete. Transfer all important pattern markings, such as cutting lines, placement lines, dots, and notches onto your pattern pieces or templates.

The cutting lines for the pattern pieces in this book are solid lines. There are inner dashed lines on each pattern piece to indicate the seam allowances. Sew all seams with ½-inch seam allowances, unless indicated otherwise.

The cutting instructions list the correct number of pieces to cut for each project. Each pattern piece is also marked with this information.

For many projects, no pattern pieces are necessary. In these cases, the instructions indicate the measurements to cut directly from the fabric or from paper to make each pattern piece. In these instances, measurements in the cutting directions include the seam allowances.

CUTTING THE FABRIC

The pattern pieces in this book include directional arrows indicating the straight grain of the fabric. For projects that do not have pattern pieces, be sure to cut each piece on the straight grain whenever possible.

To save time, cut out all the pattern pieces from the fabric, the lining, and the interfacing at the same time.

Sewing Basics

PRECISION SEWING TECHNIQUES

Accurate seam allowances are a must for precision sewing. Even a discrepancy as slight as ¼ inch in several seam allowances can make a big difference when joining different pattern pieces. Measure the distance from the needle to the outside of the presser foot on your sewing machine to see whether it is actually ¼ inch. If it is not exactly ¼ inch, measure ¼ inch from the needle and place a piece of masking

tape at that point. If you like guiding seams against a raised edge, try gluing a piece of Dr. Scholl's Molefoam on the arm of your machine to create a precise ¼-inch seam allowance.

EDGE STITCHING AND TOPSTITCHING

Many of the projects call for edge stitching, topstitching, or both. Edge stitching is made by stitching exactly beside the folded edge of the project section. As you edge stitch, it helps to watch the needle, rather than the foot, stitching slowly to produce a straight and even line of stitches.

Topstitching is usually done on the right side of the fabric, and it's decorative and practical for holding seams and interfacings in place. It also keeps edges flat. The instructions for the projects indicate when to topstitch ¼ inch or ½ inch from the edge of the fabric.

MACHINE APPLIQUÉ

Machine appliqué is used for projects such as the Appliquéd Fish Lunch Bag on page 170 and the Bottle Bags on page 65. You can do satin stitch machine appliqué on any sewing machine that has a zigzag stitch setting. Use an open-toe appliqué foot or a presser foot with a channel on the bottom that allows a ridge of stitching to feed evenly underneath it. Insert a size 70 universal needle into the sewing machine. Match the top thread in the machine to the appliqué pieces and use a fine, machine embroidery-weight, white cotton thread in the bobbin. Set the machine on the zigzag width specified in the instructions and a very short stitch length. It's helpful to test the zigzag effect on a scrap of fabric first. Satin stitches should create an even band of color. If this does not occur, try loosening the top tension slightly, so that a small portion of the top thread is pulled slightly to the wrong side of the fabric. Here are some general guidelines for creating smooth satin stitch machine appliqué every time.

1. To prepare the appliqué shapes, iron a piece of webbing onto the wrong side of the fabric, following the manufacturer's directions. Trace the shapes onto the paper side of the webbing and cut them out, as shown in **Diagram 1.**

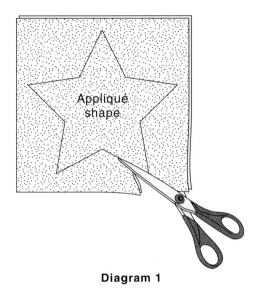

Diagram 1

2. Peel off the paper backing, position the shapes on the right side of the fabric, and fuse them with an iron on the wool setting, as shown in **Diagram 2.**

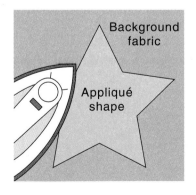

Diagram 2

3. Match the top thread in your machine to the color of each shape and satin stitch around the edges, covering the raw edges with a smooth line of stitches.

Braiding

Braiding is used for projects such as the Christmas Wreath on page 208 and the Farmer-and-Animal Sweatshirt on page 217. To braid, follow these easy steps.

1. Following the project instructions, join the tops of the three sections of the braid together. Fold strip C over strip B, as shown in **Diagram 3.**

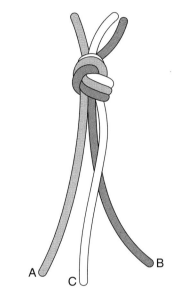

Diagram 3

2. Fold strip A over strip C, as shown in **Diagram 4.**

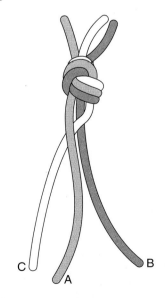

Diagram 4

3. Next fold strip B over strip A, as shown in **Diagram 5**. This establishes the braiding sequence. Pull each strip firmly to form a taut braid.

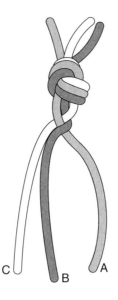

Diagram 5

4. Continue braiding strips A, B, and C together until the braid is approximately 3 inches from the end of the strips, as shown in **Diagram 6**.

Diagram 6

5. Secure the ends of the braid with a knot, a rubber band, string, or heavy thread to prevent unraveling.

Embroidery and Hand-Sewing Stitches

To work the sewing and embroidery stitches used in this book, find the stitches you need and follow the stitching sequences, as shown in the diagrams below.

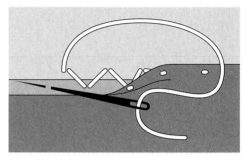

Blind Stitch

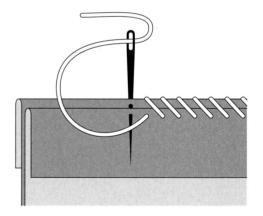

Whipstitch

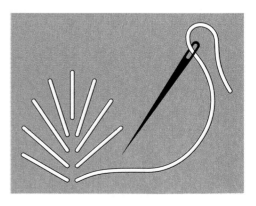

Straight Stitch

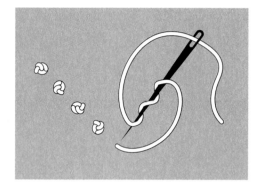

French Knot

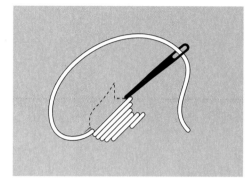

Satin Stitch

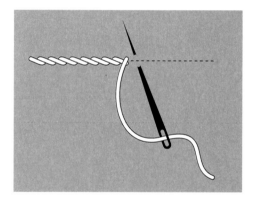

Outline/Stem Stitch

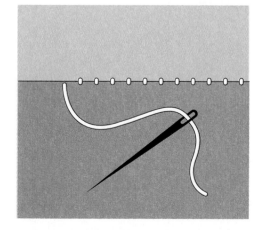
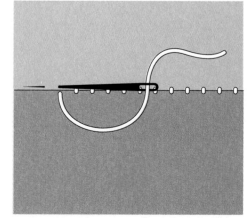

Slip Stitch

Buyer's Guide

Concord Fabric
Division of Concord House
1359 Broadway
New York, NY 10018
(212) 460-0300

Polished Apple fabric from the Town and Country collection (designed by Joan Kessler) for the Bow, Rosette, and Butterfly Pillows on page 80

M & J Trimming
1008 6th Avenue
New York, NY 10018
(212) 391-9072

Gold trim and gold-and-burgundy appliqués for the Christmas Show Towels on page 184

Waverly
79 Madison Avenue
New York, NY 10016
1-800-423-5881

Newstead Chintz fabric in the color parrot from the Bermuda collection, pattern number 660150, for the Duvet Cover and Pillow Shams on page 99

Wimpole Street Creations
P.O. Box 540585
North Salt Lake, UT 84054-0585
(801) 298-0504

Heart-shaped cutwork appliqués and Battenberg lace gingerbread boy and girl for the Battenberg Lace Dress on page 214; Battenberg lace triangles for the Battenberg Lace Camisole and Tap Pants on page 234